# Italian Americans
# before Mass Migration:
# We've Always Been Here

## Selections from the
## 37th Annual Conference
### of the
## American Italian Historical Association

November 4–6, 2004
Annapolis, Maryland

Edited by
Jerome Krase
Frank B. Pesci, Sr.
Frank Alduino

#2269655532

Founded in 1966, the American Italian Historical Association is an interdisciplinary group of scholars and lay people who share an interest in investigating relationships among Italian Americans, Italy, and the Americas. Its members encourage the collection, preservation, study, and popularization of materials that illuminate the Italian American experience. The Association promotes research through regional and national activities, including the annual conference and the publication of its proceedings.

*Library of Congress Control Number: 2008925393*

Printed in the United States.

Published by
AMERICAN ITALIAN HISTORICAL ASSOCIATION
John D. Calandra Italian American Institute
25 West 43rd Street, 17th Floor
New York, NY 10036

Volume 37
ISBN 0-934675-56-2 softcover
ISBN 0-934675-59-7 hardcover
ISSN 0743-474X

THIS VOLUME IS DEDICATED TO DR. SALVATORE MONDELLO

A founding member of the American Italian Historical Association and pioneer of Italian American studies, Professor Salvatore Mondello's professional life and academic achievements, inspired as they were by Dr. Leonard Covello, are indicative of his dedication to scholarship and his early unflagging efforts to bring to fruition the purposes of the Association.

Sal was a very private person. Few people knew him well. Those who did, knew what everyone can learn now from his autobiography. His personal life reflected the ideals of his Sicilian upbringing: a zest for life, the love of family, treating friends and colleagues with respect, doing the honorable thing, and working hard for worthwhile accomplishments. Understandably, Sal was a joy to know and work with.

In life, Sal's humility masked the significance of his achievements. But, Sal and his work will remain with us for many years to come and serve as an inspiration for those who would continue the work in Italian American studies that was started many decades ago in the Little Italy of East Harlem by those in the vanguard.

LUCIANO J. IORIZZO

*Professor of History*
*Emeritus SUNY/Oswego*

# TABLE OF CONTENTS

# ACKNOWLEDGEMENTS

*Italian Americans Before Mass Migration: We've Always Been Here* is the latest edition in an annual series that has become a mainstay in courses in Italian American studies. The educational goal is to provide a readable collection of papers, which constitute the proceedings of the 37th Annual Conference of the American Italian Historical Association (AIHA), that are informative, interesting, and stimulating.

These proceedings are the result of the AIHA Conference held in Annapolis, Maryland on November 4–6, 2004. Annapolis was the home of William Paca, Italian American patriot, statesman and politician. Planning for the conference began in May of 2003 during an AIHA Executive Council meeting in New York City. We took on the co-chairmanship of the conference, its planning and its final preparation.

Before going any further, we must mention the cooperation of the Honorable Thomas V. "Mike" Miller, long-time President of the Maryland State Senate, for his deep personal interest in the Conference. A history buff himself, Senator Miller made the newly constructed, state-of-the-art Miller Senate Office Building available to AIHA *pro bono* for its sessions and opening night reception.

The Conference was a rousing financial success thanks to generous contributions from John Marino of NIAF; Dr. Dona DeSanctis of the Order Sons of Italy in America; former Maryland State legislator, Frank Komenda; and former Maryland House Speaker Pro Tem Gary Alexander, Esq. Special thanks go to former Maryland legislator and photographer, Hon. Royal Hart, for the Conference program cover; Dolly Della Noche-Bekowitz, President, Order Sons of Italy, Maryland Grand Lodge; Frank Panessa, President, OSIA, Annapolis Lodge; Brandywine Press; Annapolis lobbyist Jack Neil; Dr. Thomas Florestano, President Emeritus, Anne Arundel Community College; Christopher DeJulio of DeJulio Homes, Inc.; The Center for the Study of Local

Issues, Anne Arundel Community College; The Department of History and Political Science, Anne Arundel Community College; Annapolis Attorney Robert Bohan; Martin Stiglio of Instituto Italiana di Cultura, and Nicholas Ciotola, coordinator, Italian American Programs, Senator John Heinz Pittsburg Regional History Center.

Thanks are also extended to former Maryland Governor Robert Ehrlich, Jr. who greeted the AIHA officers and members of the executive board in the foyer of the Governor's Mansion, and made a point of introducing his press secretary who happens to be an Italian American.

Thanks also to Al Dolgoff of Stevensville, Maryland, former CEO of Data Systems Marketing, and the Garibaldi-Meucci Museum of Staten Island, New York for their collection display.

Appreciation is extended to Dr. Martha Smith, AACC President; Dr. Andrew Meyer, Vice President for Learning at AACC; Dr. Jean Turner-Schreier, Dean of Arts and Sciences at AACC, and to Anthony Manzanares of AACC for the program design and Dr. Rebecca Kajs for her editorial assistance.

Special thanks to Dr. Jerome Krase, Emeritus and Murray Koppelman Professor, Sociology Department, Brooklyn College, CUNY, for his patience, organization and professionalism in putting together the Conference program and editing these proceedings.

Finally, thanks to Andrea Alduino, Cecilia Pesci Finsted, Dorothy Pesci, Anthony Alduino, Kathryn Alduino, Jennifer Washington, Gene and Nancy Avallone of Annapolis, and John Alduino for their assistance during registration periods and session breaks.

FRANK ALDUINO, PH.D.

*Professor of History*
*Anne Arundel Community College*
*Arnold, Maryland*

FRANK B. PESCI, SR., PH.D.

*Adjunct Professor of*
*Political Science*
*Anne Arundel Community College*
*Arnold, Maryland*

# INTRODUCTION

Friends/Amici, as have some of you, I have had a long "working" relationship with the American Italian Historical Association. For example, I have co-chaired AIHA meetings in Providence, Rhode Island (1985), Lowell, Massachusetts (1995), and two in New York City (1993 and 1998). Therefore I believe I can be trusted, as I speak from experience, when I state that our 37th Annual Conference, "Italian Americans Before the Mass Migration: We've Always Been Here" held on November 4–6, 2004 in Annapolis, Maryland was one of the organization's most successful, and memorable, events. Frank Alduino and Frank Pesci put together a marvelous venue with an amazing array of presentations. If not for Mother Nature's knocking out the power on the morning of the first day of the meetings, it would have been perfect. For this conference, my main responsibility was the academic programming. I invited, and with the sage advice of others, selected submissions for inclusion in the final program. I was extremely gratified by the number and quality of offerings that speaks well for the current state and reputation of the American Italian Historical Association. As someone who has also already co-edited five of AIHA's annual volumes (18, 26, 28, and 31), I also believe that the "Selections from the Conference Proceedings" presented here will also deserve an accolade or two.

At the lively sessions in Maryland's capital, there were almost 200 attendees from the academic, political, scholarly, and public spheres. More than one hundred presenters of one sort or another appeared before the assemblage, and more than fifty papers submitted for inclusion. After a long and difficult review process, twenty-two have been selected for publication here. In order to bring disparate, but equally important elements, of scholarship together for this volume, we have innovated with the design of the format. First, the selections made from three different pools of presentations; papers which were "on topic," and second, those which were "off topic," or not reflecting the central theme of the meeting. The third section is a collection of poetry in both English and Italian that represents not only our association's more creative side but also what might be called AIHA's "second language." In this volume the co-editors, Frank Alduino, Frank Pesci and I, also decided to represent as much of the proceedings as possible by including Abstracts and Notes on Presenters, at least those which were submitted to us, of those who presented at the conference in Annapolis. They can be found in the Appendix.

Part I, Italians Before the Great Migration, contains the "on topic" papers that were highlighted during the annual meeting. They provide us with a wide range of subjects and disciplinary approaches. Stefano Luconi is a frequent contributor at our meetings and his "Italian Americans for Ulysses S. Grant: The 1872 Campaign as a Case Study of Political Mobilization before Mass Migration" lives up to his reputation as a first rate scholar. His paper establishes that ethnic voting was a characteristic of Italian American political mobilization. Luciano J. Iorizzo, entered into the fray over whether an Italian American can be credited as a signatory of the United States of America's founding document in "The Case for the Ethnic Identity of William Paca: Signer of the Declaration of Independence." Iorizzo admits that at present the findings are inconclusive and a final judgment must wait for the results of further study. After all of the acrimonious debate, as well as genuine and ingenuous posturing over the Colombian Quincentenary, Fred Misurella explains in "Why Columbus Matters: The Evolution of an Icon in Literature and History," that despite the warts and all "Columbus remains important as a representative of global humanity struggling to understand and control its geological home." "The Italian Element in the New Smyrna Colony and St. Augustine, Florida, 1768–1800" is the subject of Michael Di Virgilio's paper. He found that although a pan-Italian identity never emerged, the descendants of the Italians were important in the history of Florida. David Coles and Frank Alduino collaborated to present "John Garibaldi: An Italian American Soldier in the Stonewall Brigade." They provide much needed attention to Italian immigrant soldiers who served the Confederacy; a subject that has been virtually ignored.

In the same theme of little noticed subjects is "Count Paolo Andreani in America: No Longer a 'Forgotten Traveler'." In this paper, Cesare Marino introduces Count Paolo Andreani who came to America during the late 1790s and who was one of the lesser known and understood early Italian visitors. Mary Ann Mannino, discusses the life and work of Sister Blandina Segale in her essay "Italian Women's Lives: Do What Presents Itself." An Italian immigrant, Sister Blandin was a missionary, frontiers woman and one of the earliest Italian American woman writers. Few of the participants at our conference would know that there was a relationship between "Giuseppe Garibaldi and Henry Adams." This is corrected by Henry Veggian as he uses examples of Adams' writings to show how Adams changed the representation of Italy in America and rendered Garibaldi as a tragic figure. Emelise Aleandri writes about "Italian Entertainers in New York City before Mass Migration" which, she shows, had different and varied reasons for their existence as opposed to those after mass migration. Finally in this section, we have a paper by Ernesto Milani. "Genoa, Wisconsin and the Civil War: The Guscetti Brothers Fight for their New Country." This work traces the long and little known history of Italian immigration to this town on the Mississippi River.

In Part II, Literature and Ethnic Identity, are the "off topic" papers that might at first glance seem incestuous to some as they have a special focus on two of the American Italian Historical Association most prominent members, Helen Barolini and Robert Viscusi, who have more and less recently made names for themselves in American literature. Barolini's work, *Umbertina*, is analyzed and celebrated by both Mary Jo Bona and Josephine Gattuso Hendin. Among other things, Bona, argues that Barolini became the well respected writer she could be by donning many linguistic hats, and blurring boundaries between genres. Hendin adds that Barolini also shows how difficult it is for a woman to seize control her of life, and reject fatalism. Elisabetta Marino investigates "Psychoanalytic Themes" in Viscusi's *Astoria* which she argues is the means through which he manages to heal and recompose his own, and perhaps others' "fragmented self."

Michael T. Ward, researched a sample of issues of *La Tribuna Italiana* between 1914 until 1940 and discusses its significance to the immigrant populations of Texas and surrounding states. In the paper he finds both reverence for the *patria* and love of the New World. Finally, my own "Seeing Ethnic Succession in Little and Big Italy" attempts to demonstrate how Italian American neighborhoods in United States are similar to Italian neighborhoods in Italy in the way that they have been changed by the invasion of new and different ethnic groups.

Part III, Poetry, provides us with a collection of poems that span both a wide range of human emotions and humanistic sensibilities. They are lovingly presented here in both English and in Italian and are a welcome addition to the sometimes rather stolid social science and humanities fare that precedes them on these pages. We the editors are especially thankful to Maria Elisa Ciavarelli for her efforts to bring the poets and their poetry together at our Annapolis conference. We are even more so grateful for her diligence in providing such excellent translations. It is impossible to provide due justice to these works with summaries so they must stand for themselves as a listing of authors and titles here: Maria Fama, "Fireworks on July 4, 2004," "Civil Rights"; Antoinette Libro, "In and Out of Touch," and "Afterward"; Rachel Guido de Vries, "Brother Poem," and "Stories from the Fire"; Albert Tacconelli, "My Father's Gladioli"; Mary Ann Mannino, "The Day You Left Me," and "Meditation on Divorce and Other Losses."

JEROME KRASE, PH.D.

*Emeritus and Murray Koppelman Professor*
*Brooklyn College*
*The City University of New York*

# PART I

# ITALIANS BEFORE THE GREAT MIGRATION

# Italian Americans for Ulysses S. Grant: The 1872 Campaign as a Case Study of Political Mobilization before Mass Migration

Stefano Luconi
University of Pisa, Italy

By the time Republican President Ulysses S. Grant sought reelection to the White House in 1872,[1] a negligible number of Italians had settled in the United States. Although no official data about expatriates were collected in Italy until 1876, the U.S. Federal government began to keep statistics about immigrants in 1820.[2] Between this year and 1870, 25,518 Italians moved to the United States.[3] Unlike their fellow ethnics during the period of mass migration, who were generally illiterate and unskilled southern laborers, these early arrivals were educated and skilled people from the northern regions. They included several political refugees seeking sanctuary from the upheavals of the *Risorgimento*.[4] According to the 1870 Federal Census, the largest Italian settlements were New York City with 2,794 immigrants, San Francisco with 1,622, and New Orleans with 1,571. No other U.S. city was home to more than 1,000 Italians.[5]

Few of these newcomers had become U.S. citizens and were, therefore, entitled to vote. Nonetheless, Italian American leaders did not refrain from trying to persuade their fellow ethnics to go to the polls and cast their ballots for the Republican Party in 1872. Focusing on the largest Italian American community at that time, New York City, this paper examines these early attempts at encouraging Italian American political mobilization and analyzes the strategy that was used to lure Italian American voters into the Republican camp.

Most active in the registration drive of Italian Americans was the Italian Citizens of New York Society. This organization intended to inspire Italian Americans to vote and, to this purpose, offered naturalized citizens the services of an attorney who helped them cope with electoral bureaucracy.[6] The lawyer, who worked *pro bono*, was Italian-born Luigi Tinelli. A prominent member of New York society, Tinelli had been a pioneer entrepreneur in silk manufacturing. He also had served as a U.S. consul in Oporto, Portugal, from 1841 (the very year he had become a U.S. citizen) to 1850; had fought for the Union during the Civil War—first in the Thirty-ninth New York Volunteer Infantry or "Garibaldi Guard" and subsequently in the Ninetieth New York Volunteers—and had been among the founders of the *Società di Unione e Fratellanza Italiana*.[7] This latter association was one of the first Italian American mutual aid societies in New York City and promoted the cause of Italian independence and unity in the United States.[8] A former Whig, Tinelli joined the Free Soil Party after John Clayton, the U.S. Secretary of State in the administration of President Zachary Taylor, dismissed him from the position of U.S. Consul in Oporto and replaced him with Horace Smith, a politician from Pennsylvania. When the Free Soil Party merged with the GOP in 1856, he became a staunch Republican.[9]

Tinelli was not without political ideals. Indeed, he was among the insurgents who vainly pressured King Charles Felix of Sardinia into granting a constitution in 1821 and left Lombardy in 1836 after being sentenced to twenty years in prison for his involvement in an anti-Austrian conspiracy of the *Giovine Italia,* the organization Giuseppe Mazzini had founded five years earlier to promote the independence and political unification of the Italian peninsula under a republican government.[10] Once in the United States, however, Tinelli learned the mechanics of the spoils system and did not refrain from trying to profit by its benefits. Actually, his post-1860 steadfast Republican loyalty resulted in part from his longing for another consular appointment that would relieve the financial troubles he had run into since his return from Portugal in 1851.[11]

Tinelli's partisan allegiance ultimately influenced the political orientation of the Italian Citizens of New York Society. When this association planned to give Italian Americans more clout in local politics by encouraging them to turn their votes into a solid bloc that could be delivered to any party in return for benefits for the community and its members, Tinelli endeavored to place the club into the Republican camp. In a heated meeting held less than two months before Election Day, he openly and strongly supported Grant on the grounds that the incumbent president had reduced the Federal debt and had reached a peaceful agreement with Great Britain with the 1871 Treaty of Washington. This treaty had resolved the controversy over the U.S. claims against three Confederate cruisers—*Alabama, Florida,* and *Shenandoah*—all built in England that had caused damage to Union property during the Civil War.[12] Although charges of corruption and misgovernment had already been brought against the Grant Administration with specific reference to the president's failure to promote a reform of the civil service,[13] Tinelli dismissed them as innuendos and nonsense. He also added that, in any case, he would never vote for Horace Greeley, Grant's opponent for the White House, who ran on the Liberal–Democratic fusion ticket. In Tinelli's view, Greeley was biased against Italy and her people and, thereby, did not deserve the Italian American vote.[14]

This latter argument won the day for Tinelli and the members of the Italian Citizens of New York Society, who, at their meeting, unanimously endorsed the Republican ticket in the presidential race. A few days later, a delegation of the club even asked for the resignation of the president of the organization, Mario Cella, because of his Democratic leanings.[15]

Actually, Greeley's anti-Italian attitude was a paramount issue in New York City's Little Italy during the 1872 election campaign. Another Italian American ethnic club, the *Associazione Donnarumma,* endorsed Grant because Greeley had "offended the Italians."[16] Greeley visited Europe in 1850 and 1851, and published the impressions of his "Grand Tour" in several articles for his magazine, the *Daily Tribune,* that he later collected in a volume entitled *Glances at Europe.* His stay in Italy was rather unimpressive. He stressed the economic underdevelopment of the country compared to Great Britain and France, the prevailing poverty of the population, the loss of the virtues that had characterized the peninsula at Roman times, the insane spirit of local jealousy of the Italian people, and the difficulties in the process of political unification because of these rivalries.[17]

Although such remarks were not particularly flattering, they were also quite conventional.[18] In addition, Greeley had also pointed to the Kingdom of Sardinia as an example of human freedom, which contributed to win many American admirers for the dynasty that promoted the unification of Italy.[19] He had also let the *Daily Tribune* publish several emotional dispatches from Rome by Margaret Fuller, an American journalist who praised Mazzini and the fight for Italy's independence during the 1848–49 revolutionary uprisings and who urged her U.S. readers to mobilize in support of the Roman Republic and the Republic of Venice in their struggle against the French and Austrian armies.[20]

Yet Giovanni Francesco Secchi de Casali—an immigrant from Piacenza—seized upon Greeley's critical observations to launch an anti-Greeley campaign among Italian American voters. A former Whig turned Republican like Tinelli, with whom he had cooperated in organizing the original nucleus of the "Garibaldi Guard" during the Civil War, Secchi de Casali was the publisher of *L'Eco d'Italia,* a New York City-based biweekly that was the leading Italian-language newspaper in the United States at that time.[21] In a series of six article that appeared between September 7 and 28, *L'Eco d'Italia* extrapolated a few passages from Greeley's work in order to present him as a bigot who detested Italy and her population. The accusations that Greeley had not mentioned a single living Italian artist, had not written enough about his visit to the Uffizi Gallery while in Florence, and had not even mentioned Galileo Galilei or the local university in his pages about Pisa easily revealed the expediency of the animus of *L'Eco d'Italia* in holding Greeley up to Italian American public scorn. As many Italian immigrants were political refugees who had fought in the battles of the *Risorgimento,* the newspaper also played on their patriotic sentiments and pride in order to further denigrate Greeley in their eyes. It argued, for example, that Greeley had maintained that Italians were more "handy with their knives in the dark" than brave enough to look "down the throats of loaded and hostile cannons in fair daylight."[22]

The stiletto stereotype and charges of cowardice were to haunt Italian Americans at least into the World War II years.[23] Yet they had already aroused the resentment of the U.S. population of Italian origin by the mid-nineteenth century. As early as 1843, for instance, Orazio de Attellis, a mason and a Jacobin who had participated in the 1820 military uprising against the Bourbons in Naples, wrote an angry letter to the Philadelphia *Public Ledger and Daily Transcript* protesting the newspaper's characterization of Italians as coward backstabbers.[24] Furthermore, in the early 1850s, Tinelli himself wrote a few articles for the *European Mercury,* a weekly newspaper published in New York City, in order to defend Italians against ethnic prejudice in the United States.[25] More specifically, an Italian immigrant to New York City, Amilcare Roncari, harshly criticized Greeley in the local English-language press as soon as the *Daily Tribune* published the letters from Italy by its own editor.[26]

Secchi de Casali, therefore, expected to strike a sensitive chord within the Italian American community when *L'Eco d'Italia* exaggerated Greeley's comments on Italy and her people. To this purpose, he even published an interview with Grant in order to demonstrate the president's appreciation of the Italian people as opposed to Greeley's supposed hostility. In a conversation with an anonymous reporter of *L'Eco d'Italia,* Grant sang the praises of the Italians for their free government, the prestige of their diplomats, and the strength of their army that was "second to none in Europe." If Grant had ever uttered such words, they were just blatant exaggerations to win the favor of Italian American voters. As Grant allegedly pointed out, the Italian ambassador to Washington, Count Luigi Corti, was indeed a member of the arbitral tribunal that was to assess Great Britain for the damages caused by the three Confederate ships. Yet such a role was hardly adequate proof of the high standing of Italian diplomats. Furthermore, six years earlier, the Italian armed forces had suffered devastating defeats from the Austrian empire by land and sea at Custoza and Lissa in the so-called Third Independence War.[27]

*L'Eco d'Italia* resorted to other ethnic issues in its campaign for Grant among its own readers. Specifically, it stated that the Catholic Church, in general, and the Jesuits, in particular, had endorsed Greeley's candidacy.[28] It had been only two years since the Kingdom of Italy had annexed Rome. Pope Pius IX was one of the fiercest opponents and antagonists of the recently established Italian State and anti-clericalism was prominent among several Italian Americans because of their widespread support for the political unification of their native country.[29] Against this backdrop, too, Greeley's alleged identification with Catholic organizations was most likely to become another shortcoming for the Liberal-Democratic candidate in New York City's Little Italy. Actually, *L'Eco d'Italia* extended the innuendo of Catholic backing to other politicians on the Democratic ticket, most notably to former Congressman and Democratic gubernatorial hopeful Francis Kernan.[30] Furthermore, bringing up the "Roman Question," namely the dispute over the end of the pope's temporal sovereignty, could potentially score another point in Grant's favor because, under his administration, Washington was the first government to recognize the Italian annexation of Rome in 1870.[31] Grant also had the reputation of being anti-Catholic.[32]

Ethnic rivalries added to religion-tinged political controversies in providing another potential issue to make the Democratic Party anathema to Italian American voters. A large number of Irish immigrants within the Democratic ranks contributed to the Catholic characterization of this party. By contrast, Irish Americans were staunch advocates of the temporal claims of the papacy, an attitude that *L'Eco d'Italia* never failed to overstress.[33] Having resettled across the Atlantic in the wake of the potato famine of 1846 and having mastered English, unlike the members of other ethnic groups, the Irish had also had enough time to gain control of the machine of the Democratic Party. This was especially true in Boston and New York City where the Irish endeavored to keep out new immigrants considered prospective competitors in American politics and society.[34] Actually, just one year after the 1872 presidential election, Tammany Hall chose its first Irish-born leader, "Honest John" Kelly.[35] Furthermore, one might easily suggest that Irish descent on his mother's side helped Francis Barretto Spinola's successful rise through the ranks of the Democratic Party in New York City after the Civil War, a rise that climaxed with the election to the U.S. House of Representatives in 1886 as the first Italian American to serve in Congress.[36]

It is well known that when Fiorello H. La Guardia decided to enter politics in the 1910s, he joined the Republican Party because the Irish controlled the Democratic hierarchy of Tammany Hall.[37] Yet Italian-Irish political antagonism had already manifested itself in New York City in the early 1870s. The establishment of the Grant and Wilson Central Club of United Nationalities offers a case in point. Promoted by Tinelli among others, this organization intended to forge a coalition of New York City's ethnic voters to support the Republican presidential ticket. All major immigrant minorities were invited to join the inaugural meeting that, after electing Tinelli to the position of vice president of the association, endorsed Grant and his running mate, Henry Wilson. Representatives of Italian, German, French, Hungarian, Swedish, Polish and even Bohemian clubs attended the rally. Only the Irish were not invited and did not show up.[38] They did not participate in subsequent meeting of the Grant and Wilson Central Club either, although organizations of additional nationality groups such as the Swiss and the Belgians joined it.[39] No significant Irish presence was reported even after the Club became a permanent association under the name of Society of United Nationalities in the wake of Grant's re-election.[40]

*L'Eco d'Italia* brought up other issues against Greeley. Most notably, it charged him with being a turncoat because of his shift of political allegiance. A maverick Republican, Greeley was the presidential candidate of the Liberal wing of the GOP, which Grant had antagonized because of the corruption of his administration and his controversial Southern policy.[41] But Greeley also accepted the presidential nomination of the Democratic Party that he had long criticized over the years.[42] His best-known remark was "All Democrats may not be rascals but all rascals are Democrats."[43] Greeley, however, was not the only one to switch party affiliations in 1872. John Adams Dix, the Republican gubernatorial candidate in New York State, was a former Democrat who had served as Secretary of the Treasury in the last few months of the administration of James Buchanan.[44] But this shift of partisan affiliation did not prevent *L'Eco d'Italia* from endorsing Dix, a further demonstration that the accusations of the newspaper against Greeley resulted primarily from political expediency.[45]

This kind of criticism, too, included a component that endeavored to appeal to Italian Americans' sense of ethnic pride. Indeed, *L'Eco d'Italia* contrasted the unstable alignment of the partisan cleavage in the United States with the supposedly consistent stand of Italian politicians. It pointed out that, unlike their colleagues in the United States who did not refrain from shifting their allegiance, in Italy a Republican would never turn into a Monarchic and a Monarchic would never become a Republican.[46] This argument was disingenuous because the so-called *trasformismo*—the practice of transforming opponents into supporters and forging alliances that blurred the distinction between "Right" and "Left"—had been a notorious feature of Italian politics since the establishment of the *connubio,* namely the parliamentary coalition between Camillo Benso Cavour and Urbano Rattazzi that was instrumental in letting the former become prime minister of the Kingdom of Sardinia in 1852.[47]

It is difficult to evaluate whether—and, if so, to what an extent—this ethnic strategy was successful in carrying the Italian American electorate for Grant. According to an estimate by Giuseppe Sormani, the editor of *Il Commercio,* a newspaper published in Milan, *L'Eco d'Italia* reached about 1 percent of New York City's population of Italian descent in the mid-1880s and, therefore, had a much limited influence within the local "Little Italy."[48] By that time, however, Felice Tocci had replaced Secchi de Casali as editor and *L'Eco d'Italia* faced competition from *Il*

*Progresso Italo-Americano,* which Carlo Barsotti had founded in 1880. Thus one may reasonably suggest that *L'Eco d'Italia* enjoyed greater prestige and authoritativeness in 1872 than it would a decade later.[49]

After the 1872 ballots were counted, *L'Eco d'Italia* reported that not only in New York City but also in San Francisco and Philadelphia voters of Italian extraction bolted to the Republican Party because they had rejected Greeley's candidacy on ethnic grounds.[50] The newspaper also contended that a large majority of Italian Americans in New York and other big cities had actually cast their ballots for Grant on Election Day.[51] Yet, on the one hand, the reliability of these statements is questionable in view of the partisan bent of Secchi de Casali's biweekly. On the other hand, voting statistics for the 1872 election included no ethnic breakdown that could help check such assertions against quantitative data. In particular, Italian Americans were so few in New York City in 1872 that no precinct had a concentration large enough to assume that the election returns for this district were representative of the vote of the local Italian American community. Nonetheless, the *New York Times,* too, reported that "the Italian vote, numbering a few thousand, was cast in the majority for Grant and Wilson."[52]

Scholarship has suggested that Italian immigrants to the United States and their offspring were long lukewarm toward politics and began to join the participating electorate in a sizeable number only in the late 1920s. In particular, with specific reference to New York City, Samuel L. Baily has argued that:

> relatively small numbers of Italians became involved in local politics prior to World War I. [ . . . ] Most southern Italians shunned politics during this period because of their lack of familiarity with the political system, their traditional distrust of government, their localism and, for many, the presumed temporary of their stay in New York.[53]

In this view, it was Alfred E. Smith's 1928 bid for the White House on the Democratic ticket that eventually mobilized Italian Americans politically. A politician of Irish ancestry and Catholic faith, Smith was the first presidential candidate of either major party who did not belong to the WASP establishment and, therefore, elicited a remarkable sense of identification among immigrant minorities.

In other words, Italian American voter turnout remained low until the emergence of ethnic issues was instrumental in bringing the eligible Italian American electorate to the polls.[54]

Catholic missionaries in the United States pointed out that the Italian American vote was key to the outcome of elections in New York City in 1914.[55] But, just one year later, as few as 15,000 individuals of Italian extraction went to the polls, although New York City's total Italian American population was more than one-half million people.[56] The same ratio of Italian Americans had cast their ballots in 1911, and only 3,000 had done so two years earlier.[57]

One may reasonably expect that the nineteenth century educated northern patriots who had fought for Italy's independence before going to the United States into exile were more politically sophisticated and interested in casting their ballots than their illiterate southern fellow countrymen who came en masse to North America a few decades later in search of those job opportunities that were missing in their native country. Immigrants from southern Italy also lacked any voting experience in their motherland because they could not meet the property requirements to quality for suffrage. Indeed, only 2 percent of the Italian population was eligible for the vote before 1882.[58] Yet this analysis of the 1872 presidential campaign in New York City's community has shown that the ethnic determinants of voting behavior were already key to encourage Italian Americans' participation in elections and to shape their party choice at the polls prior to the mass immigration in the late nineteenth century, when a sizeable influx of immigrants from Italy made the newcomers from this country a significant cohort of the eligible electorate. Conflicts and competition with the Irish were to gain momentum in the Little Italies and to influence the Italian American vote during the early decades of the following century.[59] Nonetheless, by the early 1870s, this and other ethnic issues had already begun to make inroads into the Italian American communities and to be exploited in order to bring out the Italian American vote and to win it over.

## NOTES

1. For the 1872 presidential campaign, see William Gillette, "Election of 1872," *History of American Presidential Elections, 1789–1968*, ed., Arthur M. Schlesinger, Jr. and Fred L. Israel, 9 vols. (New York: Chelsea, 1985), 4:1303–30. For Grant's campaign, see Jean Edward Smith, *Grant* (New York: Simon & Schuster, 2001), 547–52.

2. Dora Marucco, "Le statistiche dell'emigrazione italiana," *Storia dell'emigrazione italiana: Partenze*, ed., Piero Bevilacqua, Andreina De Clementi and Emilio Franzina (Rome: Donzelli, 2001), 62–64.

3. Humbert S. Nelli, *From Immigrants to Ethnics: The Italian Americans* (New York: Oxford University Press, 1983), 41.

4. Joanne Pellegrino, "An Effective School of Patriotism," *Studies in Italian American Social History: Essays in Honor of Leonard Covello*, ed., Francesco Cordasco (Totowa, New Jersey: Rowan and Littlefield, 1975), 84–104; Rudolph J. Vecoli, "Negli Stati Uniti," *Storia dell'emigrazione italiana: Arrivi*, ed., Piero Bevilacqua, Andreina De Clementi and Emilio Franzina (Rome: Donzelli, 2002), 55–58.

5. Nelli, 62. For sketchy information about New York City's early Italian immigrants, see Donna R. Gabaccia, "Peopling 'Little Italy,'" *The Italians of New York: Five Centuries of Struggle and Achievement*, ed., Philip V. Cannistrato (New York: New York Historical Society and John D. Calandra Italian American Institute, 1999), 46.

6. "Cose locali italiane," *L'Eco d'Italia* 25 Sept. 1872, 2.

7. Federal Writers' Project, *The Italians of New York* (New York: Random House, 1938), 12; Howard R. Marraro, "Lincoln's Italian Volunteers from New York," *New York History* 24.1 (1943): 57–58, 63–64; Remigio U. Pane, "Italian Expatriates and the American Civil War," *The Italian Americans Through the Generations*, ed., Rocco Caporale (Staten Island: American Italian Historical Association, 1986), 36–38; William L. Burton, *Melting Pot Soldiers: The Union's Ethnic Regiments* (New York: Fordham University Press, 1998), 169–75; Francesco Durante, *Italoamericana: Storia e letteratura degli italiani negli Stati Uniti, 1776–1880* (Milan: Mondadori, 2001), 385–86; Frank W. Alduino and David J. Coles, "'Ye Come From Many a Far Off Clime; And Speak in Many a Tongue': The Garibaldi Guard and Italian American Service in the Civil War," *Italian Americana* 22.1 (2004): 48, 54.

8. Howard R. Marraro, "Italians in New York during the First Half of the Nineteenth Century," *New York History* 26.3 (1945): 291.

9. Marco Sioli, "Nella terra della libertà: Luigi Tinelli in America," *I Tinelli: Storia di una famiglia, secoli XVI-XX*, ed. Marina Cavallera (Milan: Angeli, 2003), 89–90.

10. Giuseppe Castelli, *Figure del Risorgimento lombardo: Luigi Tinelli (Da Mazzini a Carlo Alberto)* (Milan: Ceschina, 1949), 28–33, 43–84; Howard R. Marraro, *Relazioni fra l'Italia e gli Stati Uniti* (Rome: Edizioni dell'Ateneo, 1954), 136; Giancarlo Peregalli, "L'emigrazione politica forzata: Luigi Tinelli attraverso una sua lettera," *Emigrazione e territorio: Tra bisogno e ideale*, ed. Carlo Brusa and Robertino Ghiringhelli, 2 vols. (Varese: Lativa, 1995), 1:305–16; Franco Della Peruta, "Luigi Tinelli e la Giovine Italia: 1831–1833," *I Tinelli*, 49–66; Erik Amfitheatrof, *Sinatra, Scorsese, Di Maggio e tutti gli altri* (Vicenza: Neri Pozza, 2004), 97–98. For the revolutionary and independence

14     Italian Americans for Ulysses S. Grant

movements in the Kingdom of Sardinia and Lombardy, see Giorgio Candeloro, *Storia dell'Italia moderna*, 11 vols. (Milan: Feltrinelli, 1956–1986), 2:98–119; Franco Della Peruta, *Mazzini e i rivoluzionari italiani: Il partito d'azione* (Milan: Feltrinelli, 1974).

11. Marco Sioli, "Se non c'è il conquibus si muore come cani: Luigi Tinelli a New York (1851–1873)," *Gli Stati Uniti e l'Unità d'Italia*, ed. Daniele Fiorentino and Matteo Sanfilippo (Rome: Gangemi, 2004), 141–50.

12. "Italians for Grant," *New York Times* 20 Sept. 1872, 1 (which misspells Tinelli as "Zinelli").

13. Bruce Catton, *U.S. Grant and the American Military Tradition* (Boston: Little, Brown, 1954), 171–72; Josiah Bunting, III, *Ulysses S. Grant* (New York: Times Books, 2004), 122–26.

14. "Cose locali italiane," *L'Eco d'Italia* 21 Sept. 1872, 1. For the U.S.-British controversy, see Alexander DeConde, *A History of American Foreign Policy* (New York: Charles Scribner's Sons, 1963), 257–59, 277–79, 282–83; Pia Grazia Celozzi Baldelli, *Power Politics, Diplomacy, and the Avoidance of Hostilities Between England and the United States in the Wake of the Civil War* (Lewiston, New York: Edwin Mellen, 1998). For Greeley's campaign, see Henry Luther Stoddard, *Horace Greeley: Printer, Editor, Crusader* (New York: Putnam's Sons, 1946), 308–16; William Harlan Hale, *Horace Greeley: Voice of the People* (New York: Harper, 1950), 333–47.

15. "Cronaca locale," *L'Eco d'Italia* 28 Sept. 1872, 1.

16. "Cose locali italiane," *L'Eco d'Italia* 5 Oct. 1872, 1.

17. Horace Greeley, *Glances at Europe: In a Series of Letters from Great Britain, France, Switzerland, etc., during the Summer of 1851: Including Notices of the Great Exhibition, or World's Fair* (New York: Dewitt & Davenport, 1851), 174–247. For Greeley's journey, see also Stoddard, 145–48; Hale, 144–46.

18. Indeed, occasional criticism of Italy can be found even in the works of such writers who overall admired this country as James Fenimore Cooper. According to this latter, for instance, Piacenza was "gloomy, crowded, and dull," the towers of Bologna looked like "the chimneys of a paint manufactory," and Italy welcomed the presence of bandits and robbers [James Fenimore Cooper, *Excursions in Italy*, 2 vols. (London: Bentley, 1938), 1:8, 18; 2:309]. See also Algerina Neri, "James Fenimore Cooper's Gleanings of Italy," *Rivista di Studi Anglo-Americani* 3.4–5 (1984–1985): 103–13.

19. Howard R. Marraro, *American Opinion on the Unification of Italy, 1846–1861* (New York: AMS, 1969), 187.

20. Margaret Fuller, *"These Sad but Glorious Days": Dispatches from Rome, 1846–1850*, ed., Larry J. Reynolds and Susan Belasco Smith (New Haven: Yale University Press, 1991); Francesca Bisutti, "The Sad Nymph of Margaret Fuller: A Description for a Besieged City," *Rivista di Studi Anglo-Americani* 3.4–5 (1984–1985): 557–64; Eve Kornfeld, *Margaret Fuller* (Boston: Bedford, 1997), 59–65; Cristina Giorcelli, "La Repubblica romana di Margaret Fuller: Tra visione politica e impegno civile," *Gli americani e la repubblica romana del 1849*, ed., Sara Antonelli, Daniele Fiorentino, and Giuseppe Monsgrati (Rome: Gangemi, 2000), 53–88; Sara Antonelli, "'È questo che fa la mia America': Il giornalismo di Margaret Fuller," ibid., 131–58; Giuseppe Monsgrati, "Gli intellettuali americani e il processo di unificazione italiana," *Gli Stati Uniti e l'Unità d'Italia*, 30. An Italian translation of Margaret Fuller's dispatches is available as Margaret Fuller, *Un'americana a Roma*, ed. Rossella Mamoli Zorzi (Pordenone: Edizioni Studio Tesi, 1986).

21. Giovanni Francesco Secchi de Casali, "Trent'otto anni d'America: XLI," *L'Eco d'Italia* 17–18 June 1883, 1; Marraro, "Italians in New York," 297–98; Giorgio Spini, "Le relazioni politiche fra l'Italia e gli Stati Uniti durante il Risorgimento e la Guerra Civile," *Italia e Stati Uniti nell'età del Risorgimento e della Guerra Civile*, ed. Giorgio Spini (Florence: La Nuova Italia, 1969), 148; Pietro Russo, "La stampa periodica italo-americana," Rudolph

J. Vecoli et al., *Gli italiani negli Stati Uniti: L'emigrazione e l'opera degli italiani negli Stati Uniti d'America* (Florence: Istituto di Studi Americani, 1972), 495–96; Bénédicte Deschamps, "De la presse 'coloniale' à la presse italo-américaine: Le parcours de six périodiques italiens aux Etats-Unis," diss., University Paris VII–Denis Diderot, 1996, 62–64; Durante, 426–27; Alduino and Coles, 47–48; Martino Marazzi, *Voices of Italian America: A History of the Early Italian American Literature with a Critical Anthology* (Madison, New Jersey: Fairleigh Dickinson University Press, 2004), 255–56.

22. "Lettere di Orazio Greeley sull'Italia e sugli Italiani," *L'Eco d'Italia* 7 Sept. 1872, 1; "Greeley, l'Italia e gli Italiani," ibid., 14 Sept. 1872, 1; "Greeley, l'Italia e gli Italiani," ibid., 18 Sept. 1872, 1; "Greeley, l'Italia e gli Italiani," ibid., 21 Sept. 1872, 1; "Greeley, l'Italia e gli Italiani," ibid., 25 Sept. 1872, 1; "Greeley, l'Italia e gli Italiani," ibid., 28 Sept. 1872, 1.

23. Salvatore J. LaGumina, "Introduction," *Wop! A Documentary History of Anti-Italian Discrimination in the United States*, ed. Salvatore J. LaGumina (San Francisco: Straight Arrow, 1973), 13. For anti-Italian prejudice in the United States in general, see also Bénédicte Deschamps, "Le racisme anti-italien aux Etats-Unis (1880–1940)," *Exclure au nom de la race (Etats-Unis, Irlande, Grande-Bretagne)*, ed. Michel Prum (Paris: Syllepse, 2000), 59–81.

24. Orazio de Attellis, "The *Ledger* and the Italians," 1843, Italian translation in Durante, 264–68. For De Attellis, see Luciano G. Rusich, *Un carbonaro molisano nei due mondi* (Naples: Glaux, 1982); Bénédicte Deschamps, "Press," *Encyclopedia of American Immigration*, ed., James Ciment (Armonk, New York: M.E. Sharpe, 2001), 831; Cinzia Cassani, "De Attellis, Orazio," *Dizionario biografico degli italiani*, ed. Massimiliano Pavan, 62 vols. (Rome: Istituto dell'Enciclopedia Italiana, 1960–2004), 33:329–332.

25. "Luigi Tinelli," *L'Eco d'Italia* 31 May 1873, 1; Castelli, 167–68.

26. Marraro, *American Opinion,* 162.

27. "Grant, l'Italia e gli Italiani," *L'Eco d'Italia* 16 Oct. 1872, 1. For the role of Italian diplomats in the settlement of the U.S.-British controversy, see Pia Grazia Celozzi Baldelli, "La diplomazia italiana e gli 'Alabama Claims,'" *Italia e America dal Settecento all'età dell'imperialismo*, ed.,Giorgio Spini et al. (Venice: Marsilio, 1976), 251–78.

28. "Rivista elettorale," *L'Eco d'Italia* 24 Aug. 1872, 1.

29. Peter D'Agostino, *Rome in America: Transnational Catholic Ideology from the Risorgimento to Fascism* (Chapel Hill: University of North Carolina Press, 2004), 46–50.

30. "Repubblicani e democratici," *L'Eco d'Italia* 11 Sept. 1872, 1. For Kernan, see "Kernan Francis," *Biographical Directory of the American Congress, 1774–1961* (Washington, D.C.: U.S. Government Printing Office, 1961), 1158.

31. Gian Domenico Rosatone, *Fraternità italo-americana* (Bologna: Patron, 1960), 163.

32. Matteo Sanfilippo, *L'affermazione del cattolicesimo nel Nord America: Elite, emigranti e Chiesa cattolica negli Stati Uniti e in Canada, 1750–1920* (Viterbo: Sette Città, 2003), 164.

33. "Progresso morale degli Italiani negli Stati Uniti," *L'Eco d'Italia* 26 Oct. 1872, 1.

34. Phylis Cancilla Martinelli, "Italian American Experience," *America's Ethnic Politics*, ed. Joseph S. Roucek and Bernard Eisenberg (Westport: Greenwood, 1982), 219–20.

35. Patrick J. Blessing, "Irish," *Harvard Encyclopedia of American Ethnic Groups*, ed., Stephan Thernstrom (Cambridge: Belknap Press of Harvard University Press, 1980), 535.

36. Salvatore J. LaGumina, "Francis Barretto Spinola, Nineteenth Century Patriot and Politician," *The Italian Americans Through the Generations*, 22–34.

37. H. Paul Jeffers, *The Napoleon of New York: Mayor Fiorello La Guardia* (New York: John Wiley & Sons, 2002), 43–44.

38. "The Political Field: Local Notes," *New York Times* 10 Oct. 1872, 5; "Club Centrale delle Nazionalità Unite per Grant e Wilson," *L'Eco d'Italia* 12 Oct. 1872, 1; "Mass Meeting

16     Italian Americans for Ulysses S. Grant

al Cooper Institute," ibid., 2 Nov. 1872, 1–2.

39. "The Grant and Wilson Club of United Nationalities–Grand Demonstration Last Night," *New York Times* 16 Oct. 1872, 1; "The Grand Mass-Meeting," ibid., 26 Oct. 1872, 3.

40. "New York and Suburban News," *New York Times* 15 Dec. 1872, 8.

41. For Greeley, see Erik S. Lunde, *Horace Greeley* (Boston: Twayne, 1981). For his initial relations with the Republican Party, see Jeter Allen Isely, *Horace Greeley and the Republican Party, 1853–1861: A Study of the New York Tribune* (Princeton: Princeton University Press, 1947).

42. David Herbert Donald, "The Republican Party, 1864–1876," *History of U.S. Political Parties*, ed. Arthur M. Schlesinger, Jr., 4 vols. (New York: Chelsea, 1973), 2:1282–83.

43. Gillette, 1317.

44. "Dix, John Adams," *Biographical Directory of the Governors of the United States*, ed., Robert Sobet and John Raimo, 4 vols. (Westport: Meckler, 1978), 3:1086–87.

45. "Repubblicani e democratici," *L'Eco d'Italia* 11 Sept. 1872, 1.

46. "Rivista americana," *L'Eco d'Italia* 21 Apr. 1972, 1.

47. Giampiero Carocci, *Destra e sinistra nella storia d'Italia* (Rome and Bari: Laterza, 2002), 3.

48. Giuseppe Sormani, *Eco d'America* (Milan: Tipografia degli Operai, 1888), 22.

49. Ernesto Gerbi and Aluisius, *L'eterna lotta* (Milan: Nuova Editrice Internazionale, 1962), 19–50; Bénédicte Deschamps, "Echi d'Italia: La stampa dell'emigrazione," *Storia dell'emigrazione italiana: Arrivi*, 322–24.

50. "Rivista elettorale," *L'Eco d'Italia* 25 Sept. 1872, 1; "Cose italiane in America," ibid., 30 Oct. 1872, 1.

51. "I cittadini italiani e le elezioni," *L'Eco d'Italia* 9 Nov. 1872, 1.

52. "The Italian Vote," *New York Times* 6 Nov. 1872, 2.

53. Samuel L. Baily, *Immigrants in the Lands of Promise: Italians in Buenos Aires and New York City, 1870–1914* (Ithaca: Cornell University Press, 1999), 209.

54. Stefano Luconi, "Recent Trends in the Study of the Political Experience of Italian Americans in the Interwar Years: From Leadership-Oriented Research to the Analysis of Voting Behavior," *Italian American Review* 5.1 (1996): 44–59.

55. Matteo Sanfilippo, "Mobilità, inurbamento e politicizzazione degli immigrati italiani in Nord America," Ecole Française de Rome, *La politisation des campagnes au XIX siècle: France, Italie, Espagne, Portugal* (Rome: Ecole Française de Rome, 2000), 190.

56. Salvatore J. LaGumina, "American Political Process and Italian Participation in New York State," *Perspectives in Italian Immigration and Ethnicity*, ed. Silvano M. Tomasi (New York: Center for Migration Studies, 1977), 89.

57. Alberto Pecorini, "Italian Progress in the United States," *A Documentary History of the Italian Americans*, ed. Wayne Moquin and Charles Van Doren (New York: Praeger, 1974), 94.

58. Maria Serena Piretti, "Tra elezioni ed elettori: Se votassero i non aventi diritto," *Contemporanea* 7.3 (2004): 437.

59. Francis X. Femminella, ed., *Italians and Irish in America* (Staten Island: American Italian Historical Association, 1985).

# THE CASE FOR THE ETHNIC IDENTITY OF WILLIAM PACA: SIGNER OF THE DECLARATION OF INDEPENDENCE

LUCIANO J. IORIZZO
PROFESSOR OF HISTORY, EMERITUS
SUNY OSWEGO, NEW YORK

William Paca was born in 1740 on his father's plantation in Baltimore County, the third child and second son of John Paca and Elizabeth Smith. They were native Marylanders of English descent. William had an older brother and subsequently five sisters. Paca had a distinguished political career. He served in the Annapolis Common Council, both the Maryland House of Delegates and Senate. This Italian American was a delegate to the Continental Congress, a signer of the Declaration of Independence, and a judge for Court of Appeals for Admiralty and Prize cases. Pace was also elected Governor of Maryland from 1782 to 1785, a member of the Board of Visitors and Governors of Washington College in Chestertown, Maryland and later became a federal judge.

Many of Paca's ideas found their way into the Bill of Rights. That Paca played no small role in helping America achieve its independence is confirmed by the fact that President George Washington appointed him to the federal judiciary despite his anti-Federalist views.[1]

Paca married heiress Mary Chew in 1763. He immediately built an elegant Georgian mansion in Annapolis which he sold in 1780 and moved to Wye Island on Maryland's Eastern Shore where he built an even grander house in the 1790s. They had three children only one of whom survived to adulthood, John Philomen. Mary died in 1774. Before marrying Anne Harrison in 1777, daughter of a merchant and former mayor of Philadelphia, Paca had fathered two children by different women. Anne Paca died in

1780 and their son, Henry, the following year. William Paca died at Wye Hall, his plantation on Wye Island, on October 13, 1799 and is thought to have been buried on the grounds.[2]

Thus, we know much about William Paca, but, ethnically speaking, who was he? We know his forebears came from England. Indeed, as Robert Foerster, the Harvard economist, has shown, Italian migration to England had taken place as early as the Middle Ages, and during the thirteenth and fourteenth centuries, northern Italians comprised the bulk of the movement. After the discovery of America some say that Italian migrants continued on to the New World after having taken residence in England. Would that make them be identified as Italians in America? Probably. It is my experience that Italians who first migrated to Argentina and later came to the United States are not identified as Argentinians. They are called Italian Americans. How strong is the case that Paca who came from England has Italian roots? Let's look at the evidence.[3]

There are two schools of thought on the subject. One holds that Paca is completely English. The other claims the family originated in Italy in the vicinity of Benevento in the Campagna area. This author wrote to Gregory A. Stiverson, co-author with Phebe R. Jacobsen, of *William A. Paca: A Biography* (published by the Maryland Historical Society, 1976) asking him if there was a definitive answer to the identity of Paca's origins.[4] He answered on October 22, 2004 that there was no proof one way or the other. He went on to make the case, however, for Paca's English origins. Essentially, Stiverson's case is as follows: The first Paca in Maryland was Robert (alternate spellings included Peaker, Parker, and Packer) who came as an indentured servant in 1660. He could have had Italian origins, but the name Paca probably derived from a clerical error or a clerk writing down what he heard. In certain areas of England the terminal "R" was dropped in speech much like New Englanders do today. Packer or Parker thus became Paca. (Is it not possible that if a clerk were to make a mistake in spelling, he would be more likely to produce a word whose sound is more familiar to him than that of a foreign sound? For example, would someone from England hear Packah, or some such alternative?) Stiverson stated that he knows of no shred of evidence to "prove" the argument one way or the other. Nor should we be surprised at that since indentured servants were usually lower-class and left few records by which researchers could trace their lineage. He concluded that "alleging an Italian descent for his great-grandson, William Paca, is simply wishful thinking." [5]

Stiverson's conclusion was in keeping with his letter to Louis A. Lepis of Long Branch, New Jersey on October 31, 1975 in which Stiverson stressed that "In all probablility, the Pacas were an ancient English family . . . Absolutely no conclusive evidence has been found linking William Paca with an Italian ancestry, and in fact, it seems that this myth developed in the early twentieth century." Stiverson concluded that "anything stronger than stating that it has been alleged that William Paca is of Italian descent would be taking liberties with the facts." Stiverson promised additional vigorous research in England on the subject. Given his communication with this author in October 2004 one can assume that his additional research uncovered nothing to change his earlier assessment. [6]

It was Giovanni Schiavo who has made the strongest case for the Paca family originating in Italy. He was a pioneer in Italian American history, a prolific writer who doggedly traced the ancestry of hundreds of people. Despite his lack of formal academic preparation, he has been an inspiration to many modern day scholars of the Italian migration. Essentially, utilizing newspaper articles, interviews with Paca's family members, and other sources, he claims that the Pacas were Italian and of the "same ancestral blood of Pope Leo XIII." Specifically, Robert Paca was the first of the family to settle in Maryland coming by way of England in 1657. In 1663, he was granted lands in Anne Arundel County. (He also was credited with receiving land grants as early as 1651 for transporting nine men into Maryland and increasing his holdings in subsequent years.) He married well and had one son, Aquila, by that marriage. His will in 1681 was signed Robert "Peaker" though earlier public records identified him as Paca. [7]

Schiavo claimed that W.S. Paca of Chestertown, Maryland told him in 1938 that he was a direct descendant of William Paca whose forebears came from Italy. Indeed, the same William S. Paca had one year earlier written a letter to the editor of the *New York Times* stating that his great-great-grandfather William Paca was of Italian origin. He added also that the name "is said to have originally been spelled Pacci." Other family members vouched for their connection to Pope Leo XIII. They lamented the fact that fire destroyed the original mansion built by William Paca and the many valuable family records in it. Likewise, Schiavo was unable to uncover a letter which Paca supposedly wrote after one of his business trips to Italy and England, in which he described Italy as "his land of origin."[8]

Paca and its variations, Pacca, Pecci, Pacci, etc. is not a rare name in Italy. In fact, "there is a noble family named Pacca." Originally from Amalfi, the Pacca family in recent times resided in Benevento and Naples. "Its most famous member was Cardinal Bartolomeo Pacca . . . the faithful companion of Pope Pius VII when he was a prisoner of Napoleon." The family's allies included the Aquila family.[9]

On a web site devoted to William Paca's Italian genealogy, some contributors strongly argue for Paca's Italian roots. One chatter questions why an Englishman would name his son Aquila. He also wonders why an Englishman name "Peaker" would change his name to Paca, clearly an Italian name. Citing Vatican archives the same writer claims that Paca is relatively popular in Italy and Peaker is "almost unheard of" in England. Another contributor wrote that her family name is Peca (with the accent over the e) and "it has been well-known in our family that William Paca is a relative." She cited her grandfather who traveled to Italy and often told the family of the links to William Paca. She believed that he even put it in writing, but is unable to find the document. Since the grandfather died in 1976 she is unable to certify when or where the name change took place. She was certain, however, that the Peca family is from Chieti in Abruzzi.[10]

What is one to make of all this? Certainly, there are some obvious contradictions. Stiverson claims that Paca was probably an ancient English family. Others say it was strictly an Italian name. Stiverson identifies Robert Paca as an indentured servant who came to Maryland in 1660, but he is not altogether convincing in explaining the name change from whatever to Paca. And if the name was originally not Packer or Parker, but Peaker, the case can be made that the last name is almost unheard of in England. Schiavo claims that Robert Paca came to Maryland in 1657 (three years earlier than Stiverson's date) and was responsible for bringing men to America for which he received land grants. Such actions could hardly be undertaken by an indentured servant. Could it be possible that Schiavo and Stiverson were identifying different people?

Schiavo recommends searching in the Pacca family archives for definitive information that would resolve the issue of his ethnicity. This writer took a step in this direction and contacted Giovanni Iorizzo, a retired engineer living in Benevento and Naples. Giovanni believed, for a time, that he found the solution to the problem. He sent a document from Italy identifying William Paca as an Italian. The article came from one, Generoso D'Agnese, a journalist. This writer looked eagerly for the footnotes documenting the find. There were none. A short email to D'Agnese brought an immediate reply: his source was none other than Giovanni Schiavo. We had come full circle.[11]

The Iorizzos, Giovanni and Luciano, are not yet finished. Giovanni has spoken with numerous people who may be knowledgeable on the subject. Until now, he has not been able to find anything concrete. He is hampered by the destruction of official documents due to fires and earthquakes, but has promised to check into official municipal and church records when he has the time. Should he find any information, one way or the other, he will send it to the writer who will share it with interested parties through the *American Italian Historical Association's Newsletter.*

A final word. Apparently, William S. Paca's admission of having Italian origins has not been taken seriously by researchers other than Schiavo. What would motivate anyone, who was clearly thought to be a White Anglo Saxon Protestant in America in 1937, to own up to an Italian heritage if he did not believe it for certain to be true? What would that person have to gain? Should we not place more weight on that fact than we do on the "arguments" for or against Paca's ethnic background? One waits to see if the contents of William S. Paca's letter to the editor is confirmed or rejected by those willing to do the searching in Italy's family records and/or its municipal and church archival material.

## NOTES

1. Maryland State Archives, Annapolis, Maryland. (Biographical Series) and its link to New Dictionary of National Biography entry, 24 February 2006. See www.mdarchives. state.md.us.

2. Maryland State Archives, Ibid.

3. Robert F. Foerster, *The Italian Emigration of Our Times* (Cambridge: Harvard University Press, 1919), passim.

4. Pheobe R. Jacobsen and Gregory Stiverson, *William Paca: A Biography* (Baltimore: Maryland Historical Society, 1975), passim.

5. Gregory Stiverson to Luciano J. Iorizzo, email dated 22 October 2004.

6. Gregory A. Stiverson to Louis A. Lepis, 31 October, 1975.

7. Giovanni Schiavo, *Italian American History,* Vol. 1 (New York: Vigo Press, 1947), 481–483.

8. For William Paca's letter to the editor, see *New York Times,* 18 July 1937, for Schiavo's letter to the editor see *New York Times,* 11 July 1937.

9. Schiavo, *Italian American History,* ibid. 481–482.

10. Giovanni Iorizzo to Luciano Iorizzo, email 27 September 2004.

11. Generoso D'Agnese to Luciano Iorizzo, email 5 October 2004 and Giovanni Schiavo, *The Italian in America before the Revolution* (New York: Vigo Press, 1976), 72–73.

Columbus day will go the way of the dinosaur.

— ROBERT VISCUSI, *Oration Upon the Most Recent Death of Christopher Columbus*

## WHY COLUMBUS MATTERS:
## THE EVOLUTION OF AN ICON IN LITERATURE AND HISTORY

### FRED MISURELLA
### EAST STROUDSBURG UNIVERSITY

First-rate navigator and sailor of his time, first publicized immigrant in the New World, and first European in the Americas, Christopher Columbus lived the opportunities, disappointments, triumphs, and defeats we traditionally associate with exile and immigration. As the statue of "The Admiral" in the middle of Columbus Circle in New York vividly demonstrates, his complex character and significance stand in the center of a whirl of new and old forces that represent culture, economics, travel, progress, and tradition and that make a clear understanding of his personality and meaning as difficult as crossing the two or three lanes of New York traffic between the sidewalk and the pedestal of the statue itself.

Through the centuries, Columbus' achievements have reflected shifting and contradictory views of immigrants in American life, especially Italian immigrants who, despite the controversies over Columbus' nationality and place of birth, identify with him because of his links to Genoa. In many ways, he is the first Italian American among us. But as the "Discovery Channel" recently warned, Columbus may not have been exactly all he seemed: was he Spanish, Jewish, and/or Genovese? Historically, it doesn't matter. But the confusion of Columbus' character and accomplishments reminds us of another icon, William Shakespeare (born in England and living a little more than one hundred years after Columbus) whom some people never want to accept as the creator of those great plays, primarily because he was a poorly educated commoner, like Columbus. Such controversy makes good television and meaningless history, but it demonstrates the intrigue that figures with great accomplishments can command. When we try to understand them and the truths of their life experiences, we are seeking in an imaginative way to understand humanity—its limits and motivations—as well as make sense of our individual selves. If Shakespeare represents the side of humanity that can say "All the world's a stage" because its players love words and music, then Columbus recalls the physical, empirical side of humanity that, artifice aside, dances rather than sings, and roams the world to observe the action behind the curtain. Rewards, fame, and blessings are good, possible outcomes; but the real purpose for such people lies in testing imaginative truth through tactile experience. Since our beginnings, explorers have played a central role in mythology and art; and if they sail the sea, passing beyond the limits of human community, their characters possess automatic complexity and resonance.

In Canto XXVI of *The Inferno,* Dante places Ulysses among the false counselors because he sinned in urging his followers to disregard God's ordained limits on man's experience. As a result, Ulysses' ship sails beyond the known boundaries of Dante's imagined world (virtually the same passage Columbus would follow two hundred years later); and at the sight of the forbidden Mount Purgatory that Dante and medieval tradition placed beyond the Azores, Ulysses and his crew fall victim to the vagaries of God's weather and sink to the bottom of the sea.

Known during the 2000 years from Homer to Dante as a supreme strategist and classical hero touched by the human flaw of hubris, Ulysses represents many of the same qualities we have seen portrayed in the figure of Columbus in historical essays, poems, and biographies that reflect the social thought of our world during the past five centuries. In New York, at Columbus Circle, his statue possesses a proud, human dignity. Standing on a tall, seventy-foot high white pedestal shot through with models of the three original ships he commanded (the *Pinta,* the *Nina,* and the *Santa Maria*) and looking not much larger than the average New York pedestrian, Columbus leans on a tiller and negotiates his way through twenty-first century traffic. Taxis, buses, and cars speeding by him from four directions amid a cacophony of horn toots and screeching tires, he faces south on Broadway, looking calm and visionary, resolutely guarding some larger, private goal as he works his way down the wide avenue toward New York Harbor.

In the two centuries between Dante and Columbus, another important historical event occurred to make Columbus, hubris and all, the icon he has become at Columbus Circle. In 1456, Johannes Gutenberg used moveable type to print the Holy Bible, and the new technology quickly changed the world, speedily disseminating print, encouraging literacy, and democratizing information, publicity, and news as well as religion. As James Burke says in *Connections:* "The speed with which printing presses and their operators fanned out across Europe is extraordinary. From the single Mainz press of 1457, it took only twenty-three years to establish presses in 110 towns: fifty in Italy, thirty in Germany, nine in France, eight in Spain, eight in Holland, four in England, and so on."[1]

Throughout Europe, when Columbus returned from the West with news and proof of his discoveries, owners and operators of the new technology spread the word eagerly, as Mitchell Stephens says in *A History of News: From Drum to Satellite.* "Thus the letter press Gutenberg had developed—the invention of the century—was able to circulate a firsthand account of Columbus's voyage—the story of the century—to a significant portion of literate Europe within months of his return."[2]

Dante's *Commedia* circulated in hand-printed format, but Columbus' account of his own journey through hell, purgatory, and paradise benefited from a much wider, faster distribution that reached an economically diverse, literate audience. Columbus' letter concerning his first voyage, delivered upon his return to Europe in mid-February 1493, was printed in Spain that April then translated into Latin and printed in Rome as an eight-page pamphlet the following month. By the standards of the day, the historian Daniel Boorstin tells us, it became a best seller. Three more editions followed that year in Rome; six others appeared in Paris and the rest of Europe. And Pope Alexander VI quoted the letter in his papal bull concerning the new lands. The news had clearly arrived.

Such speed and diversity, as well as Columbus' own entrepreneurial skill in promoting himself and his work, initiated the myth of the Great Admiral and Navigator. At this key historical point in Europe, humanity seemed on the march and Columbus led the column. But a negative side to his story also spread quickly: The *Indies,* as they had been named, offered less of an economic boon than the Spanish royalty (and Columbus) had sought. Because the new land lacked exotic trading opportunities in spices and gold, accusations against Columbus and his voyages spread. Mapmakers, taking advantage of the new technology, printed updated maps of the world, but named the new lands after Amerigo Vespucci, a Florentine who arrived late. His account of his voyages, *Mondus Novus,* published in 1502, while Columbus sailed on his fourth and final voyage to the West, received more than three times the published reaction to Columbus' original letter.

In the United States, however, during the eighteenth and nineteenth centuries, Columbus' voyages retained their prominence, becoming synonymous with the hemisphere's and the country's development of social and economic forces. "[T]he name of a thief," thundered Ralph Waldo Emerson, referring to Amerigo Vespucci as a "pickle-dealer," who "in this lying world . . . managed to supplant Columbus and baptize half the earth with his own dishonest name."[3]

Exaggerated though that statement may be, it expresses Emerson's and his audience's affection for Columbus. What's more, other writers and composers of the time agreed. James Russell Lowell and Joaquin Miller wrote famous romantic poems about him, Wagner composed a Columbus overture, and Paul Claudel and Darius Milhaud wrote an *oratorio.* Walt Whitman, seeking to write America's epic in *Leaves of Grass,* echoed Emerson's idea. in "Passage to India," one of Whitman's most important poems. Columbus is portrayed as an instrument of human destiny:

> *Lo, soul, seest thou not God's purpose from the first?*
> *The earth to be spann'd, connected by a network,*

*The races, neighbors, to marry and be given in marriage,*
*The Oceans to be cross'd, the distant brought near,*
*The lands to be welded together.*[4]

Published in 1871, the poem expresses a contemporary American optimism and the country's growing affection for Columbus. For Whitman and many Americans of that day—with the Union secure, its economy on track, and the Industrial Revolution transforming the way people lived—Columbus' voyages initiated unstoppable human progress toward democracy and equality that would transcend political, social, and national boundaries. It was a historical moment when the values of Italian Renaissance humanism, boasting "man as the measure of all things"—individually and collectively—seemed in the process of fulfilling itself, with the American continent geographically and metaphorically its center. Whitman called America "The road between Europe and Asia," and in "Passage to India" he followed that description with an incantation to Columbus:

*(Ah Genoese thy dream! Thy dream!*
*Centuries after thou art laid in thy grave,*
*The shore thou foundest verifies thy dream.)*[5]

From then until 1892, when Italian Americans, together with Italian immigrants in Canada and Mexico, contributed funds to raise Gaetano Russo's statue of "The Admiral" before 10,000 people at a dedication ceremony in New York, Columbus represented new, positive qualities of the human spirit: rational, scientific intelligence, familiarity with technology, and a willingness to test intellectual constructs in real experience. At the same time, this spirit possessed faith in a Divine Creator and belief that in His eyes human individuals were good and, of course, "created equal." This grand, optimistic view regarded all human achievement as fresh, forward-looking, and inevitable, with America being the latest and most progressive example.

But this view of Columbus was short-lived, colliding with artistic modernism and the horrors of twentieth-century experience: two world wars, the Great Depression, the Holocaust, the Cold

War, nuclear fission, the ensuing arms race, and the evolving Civil Rights movement which recalled the hypocrisy of slavery in the land of freedom. Culminating in Vietnam and the consequent social upheavals of the 1960s, the uncomplicated, naive optimism that Whitman and his generation expressed collided with serious twentieth-century doubt. By 1968, when President Lyndon Johnson first proclaimed Columbus Day a national holiday, *colonialism* had replaced humanism as a political buzzword, with both the Soviet Union and the United States its most imperialistic representatives. As a result, the historic expansion of Europe into the New World, with Columbus as its icon, seemed less a symptom of the human march toward democracy and more an example of man's inhumanity to man. As the New York City Central Park web page on Columbus Circle tells us:

> It is here, however, that the facts of history collide with the nobility of the gesture that placed [Columbus] here in such a prominent place before the world . . . One can only speculate at this point in time if the explorer's courage in pursuing his vision, in challenging the terrifying unknown, in opening the Atlantic to future exploration alone justifies the tribute or whether there are other considerations, which make it problematic . . . Desperate to make good on his vow of riches he enslaved the population of his conquered territory and forced men, women and children to search for the precious metal. When the natives would or could not comply with his demands he tortured, mutilated and murdered them in such large numbers that they eventually vanished from existence. Columbus now stands atop a monument on a 70–foot granite column with bronze reliefs at a place where many of the spiritual descendents of those he enslaved and slaughtered pass on a daily basis.[6]

Which is where we stand now, at the base of that column staring upward. The 1992 celebrations, less a bang and more a whimper, hardly compared to the accounts of national and international celebrations of Columbus' discovery in 1892. As long as we concentrate on the negative effects of Columbus's voyages, the poet, Robert Viscusi will certainly be right: "Columbus Day will go the way of the dinosaur."

In 1905, Colorado was the first state to commemorate October 12 as a holiday. For the past two years in Denver, Native Americans have loudly protested the Columbus Day march, investing Columbus, and by extension the Italian American immigrants who celebrate him, with all the evils their people have suffered during the country's development. According to the *Denver Post,* Columbus Day protesters have carried signs referring to Italian Americans as "Mafia Scum" and have distributed flyers addressing "our Italian friends and the Sopranos."[7]

Such attitudes oversimplify a complex historical development, as if we forgot that in printing the Bible, Guttenberg also made possible yellow journalism, public relations spin, untruthful advertising, propaganda, bad novels, awful news, and pornography. In fact, humans on all continents have sought profit from slavery, killed, maimed, tortured, and raped each other. It is terrible history, but humanity moves forward despite those developments. At some future time when we see that clearly again, I am sure that Western Humanism, its New World representative Columbus, and the Italian American community that regards him as their primary icon, will be elevated again and be seen in a clearer and more positive, yet cautionary, light.

## NOTES

1. James Burke, *Connections* (Boston: Little Brown, 1978), 105.

2. Mitchell Stephens. *A History of News: From Drum to Satellite* (Fort Worth, TX: Harcourt Brace College, 1997), 83.

3. Quoted in Daniel J. Boorstein, *The Discoverers* (New York: Vintage Books, 1985), 244–255.

4. Walt Whitman, *Leaves of Grass,* 1891–1892 edition, (New York: More Library Series, Random House, 1993), 322.

5. Whitman, 323.

6. *New York Focus,* 2002, "Christopher Columbus at Columbus Circle." 2000 Central Park, http://www.centralpark2000.com/databasecolumbus_at_cir.html.

7. David Harsanyi, "Columbus Critics Miss the Boat," *Denver Post.* 7 October 2004.

# THE ITALIAN ELEMENT IN THE NEW SMYRNA COLONY AND IN ST. AUGUSTINE, FLORIDA, 1768–1800

MICHAEL DI VIRGILIO
INDEPENDENT SCHOLAR

In 1763, the end of the Seven Years War (The French and Indian War in colonial America), Britain acquired Florida and offered large land grants to individuals in order to establish plantation-based economies. Many of these plantation owners relied largely on African slave labor. However, two of them, Deny Rolle and Dr. Andrew Turnbull, used whites, that is non-Africans, as labor. Rolle used British indentured servants; Turnbull, believing that Mediterraneans were better suited to the climate of Florida, recruited slaves from Greece, Italy, and Corsica.

A Scottish physician, Turnbull had served, according to some, as British Consul at Smyrna in Asia Minor, where he married Marie Gracia Dura Bin, daughter of a Greek merchant. Turnbull (with partners William Duncan and George Grenville) acquired 20,000 acres of land in East Florida, primarily for the production of indigo, considered "Blue Gold" by the English for its value as dye, and for cochineal, cotton, olives, silk, and wine. He called the area seventy miles south of St. Augustine, then known as Mosquito Inlet or *Los Mosquitos,* "New Smyrna." In Livorno [Leghorn], Turnbull initially recruited young, unemployed single males. From Livorno, on June 15, 1767, he wrote Lord Shelburne that the recruits were "from the South of France and from several parts of Italy." In a late 1780s rebuttal to a critical account of New Smyrna, Turnbull indicated his perception of the Italians:

> As to the Italians, who this false narrator also says were deluded from their plentiful cornfields and vineyeards, the truth is that the doctor engaged one

> hundred of them, all unmarried men, who he found
> strangers or rather vagabonds, in the streets of Leghorn
> and who the governor, the count Bourbon del Monte,
> intended to banish from that city, their idleness and
> wretchedness making them a nuisance . . . [I]nstead of
> being in plenty, they were most miserably poor, almost
> naked, and in very distressing circumstances.[1]

In July 1767, Turnbull sent the Italian recruits to Mahon, Minorca, for approximately eight months, while he recruited elsewhere. Britain had acquired Minorca, the second largest of the Balearic Islands, from Spain in 1763 as part of the Seven Years War peace settlement.[2] Turnbull then sailed to the Aegean. At Coron, he recruited about 200 Greeks from the mountains in the Mani in the Peloponnesos who were "in flight from Turkish authorities," and recruited individuals from Candia, Crete, Citera, Melos, Santorin, Malta, and Smyrna.[3] When Turnbull returned to Mahon, according to one source, "Crowds of starving people thronged the decks as soon as his three ships dropped anchor." The population of Minorca was in the midst of a three-year famine. Turnbull also found that during this time forty-seven of the Italian men married Minorcan women.[4] Some suggest that the families of the brides of the Italians lobbied for inclusion in the venture. Whatever the case, Turnbull recruited over 1,000 Minorcans, themselves a mix of Roman, Moorish, and most significantly, Catalan. In the Minorcan population were a few Greeks who had settled in Mahon in the 1740s and a few individuals from Majorca and Spain.[5] Turnbull included as members of his colony a Roman Catholic priest, Fr. Pedro Camps, and the Augustinian monk, Fr. Bartolomeo Casanovas, both native Minorcans. Although "the introduction of Catholics into the colony was a breach of English law," some suggest that authorities relaxed the law because Minorca was under British control.[6]

Within the ranks of the recruits were bakers, blacksmiths, carpenters, caulkers (for boats), farmers, fishermen, sailors, seamstresses, shoemakers, shopkeepers, stonemasons, and tailors.[7] Although some had negotiated written contracts with Turnbull, most had made oral agreements. All of the individuals "fell under the Indentured Servant Law to serve six to eight years and were then to be freed with compensation of money and a bit of land."[8] By some accounts, the colonists were supposed to receive fifty acres of land and an additional twenty-five acres for each child. Turnbull evidently offered skilled craftsmen shorter terms of service as well as more land and better rations.[9]

As Turnbull indicated, the group of 110 Italians included individuals from both the Livorno area and throughout the peninsula, the Dalmatian Islands, Corsica, southern France, Sicily, and Sardinia. More specifically, individuals came from Bagnasco and Chivasso, in the Piedmont region; either Borgo San Lorenzo or Borgo a Buggiano, Pisa and Pescia in Tuscany; Cagliari, Sardinia; Chiavari, Genoa; Gragnella della Garsona, Modena; Florence; Albissola, Liguria; Livorno; Lussinpiccolo, an island off the coast of Istria under Venetian control; Monte San Giuliano, and Trapani in Sicily; Naples; Venice; and Villafranca, Nice.[10]

Some fifty-five Corsican and Greco-Corsican recruits, who were, according to one source, "afraid of the imminent transfer of control of the island from the Genoese to the French," may have been recruited by Turnbull's agent Edward Pumell, who possibly sent them to Mahon via Livorno.[11] Although the island of Corsica was a possession of the Genovese Republic in early 1768, the majority of the Corsican recruits were actually Greek in origin. In 1676, over 700 Greeks who were fleeing from the Ottomans traveled to Genoa. The Genovese settled them in Corsica, particularly in the villages of Cargese, Paomia, Revinda, and Salongo. Attacks from native Corsicans forced many of these settlers to move to Ajaccio while some others went to Minorca and Sardinia. When the Genovese Republic ceded Corsica to France in 1768, many Greco-Corsicans fled to Minorca, Livorno, and Sardinia.[12] The Corsican colonists recruited by Turnbull included Greeks from Ajaccio and some from Bonifacio.[13] One Greco-Corsican couple, Miguel Juan Pedro "Domingo" Acosta (or Kyriakos Costas) and Maria Dolores Parta y Ambrose, whom some say were of Italian ancestry, were born, according to historian E.P. Panagopoulos, on the Aegean island of Santorini.[14] It is interesting to note that the Corsican colonists included two Medicis from a family that was descended from the Florentine Medici family and Pedro de Medici who moved to Athens in the 1380s. The family remained in Athens until 1456 then relocated to Mani after the Turks conquered the city. Many members of this Greek family returned to Tuscany in the early 1670s. The Corsican Medici's ancestor, Athanase Medici, left Vitylo, Laconia in 1676 with other Greeks and settled in Paomia.[15]

Once Turnbull had assembled his recruits in Mahon, Beeson indicates that Turnbull "set the new colonists to work preparing grape cuttings, olives, mulberries, various seeds, agricultural equipment, and silk worms for shipment."[16] On April 17, 1768, 1,403 individuals (200 Greeks, 110 Italians, 1,093 Minorcans and other Spaniards) on eight ships left Gibraltar for Florida. Four ships arrived on June 26, 1768. The "other four vessels had been carried off course by strong currents, but they eventually reached St. Augustine little by little, arriving one after the other, during the month July, 1768."[17] More than one thousand (1,255) survived the voyage, and 148 died from scurvy or other illnesses.[18] The arrival of so many colonists was not insignificant. Griffin estimates that Florida circa 1768 had roughly 1,000 Indians, 900 Blacks, and 300 Whites.

According to one account (disputed by Florida historian Patricia Griffin), the clearing and preparation of the colony was to be done by 500 African slaves imported by Turnbull, but they perished at sea.[19] When the colonists arrived their:

> first priority was to clear the land of pines, live oaks, cabbage palm, palmetto shrub, and drain the marsh. Conditions were wretched and never improved: [there was] unbearable heat and humidity; scant time to gather food; inadequate clothing; [and] palm-thatched huts for living quarters.[20]

Many colonists quickly succumbed to exhaustion, scurvy, gangrene, and malaria. Equally discouraging was the layout of the plantation. According to Griffin, Turnbull supervised the construction of "a central complex containing craft shops, three dormitories, for the young single men, warehouses, 'stores for provision,' an indigo house, and barracks for the military detachment" and erected the Church of San Pedro. Colonists' huts and plots were spaced one third of a mile apart along the eastern edge of the plantation.[21] The adjustment to working conditions was also difficult. As historian Carita Doggett Corse observed, "The lash and irons, so frequently used in England and the other colonies, Virginia, for example, were new to them, and their hatred of their oppressors grew daily. Indian depredations and trouble with food shipments completed their disgust."[22] Turnbull employed overseers, principally those of English origin who had supervised African slaves. Corse noted that "these English overseers came from plantations where [N]egroes had been used as laborers and—in addition to being unable to understand the language of their Minorcan, Italian and Greek charges—they made themselves unpopular by their arbitrary manner and impatience at what they claimed was the stupidity and laziness of some of the settlers." Turnbull also used African slaves as overseers and "early appointed several of the Italians as sub-overseers, sometimes called drivers or corporals."[23]

On August 19, 1768, approximately 300 colonists led by Italians, particularly the overseer Carlo Forni, rebelled with the intention of traveling to Havana.[24] A contemporary Dutch topographer Bernard Romans called Forni, "an Italian of very bad principles, who was accused of a rape on a very young girl, but of so much note, that he had formerly been admitted to the overseer's table."[25] A contemporary British account noted:

> Carlo Forni, one of the overseers at 11 o'clock in the forenoon, declared himself Captain General and commander-in-chief of the Greeks and Italians, seized a vessel which had been sent with provisions, made himself master of the storehouses and firearms, confined and wounded the doctor's principal manager, declared his intention of proceeding to Havana, and gave orders to put any of his people to death who should attempt to make their escape and desert the service. Rum was given in plenty . . . and the rioters who did not consist of above

twenty, soon increased to two or three hundred. The confusion was great, the store houses were plundered, casks of rum, wine, oyl [sic] which could not be put on board the vessel were staved and all of the rioters loaded themselves with the poor doctor's slops, which he had provided for their use. They even plundered the Mahonese who did not join them.[26]

Two Italians not sympathetic to the cause told Turnbull about the mutiny. Having seized a ship, the rebels sailed south, but "a British frigate captured the escapees and brought them to St. Augustine."[27] The authorities ordered the execution of two of the rebels, Forni and Giuseppe Massiadoli, the latter of the two having been responsible for the death of an overseer named Cutter. Elia Medici, who had stolen a cow, spared his life by agreeing to execute Forni and Massiadoli—which he reluctantly did.[28] The authorities pardoned others, particularly Giorgio Stephanopoly and Clatha Corona, and returned them to the colony. Thirty-five others escaped down the coast of Florida in an open boat, but a government ship captured them four months later in the Florida Keys and returned them.[29]

In the subsequent months and years, conditions hardly improved. Three hundred adults and children died of scurvy in the first five months. By the end of December 1768, nearly six hundred (598) colonists had died. In 1769, 152 adults and twenty-two children were dead.[30] Many of these deaths were a consequence of a shortage of provisions. In March 1769, Governor James Grant wrote to the Earl of Hillsborough, secretary of the colonies: "I have always recommended to him [Turnbull] to have Six Months provisions constantly in store. Mr. Turnbull, just as I expected, finds himself, this moment very much pinched for provisions as his Supplies have not arrived exactly to the time and he writes that he has only Indian Corn for a Month at the Mosquitoes."[31] Colonists warded off starvation by cultivating their own plots and by raising their own corn, cucumbers, greens, melons, peas, and potatoes. They also quickly adopted New World subsistence strategies, gathering wild plants and nuts; keeping honeybees for honey; and fishing, when possible, for the abundant sea life, such as shellfish, and tortoises, even though Turnbull discouraged fishing during important processing and harvest times and prohibited hunting. Working conditions were also harsh. Indigo processing was a difficult and harmful task. Harvest time, according to Griffin, was a relentless around-the-clock operation, and the processing took place from June to November (through the traditional Mediterranean holiday season).[32] In September 1770, Grant wrote to Hillsborough:

> They are destitute of every convenience, [and] they are ill clothed, many of them almost naked—and are obliged to live in small Huts put up in a hurry to shelter them from the Weather upon their first arrival. Dr. Turnbull has neither money nor credit to supply them with clothes and has not the necessary Tools and Materials to build Houses for them.[33]

In 1774, Turnbull expelled Father Casanovas, who had defended the colonists against Turnbull, for "alleged insubordination to colony officials."[34] Between 1773 and 1775, a drought affected indigo production. Colonists, who again faced starvation and death, felt the effects of the drought. In 1776, forty-five adults and eight children had died.[35] By 1777, "704 adults and 260 children had died in the New Smyrna Colony" since its inception in 1768.[36] According to Griffin, records indicate that "the principal causes given for deaths were scurvy, starvation, bad water, 'dropsy,' fevers, pleurisy, gangrene, and particularly, malaria."[37] Despite the incredible hardships, the colonists, under Turnbull's general direction, created a profitable venture by 1773. Using coquina (an aggregate of coral and shells), they developed a twenty-five mile-long canal system for irrigation and transport and constructed a stone wharf adjacent to the central complex.[38] Evidence shows that Turnbull also grew sugar cane and processed it at a sugar mill in the colony and produced cochineal, cotton, rice, and barilla. In addition, Turnbull produced lumber, tar, and turpentine.[39] Turnbull especially refined his indigo production and produced a superior product. Between 1771 and 1777, the colonists produced 43,283 pounds of indigo.

In 1776, the looming American Revolution created much uncertainty in Loyalist Florida.[40] In February of that year, Florida planters produced "The Humble Address of Inhabitants of East Florida," declaring loyalty to the King. Turnbull signed "for upwards of two hundred Families of Greeks and other Foreigners on the Smyrna Settlement."[41] When an American privateer appeared off of the coast of Florida, Andrew Turnbull (Turnbull's nephew was, at this time, in charge of New Smyrna) wrote, "I cannot say what might be the consequence regarding the white people, as there is a good number of them at present a little discontented, and I am fully persuaded would join the Rebels immediately on their landing at Smyrna."[42] British authorities also held this fear. By this time, it became increasingly clear to the colonists that Turnbull did not intend to honor his contracts. Settlers were further alarmed as Seminoles increasingly made raids on the colony.

In 1776 and 1777, the colonists secretly sent representatives to St. Augustine to appeal for help from Governor Patrick Tonyn, who, on May 5, 1777, allowed approximately 600 Minorcans to be moved from New Smyrna to St. Augustine. One source noted that this figure included "50 Italians, Corsicans, and Greeks" whereas Griffin estimates that there were twenty-two Italian and eleven Greco-Corsican survivors of the colony.[43]

The Spanish founded St. Augustine in 1565. It was, according to one view, "until 1763 . . . a lonely military outpost, dependent on Spain and wealthier New World colonies for support. The town basically consisted of a fort, church, seminary, hospital, fish market, and about 129 houses and shops." By the 1770s, St. Augustine had a population of roughly 3,000.[44]

After the arrival of the New Smyrna colonists in St. Augustine, there were, according to Corse, "ten deaths a week among these unfortunates," and "no provision whatever had been made for housing or feeding these people, and sixty-five of them died (without medical attendance being offered them) after sleeping under the trees and beside old walls in the heavy rains of August and September."[45] Father Camps, who had kept baptismal records from New Smyrna that became known as the 'Golden Book of the Minorcans,' arrived in St. Augustine in November 1777 and "the church of San Pedro was translated from the settlement of Mosquito to the city of St. Augustine."[46]

Between May 7 and 20, 1777, Governor Tonyn took depositions from seventeen colonists, ten of whom were Italian, Corsican, or Greco-Corsican. These depositions revealed that Turnbull and his overseers, especially Nichola Moveritte, were particularly cruel and ruled the plantation using intimidation, force, and even murder. Turnbull put both Antonio Stefanopoli (one of the rebels) and Giosefa Marcatto in leg irons, gave them both lashes, and gave them scarce provisions when imprisoned at night. Nicola Demalachis revealed that Moveritte forced Petros Demalachis who was ill to work without food to the point of death. Overseers beat Pompey Posi's cousin Anthony Blau to death and beat Luigi Capelli, a wheelwright, for making spokes that had warped. The deposition of Beppino Pozzo di Borgo indicated that his contract included good food and five pounds sterling annually, but he never received these. Luigi Socci observed that Turnbull denied Socci's discharge after his contract expired and produced a forged ten-year contract with Socci's name and the names of witnesses, Pietro Merlin and Gaspar Trotti, whom Turnbull had forced to participate.[47]

On September 3, 1783, Spain once again acquired Florida. British subjects evacuated the colony *en masse*. Some of the New Smyrna colonists had met with Governor Tonyn who reported that "The intentions of the Minorcans were my Lord to emigrate, they had carefully consulted me thereupon, and solicited to be sent to the Major part to Gibraltar, others to Dominica and the Bahamas, to the latter of which, a considerable number have gone a few to Dominica, and some to Europe."[48] Many, however, decided to remain in St. Augustine. In mid-July 1784, the Spanish Governor Vincente Manuel de Zespedes, who had arrived in Florida the previous month, received a memorial from twenty-nine Greeks and Italians expressing their pleasure with being under Spanish rule: "We humbly beg Your Excellency to represent us to His Majesty as desirous of being recognized as natural-born subjects, and we declare our readiness as such to sacrifice our lives in the royal service and to obey with especial pleasure and zeal your Excellency's orders."[49] Under Spanish rule, the Minorcans enjoyed relative calm and prosperity in St. Augustine. By the late 1780s, Father Thomas Hassett noted that there were 469 survivors of the New Smyrna colony (241 males and 228 females) and that this included ninety-seven married couples. Together, this group owned seventy slaves.[50]

The colonists moved into various occupations. From the Italians and Greco-Corsicans, Andrea Pacetti worked as a barber; and Pietro Cotsifakis, owned "a house, a store, four slaves, and a *goleta* under Spanish register." Rocco Leonardi—who became Don Roque Leonardi, a wine merchant in St. Augustine—owned two houses, five slaves, and cattle and received (in the 1790s) more than 2,000 acres from the Spanish. On this land, he "planted grapevines and became famous for his vines and his wines." Luigi Bucciantini farmed some land, owned a small wine shop, and was, as a mariner," master of the sails." Antonio Berta owned two houses and was a storekeeper; and Pasquale Santi was a sailor and a storekeeper. Giuseppe Pozzo di Borgo was a shopkeeper, co-owned a sloop, and, according to Griffin, "was prosperous enough to own two slaves, four horses, seven canoes, four cows, and twelve acres of land." Gioacchino Mazzocchi was a mariner and worked on the *San Pedro,* the schooner owned by Pietro Cotsifakis, and often captained by Domenico Martinoli. Other Italians and Greco-Corsicans worked as mariners including Angelino Bacceri; Giuseppe Bucciani, who owned "a house, a tienda and a barraca;" Giuseppe Cobacich; Miguel Costa, who was also a "medical doctor" briefly; Sebastiano Olivieri (now Oliveros) who had become "the commander of a vessel plying between St. Augustine and Baltimore" but was lost at sea in 1804; Nicola Salada; Luigi Socci; Francesco Staccioli; and Antonio Stefanopoli, who owned a schooner. Elia Medici was a shoemaker; Pietro Drimarachi and Nicolas Stefanopoli were carpenters. Others, like Antonio Alberti and Giuseppe Battelini, worked as laborers.[51]

Some farmed. One was Antonio Uberti. Andrea Pacetti owned the Nuevo Mosquitos plantation on Guano Creek in St. Johns County, but sold it in 1804. Gaetano Rossi "owned and worked six acres of land," and Giuseppe Bonelli owned a farm at Matanzas. A few went to Georgia, Louisiana, or South Carolina, primarily to farm. For example, Gaspar Joseph Trotti, was a resident in Orange County, South Carolina by 1800, and his two sons, Frances and Lawrence Trotti, were residents in Richmond County, Georgia by 1797.

Through the first decades of the nineteenth century, the surviving New Smyrna colonists and their descendants formed a cohesive community in St. Augustine. Culturally, the community was decidedly and outwardly Minorcan. In fact, they and others collectively knew them as Minorcans. An English visitor noted in 1819 that:

> Feast Days and festivals were scrupulously observed.
> . . . With Carnival time came mirth and merry making; harlequins, dominoes, and punchinellos held high revel and gay companies of maskers went about the streets. Among them, taking the part of St. Peter, went one clad in the ragged dress of a fisherman and equipped with a mullet cast net which he dexterously threw over the heads of the not unwilling children, by such rude travesty setting forth the Apostlic fishing for men."[52] In 1821, Florida became a territory of the United States and the Minorcans adapted and adjusted to yet another change. Within a period of fifty years, a few colonists had even experienced what Gold calls a "Triple-Nation Transfer."[53]

In conclusion, it is important to note that the Italians and Greco-Corsicans at New Smyrna were unique in several respects. These individuals, largely young males, were a cultural minority who had quickly intermarried with the Minorcans. In a secret letter (dated January 4, 1772) to the Bishop of Havana, Father Pedro Camps describes his parish, then notes that "not all are Minorcans, but almost all; we have some Italians, Leghorn; of Corsicans, there are fifty, and in all these cases they have Minorcan wives and families."[54] These intermarriages created a matrilineal transferal of Minorcan culture. Further, unlike the Minorcans, who shared the same village origins, the Italians and Greco-Corsicans were a conglomerate of individuals with disparate origins, customs, dialects, and occupations. Still, there is some evidence that there was a degree of ethnic unity among those of Italian origin and descent. Initially this unity was expressed in New Smyrna, first with the rebellion of 1768 and then with godparent relationships. In St. Augustine, this unity was manifested in intermarriages and business ventures through the late nineteenth century. One can surmise that vestiges of further cultural coherence and persistence of Italian identity with New Smyrna descendants remained in later decades. For instance, World War I Civilian Draft Registration records list Cosimo Raphael De Medici, as a resident of St. Augustine who worked as a field assistant for the United States Geological Survey in Aiken, South Carolina. De Medici's first name reflects, without a doubt, a clear sense of history on the part of his parents—the addition of the "de" to the surname appeared in the early 1800s—perhaps intended to honor Cosimo de Medici, III, who was instrumental in returning the Greek Medici to Italy. Whatever the case may be, those who explore this history must understand that even though the Italians and Greco-Corsicans of New Smyrna and St. Augustine were intricately connected with the larger Minorcan community and became an integral part of Florida Minorcan history and identity.

Their Italian origins should be neither neglected nor forgotten and should be regarded as an important chapter in Italian American history.

## NOTES

1. Quoted in Giovanni Schiavo, *The Italians in America before the Civil War* (New York: Vigo Press, 1934), 154.

2. Patricia Griffin, "Blue Gold: Andrew Turnbull's New Smyrna Plantation," *Colonial Plantations and Economy in Florida*, edited by Jane Landers (Gainesville: University of Florida Press, 2000), 39–40.

3. Michael D. Virgilio, "Migration," University of Calgary, www.ucalgary.ca/applied history/tutor/migrations, 20 October.

4. Philip D. Rasico, *The Minorcans of Florida: Their History, Language, and Culture* (New Smyrna Beach, Florida: Luthers, 1990), 33, footnote 49. Also see Bruno Roselli, *The Italians in Colonial Florida: a Repertory of Italian Families Settled in Florida under*

*the Spanish (1513–1762, 1784–1821) and British (1762–1784) Regimes with a Brief Historical Outline and an Appendix on the Contemporary Colonial Press* (Jacksonville, Florida: Drew Press, 1940), *passim.*

5. Archibald Menzies, *Proposal for Peopling his Majesty's Southern Colonies on the Continent of America,* published as a pamphlet in England in 1763, noted that "There are great numbers of Greeks settled in Minorca." Quoted in Rascio, 15.

6. Rasico, "Chapter 5: British Florida before the American Revolution," printed in *The Vernon Johns Society!* 1998. wwww.vernonjohns.org/nonracists/jxbrfla.html, 20 October 2004.

7. "Menorcan History," *The Menorcan Cultural Society,* n.d., www.menorcansociety.net/history.html; Rasico, 158–169.

8. Marguerite Mathews, "History & Genealogy of Camden & Charlton Counties: The Pacetti Family of St. Augustine, Florida & Camden County, Georgia, Pacetti History," *The Crypt,* 1999, sponsored by *The American Local History Network* of *the American History & Genealogy Project* (software*),* online posting, 20 October 2004. http:www.camdencounty.org/pacetti.html.

9. Griffin, "Blue Gold," 42; see also "The Minorcans in Florida," *Mike Purdy's Home Page,* n.d., *RootsWeb,* freepages.genealogy.rootsweb.com/~pudig/Minorcans.html, 26 Sept. 2004.

10 . Rasico, *The Minorcans of Florida,* 33, footnote 49; he notes that of the forty-seven marriages of Italian men to Minorcan women between 15 February 1768 and 28 March 1768 in Mahon: there were individuals from Bologna, Cagliari, Emilia, Genoa, Livorno, Naples, Piedmont, Pisa, Tuscany, Trapani, and Venice. This information was culled from book seven, folios 44–69 of the Diocesan Archive of Minorca, *Ciudadela, "Matrimonios de Maho' de 1766 en 1777.* The individuals from Lussinpiccolo were most likely of Croatian origin; see Istrianet.org for the genealogy of Lussinpiccolo.

11. Griffin, "Blue Gold," 41; E. P. Panagopoulos, *New Smyrna: An Eighteentht- Century Greek Odyssey* (Gainesville, Florida: University of Florida Press, 1966), 50, footnote 4.

12. Panagopoulos, 40–44; see also www.corsicacorsica.homestead.com/New Smyrna colony.

13. On the Genoese in Bonifacio, see Dorothy Carrington, *Corsica; Portrait of a Granite Island* (New York: John Day, 1974), 161.

14. Roselli, 20, footnote 4; he asserts that "the entire curriculum vitae of Maria Ambrosi Costa shows her to have been a Levantine Italian rather than a Turk."

15. Virgilio," Cosimo de Medici," Online posting, ancestry.com, 20 October 2004.

16. Kenneth Beeson, "Janas in British East Florida," *Florida Historical Quarterly* 44 (1966): 124.

17. Lucie Servole Myers, "Turnbull Venture to Florida 1768," www.olivetreegenealogy.com, 10 October 2004.

18. "Menorcan History," Ibid.

19. Johann David Schoepf, *Travels in the Confederation* (Philadelphia, n.p., 1911), n.p., and Michael V. Gannon, *The Cross in the Sand* (Gainesville: University of Florida Press, 1983), 86.

20. Mathews, Ibid, "Pacetti Family."

21. Griffin, "Blue Gold," 47.

22. Carita Doggett Corse, *Dr. Andrew Turnbull and the New Smyrna Colony of Florida* (Jacksonville, Florida: Drew Press, 1919), 142.

23. Patricia C. Griffin, *Mullet on the Beach* (Jacksonville: University of North Florida Press, 1991), 33.

24. Schiavo, 152; Griffin, "Blue Gold," 44.

25. Bernard Romans, *A Concise Natural History of East and West Florida* in 1776 (New Orleans: Pelican, 1961), 271.

26. Colonial Office of British Public Records Office, as quoted in Griffin, *Mullet*, 33.

27. 'The Minorcans in Florida,"Ibid, freepages.genealogy.rootsweb.com.

28. For an eyewitness account of the execution, see *Romans*, 272.

29. Schiavo, 152; Corse, 58–59.

30. Rasico, 36; Schiavo, 157; Corse, 63; see Griffin, "Blue Gold," 64, footnote 13; Griffin notes that many of the Greeks died because they "did not carry the gene for Beta Thalassemia (Mediterranean anemia)" which protects against malaria.; see also Griffin, "Thalassemia: A Case Study of the Minorcans in Florida," unpublished manuscript, (St. Augustine Historical Society, 1976).

31. Colonial Office, Class 5, Vol. 544, 200–201, Grant to Hillsborough, 4 March 1769, as quoted in Corse.

32. Griffin, "Blue Gold," 50–55.

33. Governor Grant to Hillsborough, 1 September. 1770, Colonial Office, Class 5, Vol. 545, 33–34, as quoted in Corse.

34. Gannon, 87.

35. Beeson, 127, 129–30.

36. "The Minorcans in Florida,"Ibid, freepages.genealogy.rootsweb.com.

37. Griffin, "Blue Gold," 45.

38. Linda Walton, "Archaeologists Unearth Indigo Dyeing Site," *The Daytona Beach News-Journal*, 13 November, 1998, (www.niedworld.com), 20 October 2004.

39. Rasico, *Minorcans of Florida*, 41.

40. Griffin, "Blue Gold," 60–61.

41. Colonial Office, Class 5, Vol. 556, 113–115, quoted in Corse, 118, 1.

42. Colonial Office, Class 5, Vol. 556, 767, Andrew Turnbull to Arthur Gordon, Esq., quoted in Corse, 143.

43. "How the Minorcans Settled in British St. Augustine," *The Story of Our Parish* (a history of the Cathedral Basilica of St. Augustine), 8 September 2001, thefirstparish.org, 8 August. 2004.

44. Solana family website (members.fortunecity.com/minorcan/family.htm), 20 October 2004.

45. Corse, 164.

46. Gannon, 89.

47. Rasico, Appendix Two, 147–157; these depositions are printed in their entirety.

48. Governor Tonyn to Lord Sydney, St. Augustine, 4 April. 1785, Colonial Office, Class 5, Vol. 561, 360, quoted in Panagopoulos, 175; Corse, 191.

49. Quoted in Panagopoulos, 176.

50. Panagopoulos, 180–81.

51. Roselli, 19–51, source of most information; Griffin 157, 178, whose source is Overton G. Ganong, "The Peso de Burgo-Pellicer Houses," *El Escribano* (12) St. Augustine Historical Society, 1975, 81–99); obituary of Bartolo P. Oliveros, a St. Augustine newspaper, 5 September 1888, Stephen Renouf, 28 August 1999, www.ancestry.com, 20 October 2004; www.menorcansociety.net/articles/acosta_avicepage.html; Spanish Land Grants, Vol. 4, 48, L-9; Panagopoulos, 181.

52. Quoted in Gannon, 116–17.

53. Robert L. Gold, *Borderland Empires in Transition: The Triple-Nation Transfer of Florida* ( Carbondale: Southern Illinois University Press, 1969), *passim*.

54. Quoted in Jane Quinn, *Minorcans in Florida; Their History and Heritage* (St. Augustine: Mission Press, 975), 57.

# JOHN GARIBALDI:
## AN ITALIAN AMERICAN SOLDIER IN THE STONEWALL BRIGADE

DAVID COLES
LONGWOOD UNIVERSITY

FRANK ALDUINO
ANNE ARUNDEL COMMUNITY COLLEGE

While many Civil War studies have emphasized the multi-ethnic composition of certain Northern military units, particularly those formed in New York City and other urban centers, little attention has been given to those European-born adopted Southerners who served the Confederacy. More than sixty years after its publication, Ella Lonn's *Foreigners in the Confederacy* remains the only book-length study devoted to this subject. The few modern scholars in the field have focused on the role of German, French, Irish, or Hispanic immigrants in Confederate service. The smaller Italian immigrant community has been virtually ignored.

Most Italian immigrants living in the southern states in 1860–1861 resided in seaports such as Mobile, New Orleans, Savannah, or Charleston. At the outbreak of the war, individual Italians enlisted in a variety of military units. In addition, groups of Italians served in regiments from Louisiana and Alabama, including more than 300 in the Italian Guards Battalion of the Sixth Regiment, European Brigade, New Orleans militia. One of the more prominent Italians serving the Confederacy during the Civil War was Major General William Booth Taliaferro, who fought in Virginia, Georgia, and the Carolinas. Another colorful Italian American officer was Decimus et Ultimus Barziza, a veteran of the Fourth Texas Infantry.

Fortunately for historians, an Italian Confederate who served in one of the war's most famous Southern units left a rather extensive collection of letters documenting his military career. These letters represent the only such surviving materials written by an Italian soldier in the North or the South. John Garibaldi, born in Genoa on April 30, 1831, came to the United States at the age of twenty. According to the 1860 Federal census, Garibaldi had settled in the village of Covington, Virginia, located in Alleghany County in the Shenandoah Valley. The census taker listed Garibaldi's occupation as schoolteacher and noted that he owned personal property valued at one hundred dollars. His Confederate enlistment papers record his occupation as "mechanic." The Italian immigrant lived as a boarder in the house of Bernard Lenore and family. In 1862 he married Sarah Ann Virginia Poor; and during the course of his military service, he wrote numerous letters to her, more than thirty of which survive in the archives of the Virginia Military Institute in Lexington. Unfortunately, in his surviving correspondence, Garibaldi makes no reference to his Italian ancestry or to other issues one might expect from an immigrant soldier. Only once did he comment on his religious affiliation. In a letter, he did state that he had written to a priest and received a prayer book. From this letter, we assume that early in his life he must have been a Catholic, even though his wartime letters make no other specific comments about his faith. Not living near urban centers, he did not come into contact with large numbers of Catholic Italians, which may explain his membership in other denominations. We know that in the early 1900s Garibaldi and his wife attended a Presbyterian Church, and we know that an obituary refers to him as a "communicant" in the Methodist Church. In the ten years since he arrived in America, he had become somewhat Anglicized by the time of his enlistment and largely so in the years following the war.[1]

Garibaldi enlisted in Company C of the Twenty-seventh Virginia Infantry, which became part of the famed Stonewall Brigade in May 1861. His first surviving letter, written to his future wife in December 1861, describes his regiment's efforts to destroy a dam on the Potomac River near Williamsport, Maryland in order to disrupt the water supply to the Ohio and Chesapeake

Canal. Garibaldi describes the bitter cold. The Confederates had "no tents to sleep in neither could we make a fire in the night in order to keep from being seen by the enemy, but we [had] good overcoats and blankets enough to keep from freezing."[2] The Spartan conditions did not, however, prevent the soldiers from celebrating the holidays. The Italian notes that they:

> have had [a] right merry Christmas [with] plenty to drink [and] pretty near the whole . . . company . . . drunk. The Captain bought about 10 or 15 gallons of liquor and gave it to the company, he was right merry himself. The whole of the 27[th] regiment was almost drunk even the Colonels, they were drunk too.[3]

In early 1862, Garibaldi and the Twenty-seventh Virginia joined Thomas "Stonewall" Jackson's small army for an advance to Bath and then to Romney, Virginia. The march took place during a period of extreme cold. There was much grumbling amongst the troops with so much accumulations of snow and ice. Eventually, Jackson relented and withdrew his men southward to Winchester and winter quarters. "We suffered right smart cold weather during that time," Garibaldi comments in a letter home, "for [a] good many had no tent and they had to lay out on the wet snow beds [with] snow falling at the same time. [A] good many took sick and will never get better . . . Thank goodness I have stood up very well and never got sick yet. I was on every march, and did my duty as well as any soldier ever did."[4]

In the spring of 1862, Garibaldi and the Twenty-seventh Virginia took part in Stonewall Jackson's famous Shenandoah Valley Campaign, a campaign designed to clear the Valley of several small Union armies and to prevent reinforcements from reaching George McClellan's Federal army that would threaten Richmond from the Peninsula. During this campaign, Jackson won his greatest fame when his "foot cavalry" won a number of dramatic victories over superior numbers. One of the Confederate's few reverses occurred at Kernstown on March 23, when Jackson's hastily ordered attack failed to break a Union battle line commanded by General James Shields. In this engagement, the Twenty-seventh took part in some of the heaviest fighting and suffered frightful losses: more than one-third of the 170 men in the unit were killed, wounded, or missing. John Garibaldi numbered among the latter, falling into Union hands at the conclusion of the battle.[5]

Garibaldi spent several months in captivity at the Federal prisoner of war facility at Fort Delaware, located along the Delaware River on Pea Patch Island, downriver from Wilmington. The Italian and the other 257 Confederate captives from Kernstown numbered among the first prisoners housed in the facility, originally built to defend Wilmington from a coastal attack. By 1863, some 12,500 prisoners were crowded into the brick fortification. During the course of the war, more than 2,400 died from disease, malnutrition and neglect.[6] While he was there, John Garibaldi was spared the worst of the deteriorating conditions. After five months in captivity, he received his parole and was exchanged in August 1862. In the period following his release and before returning to active service, he probably married Sarah Poor because his letter dated October 24, 1862 addresses her as "Dear Wife."[7]

Because of the Italian's forced absence, Garibaldi did not participate in the Seven Days' Battles, the Second Manassas, or Sharpsburg campaigns. By late October 1862, however, he had rejoined his regiment while it was encamped near Bunker Hill, Virginia. "I haven't any news to tell you at this time," he reported to his wife, "[as] I haven't been in the camp long enough to learn any [but] the boys here are as lively as crickets, just as lively as if it was in time of peace, or as if they were at home." Garibaldi also noted how desertions, casualties, and disease had decimated the Twenty-seventh to "thirty-four men in our company fit for duty." He further reported:

> Our company makes up near half of the regiment; it is no more than a good company the whole regiment. They nearly all deserted or went home on a French [leave]. There is some few sick and wounded but not many. There was only twelve in the Battle of Sharpsburg in Maryland out of our regiment. The balance remained behind, and most of them never went across the [Potomac] river.[8]

By early November, Garibaldi was stationed at Camp Allen in Clarke County. He complained about a lack of writing paper and stamps, forcing him to "tear a leaf off an old book in order to write you this letter and I am bound to send it without prepayment." Garibaldi believed his regiment would soon get paid, and he planned to send Sarah most of what he received: "If I don't get [a] chance to send [the money] to you I intend to take a French furlow and fetch [it] home myself if I can." The Italian soldier added, "Dear I am lonesome for you and would like to be with you, but I hope that the Lord will spare my life long enough to come home again and to see peace restored once more in our country."[9] Later that month, Garibaldi reports he had been promoted to sergeant because of several other non-commissioned officers' "straggling out of the company without permission." He also expresses his concern over not having received a letter from his wife since his return to the regiment. "You are the only one that I care for in this world," he tells her. "A day is not passing without thinking of the one I left behind." More ominously, Garibaldi notes that the men had received orders "to cook a day's ration[s] and be ready to march in the morning by day light."[10]

The Stonewall Brigade did in fact leave its camps in the Shenandoah Valley near Bunker Hill the next day for the long march southeast to Fredericksburg, Virginia. There, Robert E. Lee assembled his Army of Northern Virginia to prevent Ambrose E. Burnside's Union Army of the Potomac from crossing the Rappahannock River. Fortunately for the Virginians, the brigade experienced little combat in the subsequent battle of Fredericksburg, assisting only in repelling a Yankee attack that briefly penetrated a portion of the Confederate lines.[11]

Garibaldi's regiment remained in winter camp near Fredericksburg during the early months of 1863. The news in his letters from this period deal with sending money home and receiving items from his wife, items such as soap, pepper, thread, and socks.[12] By late March, Garibaldi reports that "every indication seems that we are on the verge of [a] move as we had order[s] to pack up all our extra bagages [sic] that we can not carry on our shoulder and send it away to Richmond. The days are getting long and the weather dryer and it shall soon [be] pleasant enough to admit of active movement." He adds, "Although there is a heap of talk about fighting, I think that there wouldn't be as much fighting as there was last summer. There may be a fight or two here and if we whip them I think they [will] give it up provide[d] we don't go to Maryland. But if we go there I think we shall [have] some tall fighting to do."[13]

Though the Stonewall Brigade did not see combat in late March as Garibaldi had anticipated, they would be heavily engaged in the Chancellorsville campaign in late April and early May. The campaign commenced when Major General Joseph Hooker moved his Army of the Potomac across the Rapidan and Rappahannock Rivers (west of Fredericksburg) in an effort to flank Lee's Army of Northern Virginia. On April 30, Garibaldi wrote to Sarah that his unit was "on the battle field drawn up in line of battle this evening and that the cannons began to roar this evening. How we will come out I am not able to tell you, but I hope that we will be able to whip them."[14] Several days later, the Twenty-seventh Virginia took part in Stonewall Jackson's famous May 2nd flank attack, which surprised and threatened to destroy the Union army, and in heavy fighting the following day. In all, the Twenty-seventh lost seventy-three men—killed, wounded, or missing while the entire Stonewall Brigade suffered nearly 500 casualties. In several letters, John Garibaldi left a detailed account of the campaign. In one, he describes Jackson's flank march, stating that the Confederates took "a small county road [and] marched about twelve miles leaving the enemy at our right, and got in the rear in the evening . . . There the fighting commenced... [we] drove the enemy for about two or three miles, [and] drove the Yankees out of their breastworks . . . and took several batteries and a good many prisoners." In another letter the former teacher tells his wife that "we have been engaged in a hot battle since I last wrote you and with the help of God I came out safe but out of about forty of our company that went in to the fight last Sunday there was only about thirty came out safe." He added:

There was six hundred and fifty . . . killed out of our
brigade and wounded. Our brigade went into battle
twice, and the second time charged over the yankee
brest works and ran the yankees away from there. Men
fell on both side[s] of me and had it not been that God
was with me I believe I'd fell too . . . We got in the rear
of the yankees saturday and we were fighting nearly
all night saturday and all sunday. We got thirty pieces
of artillery. I can't tell you how many small arms but
we have got any number of them. There was yankee
knapsacks enough left on the ground to supply our
whole army. The blankets were laying there in piles
and were trampelled over by our men in the mudd. I
never saw so much waste of property in my life. The
enemy was laying behind their breastworks sunday
morning with their knapsacks off and blankets and
when they saw us coming they ran away leaving every
thing behind them.[15]

But the subsequent death of Stonewall Jackson cast a pall over
the Chancellorsville victory. In a letter dated May 11, Garibaldi
describes Jackson's death:

He did not die on account of his wound, he die[d] of
the newmony [pneumonia]. He was wounded . . . it is
said by our men. When the enemy was making them
charges on us he accidently or some how or other
happened to be between our men and the enemy in one
of them charges with several other Generals, and they
road towards our lines. At the approach of the enemy
and of his musketry and our men hearing such noise
through the bushes thought it was the enemy's cavalry
and they fired into them wounding two Generals and
a Colonel. Yesterday there was an escort of honor of
about two hundred and fifty [men] detailed out of our
Brigade to accompany General Jackson's corpse to
Richmond and I was one among them, but before we
could march down to Guinea Station . . . the remains
of our general had been removed on the Rail Road and
so we were about an hour too late.[16]

Shortly after Chancellorsville, Robert E. Lee reorganized Jackson's army and embarked on an invasion of Pennsylvania. In mid-June, during the early stages of the campaign, the Stonewall Brigade took part in the overwhelming victory at Winchester, Virginia. Afterwards, Garibaldi wrote that "five yankee regiments gave [in] to our brigade and surrendered. They sta[c]ked arms for us, hung their accoutrements and gave themselves up to us as prisoners of war. Our brigade alone took six of their flag[s]."[17] At Gettysburg, the brigade fought on the Confederate left, taking part in assaults on Culp's Hill on the second and third of July. By this time the Twenty-seventh Virginia numbered only 129 men. The Brigade suffered almost fifty casualties, including seven killed, thirty-four wounded, and six missing.[18] After the campaign, Garibaldi described his experiences to Sarah:

> We crossed the Potomac river on the 18 of June. We have been nearly up to Harrisburg the capitol of Pennsylvania. We then came back and met the enemy at Gettysburg Pennsylvania and fought for three days. We whipt him badly the first day, and [they] fell back, took up a strong position and threw entrenchments and repulsed us. We then fell back ourselves and took up a position but the enemy refused to attack us. After staying there a day without being attacked we fell back across the mountains where we are now about thirteen miles from the Potomac.[19]

In a subsequent letter, Garibaldi recalled that the people of Pennsylvania "seem to be very unconcerned about the war, very seldom [do] they see a soldier, and they hardly know what war is, but if the war was to be carried on there as long as it was carried on in Virginia they would learn the effects of it, and perhaps would soon be willing to make peace like we are."[20]

The late summer and fall of 1863 saw much maneuvering and some fighting between the Army of Northern Virginia and the Army of the Potomac, but no combat surpassed the scale of Chancellorsville or Gettysburg. During the early months of 1864, Garibaldi and the Twenty-seventh remained in camp south of the

Rapidan River and west of Fredericksburg, Virginia. Clothing deficiencies and shortages of food sapped the men's morale. In January, Garibaldi comments that the unit's meat ration "has been reduced to a quarter of a pound of bacon per day, or three quarters of a pound of beef, but they are giving us lard in place of it."[21] In the same letter, the Italian soldier commented on his future in the military. While his term of service would be completed in the spring, he doubted that the Confederacy would allow any men to be discharged. "But if," he adds, "they give us the chance to reenlist and join any command we please, I have concluded to come West [apparently to the Shenandoah Valley]. It seems to me that the war is going to be a long one."[22] Despite the lack of food and clothing and his concerns over the war's length, Garibaldi still hoped for a Confederate victory. In late April 1864, shortly before the beginning of active campaigning, he wrote to his wife that if "we only whip Grant it would be very encouraging to us and very discouraging to the enemy. I think we will soon have a trial of it, and I am pretty confident that if General Grant comes over the Rapidan River to fight us over here in our breastworks he will get pretty badly whipped."[23]

The long-awaited opening of Grant's Overland Campaign in early May 1864 saw Garibaldi and his brigade heavily engaged in the fighting at the Wilderness and at Spotsylvania. On May 12, the brigade took position in the Confederate "Mule Shoe" salient in the lines near Spotsylvania. On that day Winfield Scott Hancock's Second Corps struck the Southern lines in a devastating assault that overwhelmed Edward Johnson's Division and Stonewall's Brigade. The attack, which led to some of the most brutal hand-to-hand fighting of the entire war, resulted in the capture of several thousand Southern troops, including eighty men from the Twenty-seventh Virginia. John Garibaldi, who would fall into Union hands for the second time in the war, numbered among the latter. Meanwhile, the fight at Spotsylvania had so decimated the Twenty-seventh Virginia that its remnants were consolidated with thirteen other regiments into a temporary brigade. The debacle had essentially ended the history of the famed Stonewall Brigade.[24]

Sent first to a prisoner collection point at Belle Plain, Virginia, Garibaldi's captives eventually transferred the Italian prisoner once more to Ft. Delaware, where he had been held in 1862. He remained there for several months before his exchange in late September or early October 1864. By the middle part of the latter month, his name would appear on a list of paroled prisoners at Camp Lee near Richmond. It is assumed that he returned to his unit in time for the final battles in the Shenandoah Valley and in the outskirts of Petersburg, though his service records give no indication of his status.[25] No final parole has been recorded in his compiled military service, indicating that he was not present at Appomattox. In his last letter written shortly before his capture, he writes that he is "pretty tire[d] of this war by this time but there is no chance for us unless the war stops for we shall all have [to] keep fighting until [sic] the yankees give . . . up or until we shall be subjugated.[26]

For a time after the war, Garibaldi taught school and farmed at Buffalo Mills in Rockbridge County, Virginia. By 1904 he had moved to Lexington, where he joined the Lee-Jackson Camp of the Confederate Veterans and became "a familiar and highly respected figure at all Confederate reunions." He also received a pension from the state for his Civil War service. Garibaldi died of paralysis at the home of his daughter at Big Island, Bedford County on September 8, 1914. A funeral was held on the morning of September 10, with four of the veteran's five children attending. Reverend P. F. Arthur of the local Methodist Church presided at the ceremony, which was followed by internment in the family plot in the Stonewall Jackson Cemetery in Lexington.[27]

An historian of the Twenty-seventh Virginia referred to the Italian American simply as "A Brave Soldier."[28] It is unfortunate for later historians that the Garibaldi letters, apparently the only significant surviving collection of letters from an Italian or Italian American soldier in the Civil War, make virtually no mention of the author's ancestry or of the problems facing immigrants in the Union or Confederate armies. The very absence of such comments, however, may in themselves be revealing. With such a small antebellum Italian population spread throughout the United States and with only a few places like New York and New Orleans boasting even a modest concentration of Italians, immigrants like Garibaldi probably accepted the need for quick assimilation into the mainstream population. His letters are full of comments typical of Civil War soldiers. He wrote about family, food, living conditions, the progress of the war, the movements of his unit, and combat operations—all similar to those written by many native-born combatants. Just ten years after his immigration to the United States, the native of Genoa seemed, at least in his correspondence, to have been comfortably acclimated to the dominant American culture and society.

Mass Italian immigration into the United States did not occur until the decades following the Civil War. Thus historians have tended to ignore the eleven to twelve thousand Italians living in America in 1860. If mentioned at all, they are usually connected with colorful Northern units like the Garibaldi Guard, which included only a relatively small number of Italians. Those Italians living in the seceded states have been almost completely neglected. Yet largely because of the cosmopolitan make-up of southern cities like New Orleans, Mobile, Savannah, Charleston, Memphis, and Richmond, Italians and Italian Americans, as well as other immigrants, did serve their adopted nation in numbers greater than might be expected. Yet the story of immigrants in the Confederacy remains at least partly untold because some Southerners, even during the war, viewed the struggle as native-born Confederates fighting largely foreign-born Union armies. Confederate nurse Kate Cumming criticized this view during the latter part of the war: She noted that:

> if the native [S]outherners, who when the war was first inaugurated, used to . . . cry 'secession and war to the knife,' had come forward as I know foreigners had done, we would not now be in need of the late earnest appeal for men . . . And I not only think it bad taste, but unfeeling, in any of our people to draw distinctions at the present time, when we all know

how nobly foreigners have poured out their blood in our defense.[29]

John Garibaldi, and hundreds of others in the South's small Italian population did their share for the Confederacy.

## NOTES

1. Population Schedule for Alleghany, Amelia, Amherst, and Appomattox Counties, Virginia. Roll 1332, National Archives Microfilm Publication, Microcopy No. 653, Population Schedule of the Eighth Census of the United States, 1860. Obituary clipping, apparently from the *Rockbridge County News*, 10 September 1914, in Garibaldi Collection, MS #284, Virginia Military Institute Archives, Lexington, Virginia. Hereafter Garibaldi Collection refers to this source.

2. Garibaldi to "Dear Miss," 30 December 1861, Garibaldi Collection. A photocopy of this letter is in the Garibaldi Collection, while the original is in private hands. Typescripts of the Garibaldi letters are available on the VMI Library's website at http://www.vmi.edu/archives/Manuscripts/MS284.html.

3. Garibaldi to Miss.

4. Garibaldi to "Dear Sir," 28 January 1862.

5. James I. Robertson, *The Stonewall Brigade* (Baton Rouge: Louisiana State University Press, 1963), 70–77. For a good overview of the campaign see Robert G. Tanner, *Stonewall in the Valley: Thomas J. "Stonewall" Jackson's Shenandoah Valley Campaign, Spring 1862* (revised ed. Mechanicsburg, PA: Stackpole Books, 1996). For the engagement in which Garibaldi was captured, see Gary L. Ecelbarger, *"We Are in For It:" The First Battle of Kernstown* (Shippensburg: White Main, 1997), 76–206.

6. David S. Heidler and Jeanne T. Heidler, eds., *Encyclopedia of the American Civil War* (2000, reprint ed., New York: W.W. Norton, n.d.), 727–728.

7. John Garibaldi to "Dear Wife," 24 October 1862, Garibaldi Collection. For a good study of Fort Delaware during the Civil War see Brian Temple, *The Union Prison at Fort Delaware: A Perfect Hell on Earth* (Jefferson, N.C.: McFarland Press, 2003).

8. Garibaldi to wife, 24 October 1862. Throughout this text, any errors in Garibaldi's letters are reproduced as written so that the use of *sic* is unnecessary.

9. Garibaldi to wife, 2 November 1862.

10. Garibaldi to wife, 20 November 1862.

11. Lowell Reidenbaugh, *27th Virginia Infantry* (Lynchburg: H.E. Howard, 1993), 74–76; Robertson, *The Stonewall Brigade*, 172–175; Francis Augustin O'Reilly, The Fredericksburg Campaign: *Winter War on the Rappahannock* (Baton Rouge: Louisiana State University Press, 2003), 198–245.

12. Garibaldi to wife, 4 January 1863, 18 January 1863, 27 January 1863, 26 February 1863, 24 March 1863, Garibaldi Collection.

13. Garibaldi to wife, 29 March 1863.

14. Garibaldi to wife, 30 April 1863.

15. Garibaldi to wife, May 9, 1863, ibid. Robertson, *The Stonewall Brigade*, 182–193; Reidenbaugh, *27th Virginia Infantry*, 78–82. Perhaps the best secondary account of the entire campaign is Stephen W. Sears, *Chancellorsville* (Boston: Houghton Mifflin, 1996); see particularly 225–307.

16. Garibaldi to wife, May 11, 1863, Garibaldi Collection.

17. Charles S. Grunder and Brandon H. Beck, *The Second Battle of Winchester, June 12–15, 1863* (Lynchburg: H.E. Howard), 28–65.

18. Garibaldi to wife, June 16, 1863. Reidenbaugh, *27th Virginia Infantry,* 85–88.

19. Garibaldi to wife, 10 July 1863, Garibaldi Collection.

20. Garibaldi to wife, 19 July 1863.

21. Garibaldi to wife, 9 January 1864, Garibaldi Collection.

22. Garibaldi to wife, 9 January 1864, Garibaldi Collection

23. Garibaldi to wife, 22 April 1864.

24. Reidenbaugh, *27th Virginia Infantry,* 92–102; Robertson, *Stonewall Brigade,* 209–226. The best general studies of the fighting that decimated the Stonewall Brigade are Gordon C. Rhea, *The Battles of Spotsylvania Court House and the Road to Yellow Tavern, May 7–12, 1864* (Baton Rouge: Louisiana State University Press, 1997), 189–265; and William D. Matter, *If It Takes All Summer: The Battle of Spotsylvania* (Chapel Hill: The University of North Carolina Press, 1988), 183–207.

25. John Garibaldi Compiled Service Record, National Archives, Washington, D.C.

26. Garibaldi to wife 22 April 1864 Garibaldi Collection.

27. Obituary clipping, 10 September 1914.

28. Reidenbaugh, *27th Virginia Infantry,* 145.

29. Quoted in Ella Lonn, *Foreigners in the Confederacy* (Chapel Hill: The University of North Carolina Press, 1940), 477.

*His name was Count Andriani [sic]. Does anyone know
anything of the result of the Count's investigations?*
— Thomas L. McKenney, 1827

## Count Paolo Andreani in America:
## No Longer a 'Forgotten Traveler'

### Cesare Marino
### Smithsonian Institution

From 1790 to 1792, a young, aristocratic naturalist-explorer
from Milano—already famous in Europe for having successfully
executed the first manned, hot-air balloon flight in Italy on March
13, 1784—visited the United States of America and the Dominion
of Canada. He met with the leading political and intellectual
figures of the two countries, traveled extensively along the Atlantic
Coast, through Pennsylvania and New York State, explored the St.
Lawrence River and Niagara Falls, and ventured into the interior
region of the Great Lakes. This first, intense American stay was
followed, after a fourteen-year hiatus, by a second and longer
voyage to the Caribbean and again to North America in the years
1806 to 1812. Afterwards, the restless and eclectic Italian traveler
returned to Europe. He wandered from city to city and finally took
up residence on the French Riviera. Exiled from his hometown of
Milano, due to the large debts he had accrued in the course of his
unsettled and dissipate life, he died in 1823. His name was Count
Paolo Andreani, and until recently he was one of the lesser known
and least understood of the early Italian visitors to America.

A *precocious literato* with a peculiar, personalized command
of Latin, Italian, French, and Spanish (English was not his
forte), Count Andreani, an eccentric, was a member of the
Republic of Letters with a passion for science, field research,
and experimentation. He was a seasoned traveler, explorer,
mountain climber, flight pioneer, and outspoken social critic. A
prolific writer, Andreani meticulously recorded the itineraries,
experiences, impressions, and scientific and ethnographic

observations of his early European and subsequent American, Canadian, and Caribbean wanderings in several handwritten diaries and letters of which only a few survive. For many years, the existence of Andreani's diaries, the exact sequence and routes of his travels and explorations—particularly those in the New World—and the results of his extensive scientific, geographical, and ethnographic studies have eluded archivists and historians. In 1938, noted historian G. Hubert Smith, intrigued by the persistent lack of sound information on this elusive Italian pioneer-naturalist in America, attempted to answer Thomas L. McKenney's century-old question: "[D]oes anyone know anything of the Count's investigations?" After a thorough search, Smith acknowledged in a paper presented at the Minnesota Historical Society that too little was known of the idiosyncratic Count Paolo Andreani. The historian concluded that the true nature and extent of Andreani's travels in America was still largely a mystery. The Italian Count thus remained, as Smith put it, "a forgotten traveler."[1]

During the last twenty years, new and extensive research conducted in Italian, American, and British libraries and archives has led to the discovery of a number of Andreani's missing diaries and several of his surviving personal letters and ancillary papers. Together, these important documents shed new light on Count Andreani's travels and his pioneering contributions to early Italian American history. Today, based on solid documentary evidence, we can finally answer McKenney's query and reverse Smith's conclusion: indeed, we do know Andreani, and he is no longer "a forgotten traveler." Two of his travel diaries in particular are historically valuable. *The Giornale* (1790) describes Andreani's excursion from New York City to the Iroquois villages south of Lake Ontario and to other sites in New York State. The other diary, the long presumed lost *Giornale dei Grandi Laghi* (1791), chronicles instead his daring canoe voyage from Montreal to Lake Superior and back.[2]

America, with its natural wonders, "savage Indians," and revolutionary spirit, attracted the attention of many eighteenth-century enlightened Italian aristocrats who sought to see for themselves this distant land and its remarkable progress. They were eager to experience first-hand this newly independent nation, meet the Founding Fathers, travel far and wide and possibly interact also with the Native American population. In rapid succession, three Milanese noblemen traveled across the Atlantic, spearheading a significant and little known movement of Italian accidental ethnographers who followed them well into the nineteenth century.[3] The first Italian who crossed the Atlantic at this time was Count Francesco dal Verme who, between 1783 to 1784, visited America and, as he put it, "its great men." Well received by George Washington and other distinguished citizens of the new Republic, dal Verme drafted a series of letters and kept a concise diary of his trip, both of which, however, were never published in their entirety in Italy. Only two centuries later they were, instead, translated and published into English by Elizabeth Cometti in 1969.[4]

Francesco dal Verme was followed by Luigi Castiglioni, a renowned botanist who, between 1785 and 1787, traveled extensively between New England and the Carolinas. Broadening the original scope of his predecessor dal Verme, Castiglioni collected early samples of American Indian cultural material, and word lists in two Indian languages (Choctaw and Cherokee); updated historical, geographical, economic, and social information on the states he visited; and, most importantly, gathered an extensive amount of botanical data. Castiglioni was also welcomed by President Washington, and other Founding Fathers and new American intellectuals who appreciated and valued the great cultural heritage of Italy and the *bella lingua*.[5] After he returned to Milano in 1790, Castiglioni published a book of his travels and a companion botanical treatise, both of which were highly praised in European scientific circles. Castiglioni's *Viaggio* and his *Trasunto* were eventually translated into English by Antonio Pace and published in 1983.[6]

Paolo Andreani, the last and youngest of these early Milanese visitors to America, was, arguably, the most adventurous, but he was also the most controversial. Andreani was born in 1763, not far from the famous *Duomo*, to one of Milano's most prominent and wealthy families.[7] After the premature death of his parents, young Paolo became the charge of his older and more stable brother Gian Mario, who tried unsuccessfully to restrain his younger sibling's exuberant and at times unruly behavior. Much to the chagrin of his older brother, Paolo, the *contino*, patronized questionable women and gambled excessively in Venice. To his credit, however, from an early age and throughout his life, Andreani invested considerable amount of time and energy in the pursuit of a scientific education and spent long hours studying and experimenting with the natural world. He spared no expense when purchasing the latest scientific instruments. So great was his passion for experimental science that, inspired by the memorable example the famous French aeronaut brothers Joseph and Jacques Montgolfier, in early 1784 Count Andreani hired three talented Milanese craftsmen and, with their help, he designed and built a large, hot-air balloon. On March 13, Andreani successfully executed the first manned balloon flight in Italy. Not yet twenty years old, the young aristocratic scientist acquired instant celebrity at home and abroad. After this heroic feat, the young Count was hailed the Daedalus of Italy and poems were written in his honor.[8]

Free from family responsibilities (he never married), he began to travel restlessly from Paris to London to Scotland (he shared this trip with James Smithson, after whom the Smithsonian Institution is named), then from Austria to Holland, to the Alps and to Sicily and nearby islands. He then traveled back again, north across the continent all the way to Ireland. Everywhere he went, he was well received by members of the European intellectual and social elite.[9] Conversely, he showed little interest in politics and reacted with satirical caution to the news of the French Revolution. Writing to Gian Mario from London, on August 31, 1789, Paolo urged his fellow Milanesi to entertain themselves at the famed La Scala rather than pay attention to the excitement in Paris.[10] His own eyes were now set across the Atlantic. The information made available in Italy by the *Gazzettiere Americano*,[11] and by the translated works of Benjamin Franklin—particularly the *Scelta di lettere e di opuscoli and the Avviso a quegli che pensassero d'andare* in

America[12]—in addition to the first-hand accounts of dal Verme and Castiglioni, had whetted Paolo's appetite for new horizons, new scientific research, and new ventures in the New World. With brother Gian Mario's blessings, Paolo carefully planned his trip by securing several letters of introduction addressed to the most prominent men in the United States and Canada. He obtained one such letter from Filippo Mazzei, the distinguished Tuscan friend of the American Revolution. Written in Italian and addressed to James Madison in March 1790, the letter stated:

> Degno e Caro Amico, Il latore della presente sarà il Sig. Conte Paolo Andreani, di Milano, che vi raccomando particolarmente. Voi sapete che io sono piuttosto scrupoloso che facile a dar lettere di raccomandazione . . . Tra i suoi studi la fisica e l'Istoria naturale sono i più favoriti. Questa è l'unica lettera che gli do; tutte le altre sarebbero superflue, poichè voi l'indirizzerete, a seconda dei viaggi che intraprenderà in America. Per mera curiosità vi dirò che il Sig. Conte Andreani è stato il solo . . . che in Italia siasi elevato in una macchina Areostatica, esperienza benissimo eseguita.[13]

In mid-April 1790, Paolo Andreani departed from Falmouth, England; after a forty-four day long ocean crossing, he landed in Halifax, Nova Scotia. Here he had his first encounter with a delegation of Cherokee and Creek Indian chiefs on their way to London.[14] The possibility of studying the American Indians and the natural sciences, particularly mineralogy, motivated his voyage to America. Writing to his beloved and ever-patient Gian Mario, Paolo intoned: "l'oggetto mio che m'indusse a passar l'oceano non fu già di visitare città che non dissomigliano dalle nostre che nella inferiorità, ma bensì di internarmi nelle parti incognite, e di visitare le nazioni de' selvaggi."[15] Andreani clearly had little interest in touring the American cities, which he felt were inferior in their history, size and architecture to those in Europe.[16] Instead he wanted to explore the unknown parts of the American continent and to visit the "savage nations." Before leaving for the frontier, however, Andreani was introduced to George Washington, to whom he personally delivered a copy of Vittorio Alfieri's "L'America Libera," a collection of five odes, one dedicated to General Washington himself.[17] Andreani also met Secretary of War Henry Knox, Secretary of State Thomas Jefferson, and James Madison, then a member of Congress with whom Andreani established a life-long friendship. The Italian Count was also introduced to several other illustrious Americans.

Having met his social obligations, Paolo Andreani undertook his first American exploration in the summer of 1790. Traveling alternatively by carriage and on horseback, in mid-August he departed from New York City, then the capital of the United States, situated at the lower end of Manhattan Island. After reaching the northern tip of Manhattan, he crossed the Harlem River via a wooden bridge and began his journey towards Iroquoia. Following the Hudson River along the Albany Post Road, Andreani meticulously recorded information about the many rocks and minerals he saw and commented on the condition of the roads, the countryside, and the taverns where he spent the night. Upon reaching Albany, he found many Dutch inhabitants, who, as he put it, had the dishonorable reputation of not being hospitable to foreigners. The Italian Count then continued north to Cohoes Falls at the Mohawk River junction; he then followed the Mohawk all the way to Fort Stanwix. From there he traveled to the Iroquois Country, making the first stop at Oneida where he was a welcomed guest of octogenarian Chief Skenandoa and the noted Reverend Samuel Kirkland. Andreani subsequently visited the Onondaga and the Tuscarora tribes. During his stay among the Iroquois, Andreani collected information on their social, political, and religious customs and compiled word lists and phrases in the Oneida and Onondaga languages. Though generally impressionistic and patronizing, Andreani's notes are of considerable ethnographic interest, particularly his detailed description of a lacrosse stick and the "ballgame"; they are among the first descriptions of this Native American game recorded by a European.[18]

From Iroquoia, Andreani retraced his steps down the Mohawk River, visited and described the mineral springs at Saratoga, and then traveled to the Shaker's utopian colony of New Lebanon, located near the border of Massachusetts. He expressed the same ambivalence for the Shakers that he had for the Iroquois. On the one hand, he criticized their outrageous ways of worship, their communistic ideals and practices, and their unnatural sexual abstinence. On the other hand, he noted their family cohesion, industry, honesty in trade, and overall disciplined life. Descending the Hudson, Andreani visited West Point and then returned to New York. As we mentioned earlier, he recorded the details of this first voyage in the *Giornale* (1790), which was only recently published in his entirety both in the original Italian transcription (C. Marino 2005) and in a new English translation (C. Marino and K. Tiro 2006).

Andreani spent the winter of 1790–1791 in Philadelphia, where Congress had recently relocated. He soon, however, found himself entangled in several political and personal controversies. Colonel David Humphreys, George Washington's secret envoy to England, had made public the contents of a private letter Andreani had sent to a friend in London. In this letter, the Italian freely criticized the United States and its leading political figures.[19] In fairness to Andreani, some of his criticism, particularly the political factionalism and personal rivalries in Congress and the pomp and circumstance surrounding President Washington, were well founded.[20] And, as if his criticisms were not enough, the Italian casanova, prompted the jealousy of American gentlemen because he enjoyed the witty hospitality of the leading ladies in the City of Brotherly Love. To complicate matters, Andreani also managed to anger many women of the Philadelphia's high society by allegedly making some offensive remarks.

By the spring of 1791, Paolo Andreani thought it wise to leave Philadelphia and immerse himself in the distant wilderness to pursue his second, more daring exploration. He traveled to Montreal, where he hired twelve seasoned, mixed-blood Canadians (known as *bois brulé* or *engagés*) and secured a completely outfitted birch bark canoe. On July 1, he embarked on a remarkable adventure.[21] In their large canoe, Paolo Andreani and his crew, which included two Indian interpreters, followed the Ottawa River route to Lake Nipissing.

By way of the French River, they entered Georgian Bay, passed Manitoulin Island, and crossed Lake Huron to Fort Michilimackinac, the British outpost where they rested and re-supplied. The second leg of this long canoe voyage took Andreani and his men through Sault St. Marie into the majestic body of water appropriately called Gitchi Gumi by the Ojibwa Indians. Navigating counter-clock wise, Andreani explored the coasts of Lake Superior. He stopped, among other places, at Thunder Bay, Ontario; Grand Portage, Minnesota; and La Pointe, on Madeline Island off the coast of Wisconsin, diligently gathering information on the Indians, the fur trade, the geography and the geology of the region.[22] It was at La Pointe, in September 1791 that Andreani, equipped with his faithful scientific instruments, was seen taking measurements of the curvature of the earth by Irish-born fur trader John Johnston who, in turn, later related to Thomas McKenney (then Superintendent of Indian Affairs) his amicable but odd encounter with the Italian naturalist-explorer. Writing in his diary, Johnston noted that Andreani had already climbed the highest mountains, including Mont Blanc. Johnston wrote, "His name was Count Andriani. Few people would suppose that these extreme points, so far beyond the bound of civilized life, and so far in the interior, had ever been the theater of such investigations."[23] British traveler John J. Bigsby recorded additional testimony of the pioneering passage of Count Andreani to a wilderness region dominated by Indians, trappers, traders and beavers. While occupying himself in astronomical observations, in addition to gathering data on the fur trade, and studying Native American tribal customs, the Italian Count might have been the first European ever to circumnavigate Lake Superior.[24]

As the cold weather rapidly approached, Andreani and his crew returned to the East via a different route. First, they crossed Lake Huron to Detroit. Then, they continued to Lake Erie, portaging at Niagara Falls, and reentering Canada. By the end of 1791, Andreani was back in Philadelphia, where, by now, his scandals had been nearly forgotten. His incredible voyage of over 2,000 miles by canoe had once again won him great acclaim and recognition. He was first admitted into the exclusive Club du Castor of Montreal and was subsequently elected a member of the prestigious American Philosophical Society at Philadelphia. But the expedition had also been expensive. By late spring 1792, Andreani prepared for his return to Europe. He arrived in the summer of that year. Thus ended Paolo Andreani's first voyage to America. Unfortunately, some of the diaries he drafted during his two-year stay were lost before he departed from America. Apparently, they fell into the frozen waters of a river when the ice suddenly broke under the weight of his horses and sled. Besides losing precious research material, this incident also almost cost him his life. Upon his return to Europe, police confiscated other papers and personal possessions in order to pay angry creditors in Milano and elsewhere. Fortunately, however, enough documents survived to enable us to retrace with adequate accuracy Paolo Andreani's first American journey. Later, the peripatetic count took yet another journey to the New World. His second trip included a forced detour to Jamaica where he witnessed the horrible slave trade, which he abhorred; he also contracted smallpox, but his strong will and the aid of a fellow Milanese helped him recover. This new adventure took Andreani to New Orleans, Florida, Washington D.C., Baltimore and again to Philadelphia. These experiences and travels have been ably covered (but only in Italian) by Emilio Fortunato, a long-time student of Andreani.[25]

Few Italian or American historians have adequately researched Andreani's explorations in the New World. Several decades after Andreani's passage to America, another Italian accidental ethnographer, Giacomo Costantino Beltrami, visited the United States and claimed the discovery of the northernmost sources of the Mississippi River; a discovery soon contested by some American writers.[26] In the summer 1823, Beltrami reached Lake Julia (in northern Minnesota) by canoe, a discovery later recognized by most historians. During that same year, Paolo Andreani, suffering from degenerative gout as well as being poor and exiled, died in Nice a few days before his sixtieth birthday. Although forgotten by history, documentary evidence reveals that, in 1791, Andreani may have reached a yet unspecified location at the headwaters of the Mississippi, thus preceding by some thirty years the travels and explorations of the better-known Beltrami. This new and interesting twist to the saga of Paolo Andreani in America is currently under investigation and will be the subject of a future paper on our no longer forgotten traveler.

## NOTES

1. G. Hubert Smith, "Count Andreani: A Forgotten Traveler," *Minnesota History*, 19, 1 (1938): 34–42.

2. For a detailed treatment of Andreani's first journey in America, and the complete translated text of his Iroquois diary, readers are referred to the newly published volume by Cesare Marino and Karim Tiro, *Along the Hudson and Mohawk: The 1790 Journey of Count Paolo Andreani* (Philadelphia: University of Pennsylvania Press, 2006.) We are grateful to Countess Luisa Sormani Verri of Milano, a descendant of Count Andreani, for authorizing the publication. For the Italian transcription of the original diary see: *Giornale 1790. Diario di un viaggio da New York ai villaggi irochesi* [etc.], a cura di Cesare Marino (Bologna: CLUEB, 2005). This writer is also currently working on a preliminary assessment of the second Andreani journal; see endnote 21.

3. Daniele Fiorentino, "Accidental Ethnographers: Italian Travelers and Scholars and the American Indians (1750–1900), *European Review of Native American Studies*, 4, 2 (1990): 31–36.

4. Francesco dal Verme, *Seeing American and Its Great Men: The Journal and Letters of Count Francesco dal Verme, 1783–1784;* translated and edited by Elizabeth Cometti (Charlottesville, VA: University Press of Virginia, 1969.)

5. See Antonio Pace's two essays, "The American Philosophical Society and Italy," *Proceedings of the American Philosophical Society*, 90, 5 (1946): 387–419; and "Benjamin Franklin and Italy," Memoirs of the American Philosophical Society, Vol. 47 (1958).

6. Lugi Castiglioni, *Viaggio negli Stati Uniti dell'America settentrionale fatto negli anni 1785, 1786, 1787; Trasunto delle osservazioni sui vegetabili dell'America settentrionale,* (Milano: G. Marelli, 1790). See also, Luigi Castiglioni's Viaggio, translated and edited by Antonio Pace (Syracuse, N.Y.: Syracuse University Press, 1983).

7. For additional biographical information see Giuseppe Dicorato, *Paolo Andreani, Aeronauta, esploratore, scienziato nella Milano dei Lumi* (1763–1823) (Milano: Edizioni Ares, 2001).

8. Andreani's magical flight was the subject of an extensive documentary collection assembled by Jotti da Badia Polesine, "Nuovi documenti intorno al Cav. Don Paolo Andreani ed alle prime esperienze aerostatiche eseguite in Italia," L'Aeronautica, Milano, No. 4 (1931): 365–370, 442–448, 513–518, 577–581, 649–655, and 745–747.

9. Three of the Andreani diaries of this first European journeys were edited, respectively, by Domenico Porzio, *Diario di un viaggio di un gentiluomo Milanese, Parigi-Londra 1784,* (Milano: Il Viale, 1975); by Emilio Fortunato, *Giornale di un viaggio; un gentiluomo milanese sulle Alpi,* (Milano: Cda & Vivalda, 2003); and again by Fortunato, *In tour aspettando Goethe,* (Milano: Viennepierre, 2004). Other diaries and letters, still in manuscript form, are in the Fondo Sormani-Andreani, Archivio di Stato, Milano (hereafter, FSA-ASMI).

10. Paolo Andreani to Gian Mario Andreani, Londra, 31 Agosto 1789, FSA-ASMI.

11. This was the Italian translation of the *American Gazetteer,* originally issued in London in 1762; it contained, as the running subtitle explained, un distinto ragguaglio di tutte le parti del Nuovo Mondo, della loro situazione, clima, terreno, prodotti, stato antico e moderno, etc. *The Gazzettiere* was published by Marco Coltellini in Livorno in 1763.

12. Franklin's Scelta is a selection of his scientific works translated from the 1773 French edition and published in Milano in 1774; the Avviso, which was made available to Italian readers in Franklin's famous *Two Tracts,* was published in Cremona in 1785.

13. Filippo Mazzei to James Madison, March 1790, James Madison Papers, Library of Congress, Washington, D.C.

14. Paolo Andreani to Gian Mario Andreani, 26 Maggio 1790, FSA-ASMI; Paolo wrote, Ho pranzato oggi con [cinque capi Indiani] dal Governatore, e come parlano un poco lo Spagnolo, da cosi ho potuto conversare seco [con] loro; see also William Sturtevant, "The Cherokee Frontiers, the French Revolution, and William Augustus Bowles", in: The Cherokee Indian Nation, edited by Duane King (Knoxville: University of Tennessee Press, 1979: 61–91). The diaries of Andreani's Atlantic crossing, his brief stay in Halifax and subsequent transfer to New York were edited by Emilio Fortunato, *Viaggio in Nord America,* (Milano: Scheiwiller, 1994). They have not yet been translated into English.

15. Paolo Andreani to Gian Mario Andreani, 16 Dicembre 1791, FSA-ASMI.

16. For Andreani's criticism of the American cities see Cesare Marino, "La citta nella natura," Storia urbana, *Fascicolo 105,* Milano, (2003): 19–31.

17. Vittorio Alfieri, *L'American Libera, Odi di Vittorio Alfieri da Asti,* privately printed by Pierre A. C. Beaumarchais at Kehl on the Rhine, 1784.

18. See Thomas Vennum, "One of a Kind Find: A Drawing of an Iroquois Lacrosse Stick is Found in an 18th Century Manuscript," *Lacrosse Magazine,* 23, 6 (1999): 60–61; the article was based on information and a translation of the original tract provided by the present writer.

19. Henry Tuckerman, *America and Her Commentators* (New York: Scribner's, 1864), 340; Tuckerman incorrectly wrote that "after visiting President Washington, Count Andriani of Milan . . . wrote an abuse book about America." Andreani may have intended to do so, but no such book was ever printed.

20. An insightful reading on this subject is the classic by Rufus Griswold, *The Republican Court* (New York: Appleton, 1867); see also a more recent article by Jay Tolson, "Founding Rivalries," *U.S. News & World Report,* 26 February 2001: 50–55.

21. The reconstruction of Andreani's voyage to the Great Lakes is taken directly from a photocopy of the original Italian journal kindly provided to this writer by Count Gaetano Belgiojoso of Milano.

22. An extract of the detailed figures Andreani collected on the fur trade were published by the Duke of La Rochefoucault Liancourt, *Travels Through the United States of North America,* etc., 2 vols., London; see Vol. 1 (1799): 325–335, chapter titled: "Accounts of the Fur-trade, extracted from the Journal of Count Andriani [sic] of Milan, who travelled [sic] in the interior parts of American in the year 1791." It is unclear how La Rochefoucault obtained a copy of Andreani's journal; the same author praised Andreani's abilities and character which, he concluded, inspired great confidence in the exactness of the information the Italian explorer had compiled at the distant trading posts.

23. Thomas L. McKenney, *Sketches of a Tour to the Lakes,* etc. (Baltimore: F. Lucas, 1827): 263. See also J. Johnston to H.R. Schoolcraft, 10 June 1828 in: *H.R. Schoolcraft, Oneota, or Characteristics of the Red Race of America* (New York: n.p., 1845): 299–301.

24. John J. Bigsby, *The Shoe and Canoe, or, Pictures of Travel in the Canadas,* 2 vols., (London: Chapman and Hall, 1850): 228.

25. Fortunato, *Viaggio in Nord America*, 53–128.

26. Beltrami related his discovery in *La Decourverte des Sources du Mississippi,* etc. (Nouvelle Orleans, B. Levy, 1824); and in Vol. 2 of A Pilgrimage in Europe and America, etc. (London: Hunt and Clarke, 1828); he replied to his critics in To the Public of New York and of the United States, (New York, 1825). See also Augusto P. Miceli, *The Man with the Red Umbrella: Giacomo Costantino Beltrami in America,* (Baton Rouge, LA: Claitor's, 1974) and Cesare Marino, "Bravo Beltrami!" *Ambassador Magazine,* 27 (1995): 6–11.

# ITALIAN WOMEN'S LIVES: DO WHAT PRESENTS ITSELF

TEMPLE UNIVERSITY

Sister Blandina Segale, missionary, frontierswoman and Italian immigrant was born in Cicagna, Italy, a small town near Genoa, in 1850. Her family immigrated to Cincinnati, Ohio when she was four. At sixteen, she joined the Sisters of Charity of Cincinnati and when she was twenty-two was assigned to teach in Trinidad, Colorado, a rough mining town where the first Sisters had arrived only two years before. Because of the difficulty in traveling in the Southwest and knowing that her contact with her family would be infrequent, Sister Blandina decided to keep a journal of her life experiences, which she intended to share only with her sister when they met again. Her sister, Sister Justina, also a Sister of Charity was stationed in Ohio. Sister Blandina's journal was written in the twenty years between 1872 and 1892 when she lived first in Trinidad, Colorado, then in Santa Fe and Albuquerque, New Mexico. The years she spent in the Southwest were times of enormous political and social change. This was the era of the Indian Wars between the U.S. government and the Apache and Ute Nations in New Mexico. In addition, there was the push of settlers westward, the building of the transcontinental railroad, which was completed in New Mexico in 1878, the arrival of "land-grabbers" and dangerous individuals such as Billy the Kid who was shot in New Mexico in 1881. Furthermore, Sister Blandina was in the West during the continued destruction of the indigenous population and the surrender of Apache Chief Geronimo. Although Sister Blandina's intention in writing was not to take a political stand on the issues of her day, a close reading of her journal reveals her values and indicates that her beliefs about the treatment of indigenous people and the role of women are rooted in an Italian cultural practice.

In a study of southern Italian women, *Women of the Shadows*, published in 1976 and based on ten years of work in the 1950s in Lucania with the Save the Children Fund, Ann Cornelisen reflects upon the abject poverty of the villages in which she lived, the unlikelihood that *la miseria* would be relieved soon and the strength, inventiveness, endurance, and courage of the women who were born and died under these conditions. She attributes the development of these qualities of resilience in the women to a "certain moral fortitude" which she believes to be the result of the conditions under which the women lived and had lived for generations. Despite much evidence to the contrary, Cornelisen is convinced that the society is a matriarchal one and that "whatever quality of life there had been in the South [and] whatever security has depended on the women" (226). One woman whom Cornelisen grew to know quite well, Chichella, comments on her own life and the lives of other southern women. Cornelisen quotes her as saying:

> As for the women. Put any label you want on it. It amounts to the same thing: we do whatever no one else has done. That's what we're taught; that's what we're supposed to do. Men work and talk about politics. We do the rest . . . That's what our lives are. We're born knowing it . . . It's a world of work. It's that simple. If you want something, you work. (Cornelisen, 227–228)

A more recent study, *Widows in White: Migration and the Transformation of Rural Italian Women, Sicily, 1880–1920* (2003) by Linda Reeder, while disputing the idea of southern Italy as a matriarchal society, supports Cornelisen's findings that Italian women are quite capable of taking advantage of every opportunity to improve their status no matter the degree of work involved and have managed to succeed quite well when they are without men. Reeder examined migration from the perspective of the women who were left behind in the rural south and for the first time took on new responsibilities such as paying taxes and enrolling children in schools. Her study finds that in the years between 1880 and 1920 "white widows," women whose husbands had gone to American, were able for the first time to start small businesses and buy consumer goods with the money their husbands sent back to the villages. Often, they enrolled in school to become literate and participate further in their own development and that of their children. Reeder acknowledges "the lives of these women testify to the complicated nature of patriarchal relations in southern Italy and point to the ways Sicilian women carved out some degree of moral and economic power within the family" (15). Reeder argues that because so many men left southern Italy in the Great Migration, as early as 1910 "a distinctly female image of national belonging had emerged in rural Italy" (4). She further claims "these women appear at the center of the great social, economic, and political changes that transformed rural life at the beginning of the twentieth century" (16). Both researchers attest to the creativity, courage and spunk of Italian women.

In discussing writing that records personal history like that of Sister Blandina, Susan Carol Hauser makes a distinction between a journal and a memoir by examining the intended audience: a journal or diary is written with only the self in mind as reader while the memoir, frequently written for publication, is intended for an audience of strangers. In many ways audience awareness governs the kinds of things that are recorded and the writer's reflections on those events. Sister Blandina Segale's record, *At the End of the Santa Fe Trail*, is unique because although it was written to be shared with only one other person, the historic value of an eye-witness account of the establishment of schools and hospitals on the frontier led to a cry for publication in 1932. It was published as originally written because Sister Blandina, eighty-three years old at the time, felt her work as a Sister of Charity kept her too busy to revise it. A journal, written to be shared with a cherished relative who could both be expected to share the writer's values and hold similar ones, became a public voice representing the writer to the world as a member of both a religious community and an Italian American one. Sister Blandina's record and interpretation of events can be placed in a tradition of life writing by Italian American women which foreshadows current examples of the genre.

Edvige Giunta, in examining recently published memoirs of Italian American women, sees these contemporary writers in Gramscian terms. Through writing they become "public intellectuals" who in revealing their own stories can promote social and political transformation. Giunta suggests that Louise DeSalvo's, *Breathless: An Asthma Journal* (1997) both reveals her personal experience with the disease and makes a political statement about the severity of the current asthma crisis in American inner cities. Likewise in *Wrongful Death* (1994) Sandra Gilbert combines a personal narrative with a political reflection on public health issues. For Giunta these memoirs "speak of and to a collective cultural and political consciousness and seek to recount stories that, while filtered through the voice of one individual, partake in the lives and voices of a community" (119). Giunta further notes that current Italian American memoirists "act as spokespersons for—and also sustainers of—historically disenfranchised communities" (119). At times the role of the public intellectual is to speak for the "silenced and disenfranchised who paradoxically, are often marginalized by the same community on whose behalf these women speak" (122).

In examining Sister Blandina's memoir, I wish to look at the ways it locates her as a strong and resilient women like those mentioned by Cornelisen and Reeder and the ways in which Sister Blandina becomes a public intellectual in her writing representing the voices of the disenfranchised Indians and Mexicans. In addition, she becomes a spokeswoman for several communities to which she belongs telling the story of the American frontier through the eyes of an Italian American nun.

Sister Blandina begins her journal by including the letter she received from her superior indicating she would be traveling to Trinidad alone, which was quite unusual for a nun at that time. Then she includes warnings from friends about the dangers she would be facing from cowboys and potential snow storms, which would be compounded because she would have to face them alone. In addition, she describes in detail a day she spent at an open house at her parent's home on December 5, 1872 just before she began her journey. She describes the many people who, at the open house, protested her leaving culminating with her mother offering to give her a one thousand dollar check in case she desired to come home and her father commanding her not to go. Sister Blandina, with the courage Cornelisen found in the Italian women she interviewed, writes: "Why should snow or cowboys frighten me any more than others who will be traveling the same way" (5)? She refuses her mother's check; tells her mother's friend, Mrs. Garibaldi, that she has "chosen her portion;" and writes that although she is pained by her father's tears, she is more pleased to be going alone than if she had a dozen chaperons with her.

Her determination and courage serve her well on her journey to Trinidad. She encounters a cowboy, and is at first prepared to die. When he addresses her, she finds that he is harmless and encourages him to write to his mother. The parish priest in Trinidad undertakes to play a joke on her in an attempt to find out "what kind of a Sister is she who was sent across the plains alone" (27). He comes to her stagecoach door as it stops outside of town and tries to convince her that a small store is the convent to which she had been assigned. Sister Blandina is not fooled and stays in the stage until she reaches her true destination.

In Trinidad, Sister Blandina's first concern is to review her Spanish so she can communicate with the Spanish speakers who have lived on the land for several hundred years before it became a territory of the United States and whom she will be teaching. She is surprised that the other sisters do not speak Spanish. Her first look at the schoolhouse reveals that is has only two small windows and a tiny door to "protect the inhabitants in case of a sudden attack from the warring Indians" (27). Ventilation has been sacrificed for security. Acquiring a bright and airy schoolhouse becomes her first objective. After walking through the town and seeing the homes of some residents and the jail, she writes: "I have adopted this plan: Do whatever presents itself, and never omit anything because of hardship or repugnance" (29). In her determination to handle any situation that might arise, she echoes the words of the southern woman, Chichella, who was interviewed by Ann Cornelisen: "As for the women. Put any label you want on it. It amounts to the same thing: we do whatever no one else has done. That's what we're taught; that's what we're supposed to do" (Cornelisen (227).

Sister Blandina's four years in Trinidad are spent teaching both Mexican and Indian students, having numerous successful confrontations with runaway horses, outlaws like Phil Schneider who murdered people along the Santa Fe Trail for their money or jewelry, and land-grabbers. Yet her most outstanding accomplishment was building a new schoolhouse with absolutely no money. She did this by standing on the roof one sunny morning armed only with a crowbar to take off the old adobes. Just as she had hoped, a Spanish woman, who was married to an Anglo, saw the nun and immediately offered to provide her with six workers and the necessary supplies to complete her project. As the new building began to take shape, Sister Blandina found other wealthy families to donate to the school. She also found several working-class families willing to work on the project in exchange for free tuition for their children. When the plastering started, Sister Blandina demanded that instead of the customary mud walls, the school should have smooth walls of lime, sand and hair. Although the plasterer was opposed to using new materials, particularly, since their use had been suggested by a woman, he agreed to do what she asked on the condition that she would take responsibility for any failure. Since all the other workers had left for the day when Sister finally won over the plasterer, Sister Blandina got a bucket and proceeded to carry the mortar to the plasterer so he could continue his work. As she was thus engaged, the Rt. Rev. Bishop Joseph Machebeuf of Denver, Colorado arrived on his visitation. In the end the walls turned out smooth and the plasterer made a lucrative living using Sister's American method of plastering and the reverend discovered the ingenuity of Sister Blandina.

Sister instituted a vigilant committee among her students whose job it was to find people in need of the sisters' help. Through this committee Sister helped an outlaw who had been shot in the thigh by a man he had murdered. As it turned out Billy the Kid was a friend of his and came to Trinidad to scalp the doctors who had refused to help his friend. When Sister Blandina heard about this, she went out to meet Billy the Kid and managed to prevent the scalpings.

In addition to recording heroic deeds, Sister Blandina's journal allows the reader to understand her beliefs about the Spanish and Indian people to whom she ministers. Her most telling remark is "Every Spaniard or Mexican I've met has an innate refinement" (38). She respects the Spanish speakers and believes that the Indians are being abused by the government. If there are any people she does not respect, they are the land-grabbers who took advantage of Indians and Mexicans. These unscrupulous speculators robbed many poor unsuspecting victims by fraudulently securing their land deeds. She recounts endless stories of injustice to Indians and Mexicans. She records that during Easter week, an elderly American couple was found murdered in their homes. The people in the town suspected the natives as the perpetrators and so small groups of men went out to capture the murderers. They found four Mexicans who refused to say they were guilty. The angry posse, believing the Mexicans were lying, lynched them and threw their bodies in an abandoned adobe hut near the convent. Two days later the real murderers were captured and confessed the crime. The true murderers were American.

Of American land-grabbers she writes: "The Mexican cannot forget that all his earthly possessions have gone into the hands of strangers. Woe to the poor native if he attempts to retaliate! He has no rights that the invading fortune hunters feel obliged to respect" (45).

Reflecting upon the American treatment of Indians, Blandina intoned:

> Rafael chief of the Ute Indians, came to tell me that his son is dead. 'Shall I throw him away like a dog?' meaning without Christian burial, 'or will you take him The white men call us dogs!' Poor creature! There are crimes which cry for vengeance . . . Generations to come will blush for the deeds of this, toward the

rightful possessors of the soil. Our government, which poses with upraised finger of scorn on any act which savors of tyranny, lowers that finger to crush out of existence a race whose right to the land we call America is unquestioned. Has custom made might right? (52).

Of the writing of official histories of the Southwest she writes:

True, Mr. [George] Bancroft did narrate in his History of the United States some of the hardships and heroic sacrifices made by the first Jesuits, but I have been told on excellent authority that bigots are determined to have Mr. Bancroft omit the praise given the first Indian missionaries when he issues the next edition ... How much is there made of Lord Baltimore giving freedom of conscience to those who lived where he controlled! Yet look at the stream of articles constantly given to the public about Plymouth Rock and the Pilgrim Fathers! 'Oh, Justice, where art thou! (56)

Sister Blandina was sent to Santa Fe in January of 1877. While there she began an industrial school for girls once again participating in the physical labor involved. She was active at St. Vincent Hospital in providing health care, especially for the poor. While in Santa Fe she successfully lobbied the New Mexico Territorial legislature for assistance in paying for medical care for the poor and persuaded the county coroner to pay for their burial. Later she was sent to Albuquerque first to teach and then in 1901 she returned to supervise the building of St. Joseph's Hospital. Although her journal ends in 1892 just before she began her assignment in Pueblo, Colorado, Sister Blandina's biographer notes that in 1905 the nun was assigned with her sister Sister Justina to begin work among the Italian immigrants in Ciccinnati: "They branched out into every aspect of social services and by 1897 had founded the Santa Maria Italian Educational and Institutional Home, probably the first such institution in the United States." After thirty-six years at Santa Maria, Sister Blandina died at ninety-one in 1941.

Her journal records the actions and thoughts of a public intellectual, which demonstrate that she followed her plan to "Do what presents itself and never omit anything because of hardship or repugnance" (29). She has the strength an compassion of the women of Italy that both Cornelisen and Reeder record.

## WORKS CITED

Cornelisen, Ann. *Women of the Shadows.* Boston: Little, Brown, 1975.

Giunta, Edvige. *Writing With an Accent: Contemporary Italian American Women Authors.* New York: Palgrave, 2002.

Houser, Susan. *You Can Write a Memoir.* Cincinnati: *Writers Digest,* 2001.

Reeder, Linda. *Widows in White: Migration and the Transformation of Rural Italian Women, Sicily, 1880–1920.* Toronto: University of Toronto Press, 2003.

Segale, Sister Blandina. *At the End of the Santa Fe Trail.* Albequeque: University of New Mexico, 1999.

# GIUSEPPE GARIBALDI AND HENRY ADAMS

HENRY VEGGIAN
UNIVERSITY OF PITTSBURGH

The conference program states that I will present a paper on "Garibaldi in America;" and while it is true that I will speak of Giuseppe Garibaldi with respect to America, my example will not draw upon Garibaldi's visits to the United States. Nor will I speak on how the majority of historians, literary critics, or cultural organizations maintain this heroic icon. Rather, this essay is concerned with a singular example of Garibaldi's life, or after-life, in the writings of the U.S. historian and novelist Henry Adams. My essay seeks to distinguish between the particular rhetorical strategies Henry Adams developed with respect to Garibaldi in *The Education of Henry Adams* (1918) and other and more conventional and heroic interpretations of Garibaldi's writings and life. The distinction is made possible by Adams' late style and its relationship to a historical tradition of Italian pessimism to which Garibaldi also belonged.

The following essay is an extract from a longer work that I have planned. In this work, Garibaldi is a subject of three distinct yet overlapping intellectual traditions. The first and most popular is the Romantic tradition that begins with the influence of Thomas Carlyle on the Italian *Risorgimento* and continues through the poetry of the Italian Nobel Laureate Giosue Carducci and the British historian George Trevelyan. The second is the tradition of Hegelian-Marxism that includes such later figures as Antonio Gramsci and Eric Hobsbawm. The third tradition is that of historical prose, which includes both the novel and historical study (with important distinctions). This last tradition begins with a study of Henry Adams and continues through what

Edward Said has described as the "Garibaldean ethics" of Joseph Conrad's *Nostromo,* Giuseppe Tommasi di Lampedusa's eminent *Gattopardo,* and the parody in Thomas Pynchon's *V.*[1] In its long, historical trajectory, my work favors the novel as the most vital discursive form of the three. Nonetheless, the project investigates connections among the three traditions on the shorter historical wavelengths where the project also elaborates affinities between them and the more local struggles.[2]

The affinity in question is that between Henry Adams and Giuseppe Garibaldi. The two men met twice (in Palermo, 1860 and in London, 1864), but two more disparate men could not be imagined. Rather, *The Education of Henry Adams* uses Garibaldi's iconic figure as a pretext for an iconoclastic rendering of history. Adams' intention is to render history intelligible without reproducing that iconic human figure. In this respect, *The Education* announces itself as directly opposed to the anthropomorphic philosophical and lyrical premises of nineteenth-century European Romanticism.

Paul DeMan recently argued most convincingly the anthropomorphic power of Romantic literary and philosophical discourse. DeMan argues in his essay "Anthropomorphism and Trope in the Lyric" that the anthropomorphic "gesture...links epistemology with rhetoric in general, and not only with the mimetic tropes of representation."[3] DeMan's thesis is dramatic in that it announces the problem by the very kinetic, physiological motion of the gesture: style appears as the hand composes the page. Beginning with an example from Friedrich Nietzsche, DeMan argues that the anthropomorphic gesture deploys its nominal power in an aggregate form. It is distinguished in this way in modern rhetoric from the singularity of the trope. The gesture "disrupts" the relation between tropes and discourse, brings their differences "into focus," and ultimately affords the gesture the potential to elaborate "prosaic, or better, *historical* modes of language power" that constitute the actual nexus between rhetoric and truth in a particular situation.[4]

Following DeMan's example, I would venture that a genetic form of the anthropomorphic gesture can be distinguished as it appears in a single literary work against how it may coalesce in a body of such works. For example, the literary text may contain a singular anthropomorphic gesture, as in Charles Baudelaire's famous line: *hypocrite lecteur, mon semblable, mon frere!* In addressing the reader as a brother, the poem implies the reader is the poet's sibling. Indeed, the poet imposes human qualities on the reader. The gesture is thus twice anthropomorphic, and this is what DeMan suggests when he writes of its aggregate power: it combines the reader with rhetoric.

In contrast to this, a series of anthropomorphic gestures may accumulate within a tradition of writing about a particular subject. Such a series may attribute a series of human characteristics to a genre such as the novel. For example, Georg Lukacs, Erich Auerbach, and Ian Watt accord to Miguel de Cervantes' *Don Quixote* a privileged position in the evolution of the modern novel. Cervantes' novel is, for Lukacs, the first example of a new modern human consciousness different from that of the classical age. It is a progenitor of the modern novels that would follow. For Auerbach, Cervantes' novel is a mutation that continues the historical momentum of post-Christian literary humanism in a different form. Following these models, other readings communicate with *Don Quixote* by rhetorical gestures, by speaking with a 'voice,' by containing a grammatical circulatory system, by offering a linguistic endoskeleton, and so on. Critical readings can thus reproduce the anthropomorphic gesture as a genealogical discourse. Such gestures can be differentiated from the manner by which Baudelaire's gestures constitute a discourse among their singular forms (each of which is, according to DeMan, already an aggregate).

The anthropomorphic gesture is an incredibly productive and dynamic rhetorical strategy that organizes both language and discourse. Its continuation through the critical act is not exclusive to modern thought. Northrop Frye famously describes in *The Anatomy of Literary Criticism* two classical trajectories for the critical act as "the aesthetic and creative, the Aristotelian and Longinian, the view of literature as product and the view of literature as process."[5] The anthropomorphic gesture certainly belongs to the latter. It is the dynamic individual in the genetic scheme and the genealogical momentum of a historical continuum and process. The incomplete significance of process is one of the historical problems carried most effectively by modern humanism from the revival of classical works during the Renaissance. In the interest of brevity, I introduce only the unique approach taken to this matter by the U.S. historian and novelist Henry Adams in his late writings on Giuseppe Garibaldi.[6]

*The Education of Henry Adams* intervened in both the individual, genetic order of the gesture and its historical–genealogical schemes. It attempted a non-anthropomorphic, historical style that began from the premise that "the object of this study is the garment, not the figure."[7] In other words, it did not reproduce, extend, or improve the human figure of Garibaldi in either the genetic properties of the work or its genealogical relation to history. In order to achieve that style, Adams had first to dismantle the figure of its Romantic and exotic cliché and all other prejudices pertinent to the nineteenth-century American perception of Italy. Adams would furthermore have to destroy the anthropomorphic gestures that claimed later to reproduce and improve upon Garibaldi's life—the "figure"—in rhetoric.

Giuseppe Garibaldi is generally treated in historical studies, ethnic studies, and literary works as a figure that invites such anthropomorphic improvement. Indeed, Garibaldi often presented his own life in those terms, particularly in his calculated staging of photographic portraits, a manner that he later came to regret. Volumes of writing about Garibaldi were added during Adams' lifetime to those iconic portraits, especially during the celebrated years 1848–1861. Those volumes included George Trevelyan's monumental three-volume study of Garibaldi's life. First published in 1909, Trevelyan's books conclude with Garibaldi's romantic legend in monumental, spectacular form. Trevelyan's precedent extends to the tremendous archival work dedicated to Garibaldi and the Italian *Risorgimento* that has resulted in a minor industry in Italy and the U.S.[8] Garibaldi and the other major figures of the *Risorgimento*—Giuseppe Mazzini, Count Camillo Cavour, Victor

Emmanuel II, Napoleon III, Prime Minister Gladstone, and others—
are cultivated to this day by that industry as the last characters
left on the stage after all the modern European nations had been
built—except one, that is, Italy. Garibaldi's heroic and iconic image
embodies the drama of that Romantic rhetorical tradition. It was
against such thinking that Adams devoted *The Education*.[9]

Henry Adams was a young man of twenty-one in the summer
of 1859. He entered Italy with his sister Mary (Mrs. Kuhn) when
the armistice between Austria and France was declared following
the Austro-Sardinian War. His sister, "not satisfied with Milan
. . . insisted on invading the enemy's country, and the carriage was
chartered for Innsbruck by way of the Stelvio Pass."[10] Adams first
witnesses Garibaldi's soldiers in the war of 1859, the *Cacciatori
delle Alpi*, as the carriage passed through to the Austrian border.

> [W]hen at last, after climbing what was said to be the
> finest carriage pass in Europe, the carriage turned the
> last shoulder, where the glacier of the *Ortler Spitze*
> tumbled its huge mass down upon the road, and Mrs.
> Kuhn gasped as she was driven directly up to the
> barricade and stopped by the double line of sentries
> stretching on either side up the mountains, till the flash
> of the gun barrels was lost in the flash of the snow.
>
> For accidental education the picture had its value.
> The earliest of these pictures count for most, as first
> impressions must, and Adams never afterwards cared
> much for landscape education.[11]

The Romantic landscape that begins with the first encounter
with Garibaldi's men continues through his sister's sublime
gasp, and concludes with the confusion of the soldiers with the
landscape. Hereafter, Adams' suspicion of the visual sense will
rigorously evacuate any trace of the "landscape education" offered
by Italy as in, for example, those images popularized by American
painters of the Hudson River School. The evacuation culminates
when Adams first encounters Garibaldi the following year.

Adams returned to Italy in the spring of 1860 and arrived
in Rome shortly before Garibaldi and his thousand attacked

Palermo. The Sicilian city of Palermo was then under a Spanish Bourbon monarchy, the Kingdom of Naples. Upon learning of the event, Adams requested a U.S. naval officer, who was a family acquaintance, allow him to visit Palermo. The officer consented and took Adams to chronicle the fight for *The Boston Courier*.[12]

The young Adams was introduced to General Garibaldi shortly after the victory of the Thousand separated Sicily from the Bourbon king of Naples. The men arrived to make an evening call on Garibaldi, whom they found in the Senate House towards sunset, at supper with his picturesque and piratic staff, in the full noise and color of the Palermo revolution. As a spectacle, it belonged to Rossini and the Italian opera, or to Alexander Dumas at the least, *but the spectacle was not its educational side*. Garibaldi left the table, and, sitting down at the window, had a few words of talk with Captain Palmer and young Adams. At that moment, in the summer of 1860, Garibaldi was certainly the most serious of the doubtful energies in the world; the most essential to gauge rightly. Even then society was divided between banker and anarchist. One or the other, Garibaldi must serve. Himself a typical anarchist, sure to overshadow Europe and alarm empires bigger than Naples, his success depended on his mind; his energy was beyond doubt.[13]

The denunciation of "spectacle" continues the evacuation of "landscape education." The prose clears the *mise-en-scene* of human clutter; the cliché of the opera and the brigand are cast aside. (Dumas had translated Garibaldi's *My Life* to French, and Adams probably first read it in that language.) Garibaldi must be defined not in terms of his own human agency, but in relation to other aggregate forces such as institutions and empires. *The Education of Henry Adams* distinguishes in this way a non-anthropomorphic, historical intelligence from the sensual encumbrance of "landscape education" or the Romantic icon's seductive energies. What is left, then, Italy or Garibaldi? The two are often confused, almost interchangeable terms for Adams, yet never entirely synonymous. In this critical respect, Adams' critique of Garibaldi departed from Garibaldi's conclusion in his autobiography.

Giuseppe Garibaldi's memoirs were not the story of his life, but a relentless polemic against it. The polemic was written with the assumption that Garibaldi's own life was the life of modern Italy.[14] To that end, Garibaldi's book was a second war of liberation—a campaign to free Garibaldi's Italy from Italy's Garibaldi. The book contains, as would be expected, a merciless critique of the foreign monarchies that once occupied the Italic peninsula, especially Austria and Spain. But Garibaldi also attacked the peoples he liberated. Garibaldi famously despised the Vatican priests who corrupted and deceived the peasantry, but he also (and infamously) distrusted the peasants who believed the Vatican's lies. He lashed out against the allegedly sympathetic monarchs of France, Sardinia, and Savoy and was suspicious throughout of any of their political maneuvers and the institutions from which they emanated. He excoriated those people who spied for foreign powers or the church and was generally indignant when confronted with the timidity of his volunteers or local brigands who deserted in the thick of battle. And finally he included Giuseppe Mazzini and the Republicans among the parties he despised most at the end of his life. About the rumors that ended his 1867 campaign to drive the Pope from Rome, Garibaldi wrote, "So the Italian Government, the priests, and the Mazzinians had succeeded in unsettling our men."[15] We must distinguish, however, between the rhetorical and the actual. In the rhetorical mode, the final object of Garibaldi's relentless critique is the heroic icon of Garibaldi as liberator and hero adored by millions around the world. In actuality, the work is often read as a critique of Italy, as we shall later see.

Garibaldi appears suspicious throughout the work of the tendency to impose the anthropomorphic, rhetorical design, that is, "Garibaldi," upon the forces at work in the Italian *Risorgimento*. It is thus possible to understand Garibaldi's memoirs as either a rhetorically subtle and self-critical work or as a polemic against the actual political failures of the *Risorgimento*. It is often impossible to separate the two.

Yet a disjunction remains. Garibaldi's critical admonitions obscure a fundamental contradiction in the writings. If the people of the Italic peninsula were so corrupt, cowardly, and ignorant, why did Garibaldi bother to drive out their oppressors and liberate them? Or, to phrase it in the rhetorical matter, how do the memoirs redress the failures and consequences of his historical actions, if at all? It is also possible that Garibaldi wrote the memoirs to salvage his own image from those very consequences, but he could have done so only by negating the connection between the icon and the nation. And this was something, which he could not entirely achieve. As a result, Garibaldi's military and written deeds stand in open disagreement, and the disjunction permits us to distinguish among the relative merits of each.

It is all too often, however, that literary rhetoric, and especially that of Romanticism, has sought to erase that difference and capture Garibaldi's actions in language. As a consequence, Garibaldi's life and actions have inspired a heroic rhetoric of popular struggle and liberation at the expense of Garibaldi's own self-effacing writings. The British novelist Tim Parks has recently written a provocative forward to a newly translated and published British edition of Garibaldi's memoirs. It offers a limited explanation why Garibaldi's icon persists even though his writings are widely ignored: "About halfway through this book you realize that Garibaldi is not read in the country whose cause he served because so much of what he says would make unwelcome reading to many sections of contemporary society. Italy has an uneasy relationship with its recent past."[16] This final sentence warrants closer attention. Can we say that Garibaldi and the *Risorgimento* belong to the "recent past" of Italian history? If we do so, we assume an evolutionary continuity of form in the modern Italian state. The implied continuity begins with the monarchical compromise of the First Republic, continues through the totalitarian accommodations of the post World War I era, culminates with the parliamentary democracy of the post-World War II years and continues to the present. It is a long history, fraught with peril for such an easy statement. Parks' argument is most dangerous when it assumes that the *Risorgimento* was only the "recent past" of a longer Italian history, when in fact modern

Italy did not exist autonomously as a nation prior to 1860, at the very earliest. Any student of Garibaldi's life and reception in the United States must question these assumptions. A similar problem of implied continuity is complicated, if not confirmed, when we consider how Garibaldi has been exalted in Romantic literary-historical rhetoric against the self-criticism offered by his memoir. *The Education of Henry Adams* ultimately elaborates the discontinuity between the man and his writings. It is certainly the most lucid rendering of Garibaldi's writing and their contentious relationship to Italian (and European) historical realities in modern U.S. literature. Adams comments on Garibaldi's memoir to this effect: "In the end, if the 'Autobiography' tells the truth, Garibaldi saw and said that he had not understood his own acts; that he had been an instrument; that he had served the purpose of the class which he least wanted to help; yet in 1860 he thought of himself as the revolution anarchic, Napoleonic, and his ambition was unbounded."[17] Garibaldi's writings confirm Adams' pessimism with respect to the value of "landscape education," with its trinkets and rhetorical icons. But Adams' estimation is something more than just an attitude of pessimism; it extends the rhetorical and historical traditions that informed the *Risorgimento*. Mazzini had criticized that pessimism in his progenitors Alessandro Manzoni and Silvio Pellico, and he often said the same, or worse, of Garibaldi.[18] Garibaldi lived, however, to see Mazzini's optimism crushed. As Garibaldi composed his memoirs, Italy fell into the hands of the priestly class and monarchs that he despised. By the end of his life, Italy was emptied of its rural populace, restricted by secret alliances, and set upon a doomed, imperial venture. His pessimism is posthumously confirmed by the terrors of Fascism and the Second World War. The political writings of Antonio Gramsci are the compliment to the former; the late masterwork *Il Gattopardo* by the novelist Giuseppe Tomassi di Lampedusa is witness to the latter. Together, the writings constitute a tradition that the American novelist Thomas Pynchon describes as "the serene river of Italian pessimism."[19]

The rhetorical tradition of Italian pessimism begins for many with Dante's exile. I would trace it from a later figure, the

Neapolitan, Giambattista Vico. While neither Dante nor Vico were pessimistic thinkers who literally expected the worst, their nationalism appeared ironically outside—and in the absence of—any actual institutional framework for a modern Italian state. Vico is the better example because he lived and wrote about the "Ancient Wisdom of the Italian Peoples" under the Bourbon Kings of Naples and influenced a great many intellectuals of the *Risorgimento*.

The secular–historical momentum of Vico's work provided the anti-monarchical justification for much later Italian Republican thought. Vico's English translators have traced a lineage from Vico to the novelist Alessandro Manzoni and finally to the political architect of the *Risorgimento*, Mazzini.[20] It was Mazzini, who, after several failed attempts, found in Garibaldi the military, political, and iconic force of a unified and secular modern Italian state. We could say of the *Risorgimento* that Rosmini provided its ethical foundations, Manzoni the aesthetic models, Mazzini the political theory, and Garibaldi the tactical iconography. From there one must distinguish them from other strains of 19th century European and American pessimism in the social and natural sciences which Adams had turned against late in his life.[21]

Adams non-anthropomorphic rendering of Garibaldi was not an example of what one historian recently described as Adams' "characteristic maliciousness."[22] Rather, Adams followed from a tradition of historical writing that the Risorgimento had inherited from Vico. (Henry Adams had inherited the style already from Michelet, Vico's French admirer). The "serene river of Italian pessimism" offered Adams formidable options to wield against the Carlyle-dominated tradition of Anglophone Romanticism that had informed the majority of writing about Garibaldi prior to *The Education of Henry Adams*.

Garibaldi's pessimism is central to the style of *The Education*. It is Adams' proof that Garibaldi's mind was capable to the task before it, but other forces, other "energies," overwhelmed it. One such energy was precisely the anthropomorphic principle of nineteenth-century Romanticism. The famously difficult and self-effacing style of *The Education*, which removes even Adams from the stage of history, is a singular attempt to achieve the non-anthropomorphic style in rhetoric. The pessimism that Henry Adams inherited from Garibaldi and the *Risorgimento* renders Adams' style as a creative, intelligent, and dramatic confrontation with the modern historical forces that defied the anthropomorphic rhetoric of Romanticism and the visual designs of "landscape education." Adams crafted a style and a dramatic historical *mis-en-scene* without attributing every significant event to the gestures of its actors. The evacuation of "landscape education," the critique of Romanticism, and the pessimistic estimation of Garibaldi ultimately make possible the distinctly American concerns of *The Education of Henry Adams* that begins with the contrast, favorable to Garibaldi, between Garibaldi and Ulysses S. Grant.

The *Education of Henry Adams* offers one final, sideshow glimpse of how Garibaldi had been consumed by his Romantic other. The last important glimpse of Giuseppe Garibaldi is a comic antithesis of the heroic man, a parody of Prometheus. Giuseppe Garibaldi arrived in London, England, in 1864 to raise money for the Italian *Risorgimento*. Henry Adams, then a young man of twenty-six years, assisted in the spectacle of Garibaldi's reception at Stafford House "in a palace gallery that recalled Paolo Veronese's pictures of Christ in his scenes of miracle, Garibaldi, in his gray capote over his red shirt, received all London, and three duchesses literally worshipped at his feet."[23] The scene renders the inherited icon of the hero. Garibaldi was ferociously anti-clerical in his politics, yet he is portrayed here as Christ with the three kings of the nativity prostrate before him. The iconography of the scene is preceded by Adams' account of the London visit of Mademoiselle Castiglione, the "famous beauty of the Second Empire." These two celebrated persons are presented as Christ and the virgin mother so as to illuminate how "an ordered social system tending to orderly development—in London or elsewhere—was beyond any process yet reached by the education of Henry Adams."[24] How then could one compose a non-anthropomorphic style of history? It was R. P. Blackmur who summarized the matter best in his unfinished *Henry Adams*: "[Garibaldi] stood for the greater thing, and the thing was inhuman. But he was also an individual, and tilted in ways that, like Rome, did not seem to fit any relation . . . [I]t was not that he lacked intelligence, but there was no way of telling if any was there."[25]

## NOTES

1. Edward Said. *Beginnings: Intention and Method.* (New York: Columbia University Press), 1975. Said's comment appears in *Beginnings*. This tradition is bound by a shared language of "force" and "energy" drawn from the science of thermodynamics. Adams was influenced by thermodynamics, and in particular its laws of energy, which were often extrapolated and distorted by other contemporary thinkers (including his own brother) to suit the social sciences. Yet Adams was too careful a reader of science and history to apply the models of one to other without discrimination. Garibaldi presented himself to Adams at the crossroads of the two, and the evacuation of his heroic figure in *The Education of Henry Adams* was exemplary of how, after the energetic models of Natural Science had been exhausted, there remained the brute facts of human history to contend with in all their anthropomorphic shame. (For an excellent overview of the influence of thermodynamics on nineteenth-century British letters; see Peter Allen Dale, *In Pursuit of a Scientific Culture,* (Madison: University of Wisconsin Press), 1990. Thermodynamics is familiar in exegeses of Adams, and I extend it through the importance of mining in *Nostromo,* Lampedusa's discussion of ballistics in the Neapolitan-Bourbon Army's rifles, and the entirety of Pynchon's *V.,* where the gaucho appears in the context of as a parody, an inversion and elaboration of Adam's famous chapter on "The Virgin and the Dynamo" in *The Education of Henry Adams.*

2. These include the early twentieth century meetings between Adams and Trevelyan and the appearance of Lampedusa's novel following the mid-century success of Gramsci's posthumously published prison writings in Italy.

3. Paul DeMan, "Anthropomorphism and Trope in the Lyric," *The Rhetoric of Romanticism,* (New York: Columbia University Press), 1984, 239.

4. Ibid, 240, 262.

5. Northrup Frye, *The Anatomy of Criticism: Four Essays,* (Princeton: Princeton University Press), 1957, 66, 326.

6. It is difficult to extend Frye's categories to Adams, but it may prove useful to situate Adams' book with respect to the Longinian "view of literature as process," while keeping in mind that Adams is, unlike Frye, concerned with "anatomy."

7. Henry Adams, *The Education of Henry Adams,* (New York: Houghton Mifflin), 2000, xviii.

8. The Yale historian Denis Mack Smith is one prominent, recent example of that industry's longevity.

9. In this respect, it is the iconoclastic compliment to his earlier book, Adams' *Mont Saint-Michel and Chartres.*

10. Adams, 86.

11. Adams, 87.

12. These were reprinted shortly after Adams' death in 1918.

13. Adams, 94. [Italics mine]

14. As I noted earlier, *The Education of Henry Adams* captures this ambiguity.

15. Giuseppe Garibaldi G., *My Life*, Trans. Stephen Parkin, (London: Hesperus Press), 2004, 158.

16. Tim Parks, Foreword. *My Life*. (London: Hesperus Press), 2004. vii-xi.

17. Adams, 95.

18. Denis Mack-Smith, *Mazzini*, (New Haven: Yale University Press), 1994, 37.

19. Thomas Pynchon, *V*, (New York: Harper Collins), 1999, 166.

20. Thomas Goddard Bergin and Max Harold Fisch. Introduction, *The Autobiography of Giambattista Vico*, Trans. Bergin and Fisch, Ithaca: Cornell University Press, 1944, 65–66. Bergin and Fisch do not mention the impact of the theologian Antonio Rosmini who introduced Manzoni to Vico. For a discussion of the latter see Sandra Bermann, Introduction, *On the Historical Novel*, Trans. Bermann, (Lincoln: Nebraska Press), 1984, 27–28.

21. Richard Hofstadter writes that the American sociologist Lester Frank Ward "regarded both the Malthus-Ricardo-Darwin lineage of pessimism and Spencerian optimism as an upper-class apologia for social oppression and misery."(*Social Darwinism and American Thought*, 78–79). The writings of Henry Adams on Garibaldi stand apart from the rhetorical traditions cited by Hofstadter and firmly within the Italian tradition, which is distinguished by its rhetorical style.

22. James Chace, 1912: *Wilson, Roosevelt, Taft, and Debs—The Election that Changed the Country*, New York: Simon and Schuster, 2004, 108.

23. Adams, 198.

24. Ibid, 199.

25. R. P. Blackmur, *Henry Adams*, ed. Veronica Makowski, (New York: Da Cappo), 1984, 47.

# Italian Entertainments in New York City Before the Mass Migration

Emelise Aleandri
Artistic Director, Frizzi & Lazzi: The Olde Time
Italian-American Music & Theatre Company

In America before the eighteenth century, except for the dance rituals of Native Americans, little if any entertainment was performed among any new immigrants because of the tremendous hardships of the struggling inhabitants. Furthermore, because the Puritans considered theatre the "graven image" forbidden in the Bible, they took a harsh stand against any theatrical entertainments. Eventually, and sometimes by subterfuge, this stranglehold on the theatre loosened through the persistence of American and English actor/managers. But, it would be a long time before Italian actor/managers arrived on the scene.

During the eighteenth and early nineteenth centuries, Italians immigrated not only because of the political and religious pressures in Italy, but also because of America's continuing need for Italian workers and craftsmanship. Eventually that need would extend to music and musicians and other types of entertainers. But who were these immigrant performers? Were they Italian residents who performed for their communities? Or were they itinerant comedians, such as those of the *Commedia dell'arte*? *Commedia dell'arte* still existed in Italy, although in its decline, a condition that might have precipitated Italian voyagers to ply their art in America.

We can only examine a few records that contain Italian names and speculate about their identities because the names of those who passed through other countries, like England, underwent alteration. For example, Taliaferro could become Toliver in England. A reference to the first Italian musical curiosity of note appears in an advertisement in New York City's September 14, 1746 *Evening-Post*. At the house of Wood Furman, one could, for two weeks, see "a curious musical machine" and "the Italian Mountebank, or fomous [sic] Quack" and many other oddities exhibited by John Brickell.[1] However, as early as 1757, and possibly before this year, traveling Italian musicians performed classical music in America, held concerts, and established music schools, all of which, we hope, countered the negative impression of Italians by Brickell. Among these early musical pioneers were two Philadelphians: composer and musician John Palma (1757) and Giovanni Gualdo, composer and teacher of the mandolin, violin, flute, guitar and harpsichord (1767 to 1769). Mr. Tioli, of Providence, was a tambourine dancer (1768); and in Williamsburg, Virginia, Francis Alberti of Faenza, a teacher of violin, harpsichord and other instruments, taught vocal and music lessons to Thomas Jefferson's future wife Martha (1748–1782).[2]

But theatre in New York City during the eighteenth century is our primary focus. Journalist Pasquale De Biasi, in Guglielmo Ricciardi's *Memoirs*, refers to a performance specifically for other Italians in 1765: Mr. Galluppi, Mr. Seminiani and Mr. Giardini presented a *commedia-ballata* (comedy ballet or dance comedy or "ballad opera").[3] Nothing else is known about this earliest Italian theatrical entertainment or where theatrical historians Italo Falbo and De Biasi got their information.[4]

On April 28, 1768, two Piedmontese brothers, who claimed they had been engineers for the King of Sardinia and performed for the royal family of Spain and the Duke of Gloucester, appeared at the Ranelagh (aka Renelaugh) Gardens on Broadway at Thomas Street.[5] In 1768, on December 9 and 12, the same "Two Italian Brothers," as they were billed, demonstrated an "elegant set of fireworks" at the Southwark Theatre in Philadelphia.[6] Seven months later, on June 27, 1769, a "Magnificent set of Fireworks by the Italians" (most probably the same two brothers) took place in New York City at the Vauxhall Gardens (later the Bowling Green Gardens) on Trinity Church property at Greenwich Street between Warren Street and Chambers Street on the shores of the

Hudson River. The fireworks shows displayed many themes, only a few of which were: rockets, Chinese fountains, Italian candles, illuminated colored wheels, stars, snakes, a Marquis' tent, the sun, the moon, the globe, a Chinese looking-glass, diamonds, flowers, triumphal arches and a wheel of fortune.[7] The fireworks of the "Two Italian Brothers" were targeted specifically for American audiences who required no knowledge of the Italian language to enjoy the show. It would take a full century before a regular, viable Italian American musical and theatrical presence took hold in New York City.

Until then, the Italian presence in the world of entertainment was, nevertheless, continuously evident. This study examines the origins, initial development and early progress of that thread and to reveal the patterns of theatrical activity prevalent until the period of the mass migration circa 1870, that coincided with the unification of Italy. After this date, many factors converged to allow a fuller Italian American participation in the entertainment field.

One such performer, during the colonial period, was Gaetano Franceschini. In April 1774, under the patronage of the St. Cecilia Society of Charleston, South Carolina, he performed a "Grand Concert of Vocal and Instrumental Music," consisting of solos, concertos on the violin, viola d'Amour and a sonata on the harpsichord at the theatre on Queen Street. He led concerts in Charleston and Philadelphia[8] until 1783, adding violins, cellos, bassoons, clarinets, oboes, flutes and horns.[9] In June 1783, Franceschini performed a benefit concert in New York City, which initiated his seasonal stay at the John Street Theatre located between Broadway and Nassau Street. Although Franceschini conducted the band at this theatre throughout the season, little else is known about this early Italian musician.[10] Another seasonal performer at this time was a Signora Mazzanti. An isolated notice stated that she gave a concert with English and Italian songs on April 24 and 28, 1774. She was the "first Italian songstress," sponsored by the gentlemen of the Harmonic Society, and "probably the first Italian woman to sing before an American audience."

Though Franceschini and probably Mazzanti were only

visitors to New York City, Nicholas Biferi, "Master of Music" and a singing teacher from Naples, was "determined to stay." In May and June 1774, he and some like-minded Italian entrepreneurs attempted to establish an "Academy of Arts" in the city. Biferi advertised that he planned to teach vocal music "after the Italian way" and harpsichord at James Wilmot's store in Peck Slip for one guinea for twelve lessons.[11] His associate, the dancing master, Pietro Sodi, taught the Dauphin minuet, the Louvre, the Allemande and the Cotillion at Wilmot's store; and Joseph Cozani gave French and Italian language lessons at Mr. Wilkes' store near the Exchange. On May 26, Biferi and Sodi gave a concert at Robert Hull's Tavern and Assembly Rooms. Biferi performed his own composition on harpsichord, and Sodi danced the Louvre and the minuet with his nine year-old daughter, who also danced a rigadoon. Sodi and his young daughter also performed a concert in Philadelphia in June. Unfortunately, like Franceschini, little is known about Biferi. Apparently, the last time he performed was on March 23, 1775 at Hull's Tavern in New York.[12]

In 1787, acrobats and jugglers first appeared in New York. After an engagement in Salem, Massachusetts in 1788, Jean Donezani's (aka Donegani) Tumblers tumbled, leaped, jumped, danced, balanced and walked on the wire at the Frenchman Mr. Corre's Assembly Room (formerly Byram's Garden, later the Mount Vernon Garden) on Broadway at Leonard Street from January 8 through February 16, 1791.[13] A seven year-old boy, named Infant Hercules, performed a variety of attitudes and postures never seen before in the city. The February 1 performance served as a benefit for Hercules, who performed a "blind fandango over eggs," while proceeds for the February 2 performance were donated to the poor.[14] But their New York run was limited. From April 8, 1791 through May 16, 1792, the Tumblers and Little Hercules held sway at the Northern Liberty Theatre in Philadelphia, then traveled on to other American and European cities.[15] Italian American historian Giovanni Schiavo speculated that Hercules was actually Donegani's son, Giuseppe, who died a rich man in Montreal in 1865 at the age of eighty-four.[16]

The next enduring performer of note is one who went by the name of Signor (Charles) Falconi the Magician. Though magicians and opera singers often adopted Italian stage names, we will operate on the assumption that Falconi, and others mentioned, were Italian. Falconi entranced audiences regularly and periodically in New York City: from June 26 through July 21, 1787 at the theatre in Corre's and at the John Street Theatre where he also entertained in 1791, 1795 and 1797. He later performed at the Assembly Rooms on William Street in June and July 1795. Tickets for his show could be purchased chez Charles Bernardi on Pearl Street. Falconi's mesmerizing acts of "Natural Philosophical Experiments" included several of the following wonders from his repertoire:

> an artful contrivance of Punchinella; a sympathetic Wind-Mill that stopped on the command of anyone of the company; Catoptric appearances by the reflection of mirrors; an artificial butterfly that replied to sentiments in the minds of the company; a small automaton in a Turkish dress that answered questions by signs and guessed the number on dice thrown by anyone in the audience; the solid gold, walnut-size head of Theophrastus of Paracelsus, shut up hermetically in a crystal vessel which answered any question by signs; Falconi made a salad grow in the hand, 2 inches in 5 minutes; Chinese talismans and shades, the Magic Swan; expulsion by electricity; a penetrating spy glass; the sagacious Mermaid; incomparable Simon; a Thunderstorm at sea with shipwreck; the dance of the witches; the conquest of the Golden Fleece; the illusion of President James Monroe; the wonderful experiment of the dove; the mysterious candle; the electrical and perpetual lamp; physical electricity; a duel between hunters with small swords; the farce *Marechal Ferrant* and the sketch *The Irish Farmer.*

Falconi continued performing in American cities until 1817.[17]

In 1791 an acrobat known only as the Young Florentine made his appearance on the New York stage.[18] From March 3 to April

11, 1794 there appeared the first notices for the Milanese scene designer Charles Ciceri from Philadelphia, who came to New York for the production of *Tammany/The Agreeable Surprise or the Indian Chief* at the John Street Theatre. His scenery and decorations were called "gaudy and unnatural but brilliant of color, red and yellow in abundance." Apparently, he was an excellent theatre machinist.[19] Falbo called him "Ciseri, [sic], a Milanese scene painter."[20] During Ciceri's tenure at the John Street Theatre, until March 6, 1795, he designed for such productions as *Macbeth*, *The Danaides or Vice Punished*, a pantomime, and *Days of Old*.[21] He resurfaced for a short time at the Park Theatre, when it opened in January 1798 at Chatham Street (later Park Row) for the productions of *As You Like It* and *The Adopted Child*. The reviewer of *The New York Daily Advertiser* paid him and his crew this compliment: "Too much cannot be said for the science of Mr. Ciceri as the machinist, and for his taste as scene-painter. They are artists, who would do honor to any country, and are a great acquisition to this [country]." The premiere of *Andre* on April 4 was his last performance there when the actor Hodgkinson ordered the curtain raised before Ciceri had the stage ready. An argument followed, and Ciceri retired from show business.[22] During 1798 and 1799, Charles Ciceri continued working elsewhere in New York City. Later he was employed by an import/export business in Paris, and returned to Italy by 1820 where he retired.[23]

In 1794, Signor Laurent Spinacuta, musician, equestrian clown, pyrotechnist and tightrope walker, was found in New York. In September 1795, his future collaborator, Signore Reano (aka Reno), had arrived and performed tight rope dancing on the slack rope as Pantaloon the Clown at Rickett's Ampitheatre, a structure built just that year by John Bill Rickett on the southwest corner of Broadway and Exchange Alley. Some kind of pestilence closed down entertainments until May 1796. From May through July 1796, Reano was joined by Signor and Mrs. Helena Spinacuta in a series of pantomimes: *Harlequin Statue or the Spirit of Fancy*, *Vulcan's Gift or the Bower of Hymen*, *Linco's Travels* and *The Power of Magic or Harlequin Everywhere* (a benefit for the

Spinacuta duo). Spinacuta played the roles of Pierro and Dorcas; Mrs. Spinacuta played Columbine and the Shepherdess and also displayed fireworks. She made her New York City debut on May 7 on a cavalcade of horses, riding two horses at full speed, a feat never yet attempted by anyone in America. Mr. Spinacuta performed in the city until 1797.[24]

Signore Gonoty (aka Gonotty) appeared from November 1795 to February 1797, first at a room in Courtlandt Street and later at the New Theatre in Brom Martling's Long Room at 87 Nassau Street at Spruce Street. His amazing repertoire of tricks included: balancing swords, pipes, keys, chairs, tables, coach wheels, plates, nails, glasses, peacock feathers, straws and many other things. He did a show with Punch and His Merry Family of Puppets as well as operated machinery that imitated fireworks without powder, fire or smoke and that represented public buildings and parks in England. Two fiddlers and a hand organ player accompanied him.[25]

Only a few other Italian entertainers performed in New York City during the rest of the eighteenth century. In 1799, for example, in the theatre on Water Street, an Italian Scaramouche danced a Fandango and put himself into two different shapes. Finally, on January 12 1799, Signore Filippo Trisobio, a professor of vocal music, visiting New York and other cities, gave a concert of Italian duets and French and English songs at the Tontine City Tavern (aka the Tontine Coffee House) at 82–86 Wall Street between Water Street and Pearl Street.[26] In sum, during the eighteenth century, the Italian show people were primarily itinerant entertainers who performed their acts for American audiences in New York and other cities on the East Coast. Variety shows that owed much to the Italian *Commedia dell'Arte*, both in structure and repertoire, were common.

The wide gap of performance notices from 1774 to 1783 was obviously because of the American Revolution. Travel to New York City was certainly limited, as it was occupied by British soldiers, who gave performances at the John Street Theatre. Giovanni Schiavo (1898–1983) notes that minor Italian actors arrived from London shortly after the Revolution, but little else is notable for this period.[27]

In the early nineteenth century, many Italians came to America due to the turmoil resulting from Italy's early attempts at political unification. But most of the Italian performers who appeared on the New York City stage during this early part of the nineteenth century were not political refugees. The numerous Italian opera singers were primarily visitors who performed mainly for American audiences, though some Italians may have also attended. The Italian language became more popular because Italians sang these operas in their native language.

The first important Italian entertainer in this new century was Signor Manfredi, a rope dancer, who first performed in 1803.[28] Recently arriving from engagements in Paris, Signor Manfredi and his company of rope dancers included: thirteen-year-old Miss Louisa, her fifteen-year-old sister Miss Catherine, Mrs. Manfredi, Mme. La Vincennes and the Signori: Francesco, Philamos (aka Philamon), Bachicino, Bernardo, Camfroni, Antoine, Ferdinand, Jacques, Patechin and McDonnell.[29] While Manfredi and his company were certainly Italians, they must have added some French performers to their company while in Paris. Their specialties were balancing and dancing on the rope. Manfredi ate supper on the rope, rose intoxicated and kept his balance. La Vincennes performed the Egyptian pyramid on the rope, and did such pantomimes as: *The Roman Museum or Harlequin a Robber through Love*, *Harlequin transformed into an English Dog*, *Harlequin Barber*, *Harlequin the Magician's Apprentice*, *Harlequin Pastry Cook*, *Harlequin Skeleton*, *Harlequin Valetudinarian*, *Harlequin Dead and Alive* (a benefit for Miss Catherine), *Columbine Invisible* (during which Mme. La Vincennes performed a "grotesque dance"), *Harlequin Protected by a Lion*, *The Venetian Masquerade* (thirteen persons posed in the Roman style), and *Harlequin Doctor*. During the latter pantomime, Manfredi played the Buffoon, Francesco the Harlequin, Mrs. Manfredi the maid Columbine, Philamos the Old Man, Bachicino the Magician and Bernardo the Patient. Their popular acts, however, were interrupted in the summer because of an outbreak of yellow fever in the city.[30] Manfredi did not appear again in New York until 1812.[31]

In 1804, the Bologna Dancers performed *Harlequin's Statue, The Witch of the Lake, Harlequin Doctor or the Apprentice Magician* and the *Fricassee Dance*, all of which included "pantomime, tricks and drolleries" by the clown Mr. Bologna and a Mr. Martin. Bologna had arrived in 1803 after performing in Covent Garden and later helped manage the Park Theatre.[32] The Bologna performance was typical of *Commedia dell'arte: Arlecchino*, the masque of Bergamo, pantomime, tricks (*lazzi*), comedy and dance.

Due to political and religious pressures in Italy, Mozart's librettist, Lorenzo Da Ponte (born Jewish under the name Emanuele Conegliano, 1749–1838) arrived in New York in June 1805. Da Ponte affords us the first approximation of the Italian-American theatre to emerge much later in the century. In 1806, he lived on Bayard Street and the Bowery and reunited with his family. In 1807, he identified himself as a teacher of Italian, living at 29 Partition Street. In order to facilitate his teaching of Italian, during these early years, he wrote little comedies and short plays for his students, "the modest and estimable young ladies of the city,"[33] which would have made him the first, recorded Italian American playwright if his plays were originally written here.

Da Ponte and his students were able to use the house of Benjamin Moore (1748–1816), Bishop of the Protestant Episcopal Church in the Diocese of New York, and President of Columbia University. Da Ponte constructed a little theatre in his home located on the Bowery from 1808–1809.[34] There he and his students from Columbia University acted Vittorio Alfieri's (1749–1803) play, *Mirra*, two nights running to an enthusiastic audience of 150 former students. Nevertheless, this ambitious attempt failed to spark much interest in continuing the project.

Da Ponte detected "a certain prejudice against dramatic performances" and, therefore, the troupe did not continue. For example, some local society ladies censured one of his female students for performing in public. The Puritan attitude toward theatrical performances may have been relaxed enough by this time to tolerate visiting foreign performers or actors in the profession, but it was still not yet respectable for women to participate in the performing arts. From 1810–1813, Da Ponte lived at 247 Duane Street, after which time he left the city and moved to Sunbury, Pennsylvania. When he returned to New York in 1819, renting a little house at 54 Chapel Street at the corner of Provost Street (today's intersection of West Broadway and Franklin Street), he lamented that during his absence the enthusiasm for the plays and the Italian language had all but disappeared.[35] Still, Da Ponte became an important figure in the theatre in the early nineteenth century.

Meanwhile, by 1808, Italian song became more popular in New York. Exile Filippo Traetta (aka Philip Trajetta, 1777–1854), the son of Tommaso Traetta, a composer from Bitonto, Bari, was born in Venice. He arrived in America in 1799 and established the first "American *Conservatorio*" of music in Boston in 1801. Several decades later, Traetta opened another music school in Philadelphia, succeeding where Nicholas Biferi had failed many years earlier in New York. From October 1808 until February 1810, Traetta, now with the Havana Opera Company, performed with other singers at the City Hotel situated at 115 Broadway between Thames Street and Cedar Street. Their repertoire included *Harlequin's Triumph in War and in Love,* a new musical farce in two acts written and set to music by Traetta and duets from operas and songs by composers Domenico Cimarosa (1749–1801), Giuseppe Sarti (1729–1802), Wolfgang Amadeus Mozart, Giovanni Battista Paisiello (1710–1816), Franz Josef Hayden, and Ignaz Pleyel. Traetta was well traveled and is reported to have been the manager of the Italian Theatre of New Orleans in 1812. His musical instruction books, *Introduction to the Art and Science of Music* in 1829 and *Rudiments of the Art of Singing* in 1843, were published in Philadelphia. He died in that city in 1854.[36]

The 1809–1810 New York entertainment season included the Cayetano (aka Gaetano Mariottini) Circus, which had performed in Charlestown, Boston, the prior season. Mariottini was the first Italian manager of a circus in the United States. His repertoire consisted of feats of horsemanship and tricks with gloves, hats and hoops; the comic scene of the drunken soldier; the title role in Don

Quixote de la Mancha on horseback; and commander of the English troops in *The Battle and Death of General Malbrook*. By 1816, Mariottini was in New Orleans where he managed the Olympic Circus; he died in 1817. In early August 1810, at Washington Hall, on Broadway at Reade Street, Domenique Vitale (aka Dominique Vitali) and his Company of artists from Italy presented a Roman Theatre of puppets who ate, drank and smoked.[37]

In 1805, Gaetano Carusi became the leader of the United States Marine Band, having been specifically recruited with many other musicians from Italy for that purpose by Thomas Jefferson. Carusi arrived with his wife and three children, among them Lewis Carusi who would establish a dancing school in Washington, D.C. In 1811, Gaetano Carusi wrote music for a production of the pantomime, *The Brazen Mask*, along with other compositions.[38]

Mr. Schinotti, a pantomimist, dancer and singer, arrived in New York City in 1823. On August 2, he debuted in the Circus in Hoboken, New Jersey. On August 29, he crossed the river to sing and dance at the Frenchman Joseph Delacroix's Vauxhall Gardens (aka Saloon) on John Jacob Astor's land, east side of Broadway near Astor Place. On September 12, Schinotti performed the pantomime, *The Rival Indians*, at the Circus at 542 Broadway.[39] After several years of absence from the theatrical scene, except for one appearance at Drury Lane in April 1824 as the Woodcutter in *Harlequin's Frolics*, Schinotti reappeared on September 3, 1827 at the Bowery Theatre, 46–48 Bowery at Canal Street. During this performance, he worked with dancer and singer Carlo Angrisani (c. 1760–1830), a basso, and the Achille French dancers in the "glittering and graceful" *The Caliph of Bagdad*. On July 4, 1828, Schinotti and his wife were featured in *The Hundred Pound Note* at William Niblo's Garden Concert Saloon (aka San Souci Theatre, formerly Columbian Garden) at 576–586 Broadway on the northeast corner of Prince Street. On January 19, 1829, Schinotti appeared as an Indian dancer in General Charles W. Sanford's Lafayette Theatre at 308–310 West Broadway at Canal Street. The theatre burned down that April.[40] He returned to the Bowery Theatre on June 6 as the apothecary in *Romeo & Juliet* and did not perform again until April 1835 at the Bowery Theatre in *The Last Days of Pompeii*. In July he played at the Richmond Hill (aka New York) Theatre on the southeast corner of Varick and Charlton Streets. Mrs. Schinotti acted as Miami in *The India Heroine*. In September Mr. Schinotti appeared in *The Unfinished Gentleman* at the Franklin Theatre, 175 Chatham Street (aka Park Row) between James and Oliver Streets.[41]

During November 1835 and December 1837, Schinotti assisted Antonio Mondelli of New Orleans. Mondelli had studied in Milan and had been working in New Orleans since 1818. He was the chief scene painter at the Camp Street Theater from 1824 to 1832 and at the St. Charles Theatre from 1835 until it closed. Mondelli had created elaborate scenic effects that cost $3,000, a princely sum of money for that time period. One particular scene had an "admirable view of the port of Cyprus with the stage completely flooded with water across which an 8 foot Greek galley sailed majestically" and "an eruption of Vesuvius so vividly recreated as to electrify the audience."[42]

In May 1824 at the Washington Hall Theatre, and in December 1826 at the Lafayette Theatre, M. Villalane and his company entertained their audiences with performances specializing in gymnastics, acrobatics and Christmas sports. A century later, these events would be celebrated as the birth of vaudeville in the United States. The troupe, consisting of Spanish, Italian, American and Chinese performers and an orchestra, sublet a house in the city for their stay.[43]

The 1825–1826 season signaled the start of major changes in the musical scene, especially as regards the visibility and participation of Italians, a change that would influence the next several decades. The season started simply enough with Signora Bartolini's concerts of Italian songs on November 25, 1825 at Bossieux's Dancing Academy at Reade Street and Broadway. She reappeared there in December 1827. Even theatre historian George C. Odell noted that the number of concerts was dwindling because of the increasing popularity of opera. Even though the opera was brought in by way of a Spanish impresario from London, Odell remarked, "Italy was a word to conjure with."[44]

From November 1825 through September 1826 at the Park Theatre and the Bowery Theatre, the Spanish singer and composer from Seville, Manuel del Popolo Vincente Garcia (1775–1832) and the company under his management, performed in New York. During 1826, the Italian scene painter Signor Sera (aka Serra) decorated the Park Theatre. Garcia opened with Rossini's *Il Barbiere di Siviglia*, performed twenty-three times and for the first time the opera was sung in Italian by Italians in New York. This event anointed the Park Theatre as the first Grand Opera House in the country. Additionally, the first season's repertoire presented *Tancredi, Il Turco in Italia, La Cenerentola, Semiramide, L'Amante astuto* and *La Figlia del Aria*.[45] The fashionably dressed society of the city patronized the opera performances and made them a financial success. The Garcia Company concluded its run in September 1826. This engagement was the first successful attempt to establish authentic Italian opera in New York.

The temporary success of Lorenzo Da Ponte's operas was vindicated. Da Ponte called Garcia's production of Gioacchino Rossini's (1792–1868) *Il Barbiere di Siviglia*, "the root from which sprang the great musical tree of New York."[46] He was right because in the twenty-first century the taste for opera and operatic concerts continues. In 1825, Da Ponte had become the first Professor of Italian at Columbia and an indefatigable promoter of Italian language and culture, turning his home into a virtual Italian cultural center. Da Ponte took his students of Italian to Garcia's rehearsals. After the success of these first performances, Da Ponte proposed to Garcia a production of Mozart's *Don Giovanni*, for which Da Ponte himself had written the libretto. It seemed that no one in the company could play the role of Don Ottavio, and Garcia hesitated incurring the additional expenses. But Da Ponte located a capable singer and with financial contributions raised from his friends and pupils, he personally paid for the production, putting Garcia in the title role. Some of his company were Italians, including Signora Barbieri, Domenico Crivelli, who later taught voice in London; and the most notable, the multi-talented basso, Carlo Angrisani, who apparently stayed in the city to perform for several years. In January 1827, Angrisani sang a duet from *Tancredi* with Mrs. Brichta at Jennings & Henry Willard's City Hotel. In April, he danced a *pas seul* at the Bowery Theatre, joined the Achille French Dancers at the Park Theatre; and, in September joined Schinotti and the Achille French Dancers at the Bowery Theatre.[47]

When the Bowery Theatre burned down in 1828, the same Mr. Sera who had decorated the Park Theatre, was called upon to redesign beautiful scenery and rich decorations for the new Bowery Theatre. In March 1829, Angrisani and Mr. Benoni were dancing with the French Corps de Ballet at the Lafayette Theatre. Angrisani also performed on October 21, 1830 in a concert at Masonic Hall, located on the east side of Broadway between Duane Street and Reade Street. But before this, his last notice, he sang in a "Grand Concert of Vocal and Instrumental Music," at the Bowery Theatre in March of 1830, with stars from the Italian Opera, including Giulia (aka Giulietta) Da Ponte, Lorenzo's niece.[48]

Da Ponte considered his niece's voice charming and had great confidence in her voice teacher Signor Baglioni, who had trained many excellent singers in Italy. Da Ponte had known Baglioni in Prague when *Don Giovanni* was performed. Da Ponte negotiated three engagements to acclimate Giulia to singing in front of an audience. Giulia and Angrisani appeared together again in April at the Bowery Theatre in the opera *L'Ape Musicale*, created by Lorenzo Da Ponte especially for Giulia's debut. While Da Ponte judged the opera to be unsuccessful, he still believed Giulia's performance was "brilliant." However, she did not pursue a singing career and never appeared in notices again. Before Da Ponte's next groundbreaking foray into the New York musical arena, a few Italian variety acts appeared: the ballet dancers Checkini (Cecchini) in 1827 and Charles and Carolina Mary Theresa (Ronzi) Vestris in 1828; and Vito's Italian Fantoccini Puppets filled a long engagement at Christmas time in 1835 at Reuben Peale's Museum at 252 Broadway.[49] Also, one of the greatest English pantomimes was featured at Peale's Museum on New Year's Day 1832. Joseph Grimaldi (1778–1836) the Clown, though English, was the son of the Italian dancing master and pantomime, Giuseppi Grimaldi. Garcia's opera company never reprised production in the city, but as we have seen, at least one of his singers, Carlo Angrisani, continued to perform; and the appetite for opera in New York's audiences had been whetted. Italian singers were heard thereafter in a continuing stream of appearances in New York and across the country.[50] Garcia died in 1832, the same year that Lorenzo Da Ponte was instrumental in bringing to the city a more permanent professional opera company from London.

The first authentic Italian opera company, under the management of Giacomo Montresor, staged thirty-five performances during the 1832–1833 season. The season opened on October 6, 1832 at the Richmond Hill Theatre, this season called "The Italian Opera House," with Rossini's *La Cenerentola*, which played two or three times a week until the program changed on October 18. The first leg of this run continued until December 5, 1832. Da Ponte served as advisor. His friend Antonio Bagioli (1795–1871), from Bologna, teacher of Marietta Alboni, was the Musical Director; the chorus leader and conductor was Maestro Carlo Salvioni; the first violinist and conductor was Michele Rapetti; artist, architect, and engineer, Mario Bragaldi was scene designer, and Alberto Bazzani was the principal costumer. The Italians in the cast included: the tenor Giovan Battista Montresor, the bassos, Luciano Fornasari, Ernesto Orlandi, Giuliano Placci; Albina Stella, Lorenza Marozzi, and Signora T. Verducci. The Italian musicians in the twenty-four piece orchestra included the Signori: Croce, Comi, Sanna, Casolani, Paggi, Conti, Gardenghi and Cioffi. The audience, dressed in "feathers and jewels," paid an admission of one dollar and fifty cents for first and second row boxes and orchestra; or one dollar for third tier boxes and pit.[51] Reviews of the Montresor Company and other details help flesh out the personalities behind this litany of names.

Montresor was deemed a fairly good tenor, superior to Garcia, but his use of the falsetto was unsatisfactory. Antonio Bagioli composed the music for "Prayer" for the young ladies of the Troy Female Seminary and dedicated it to the President of the United

States. After the Montresor Company dissolved, Bagioli became a successful voice teacher in New York. Bagioli's *New Method of Singing* was published in Philadelphia in 1839. Fornasari, the basso, would sing the role of Figaro in *Il Barbiere di Siviglia* for forty nights during his career in New York City and was regarded as a better singer than Angrisani: A critic comments on Angrisani's voice:

> intonation excellent... execution of rapid passages at all times neat and sometimes brilliant, but his progression from note to note is short and abrupt; the absence of a portamento being indicative of a bad school . . . a very good looking man with a very fine voice but there is a tremor about it continually and his progression from note to note is imperfect.

Albina Stella was a "miserable failure" and was replaced in the next performance by Emilia Saccomani who also failed to please.[52] The Company continued the 1832–1833 season with a run in February at the Chestnut Street Theatre in Philadelphia and then from April 10 until May 11 in New York, but not at the Richmond Hill Theatre. Instead they sang at the Masonic Hall and the Bowery Theatre. Their repertoire for the rest of the season included the Mercadante's *Elise & Claudio*, *L'Italiana in Algieri*, Bellini's *Il Pirata*, *Moses*, *Othello*, Rossini's *La Gazza Ladra*, *Il Barbiere di Siviglia*, and *L'Inganno Felice*. Other members of the company not already mentioned were: the mezzo-soprano Signora Adelaide (aka Edelaide) Pedrotti, Enrichetta Salvioni, Giuseppe Corsetti, Manetti, Francesco Sapignoli, Signora Brichta, Signora T. Verducci, Stephen Ferrero, Ernesto Orlandi, and Lorenza Marozzi. Signor Albi (aka Albe) assisted Bragaldi as scene painter. Among the company, Pedrotti and Marozzi were considered "the best singers."[53]

Pedrotti was a "sensation" with this reservation: "Pedrotti had faults but like many singers she hid them by the exploitation of a very interesting personality. [Her soprano was of ] good quality and great power . . . intonation . . . faultless, style good and tact excellent. [She was a person who was] handsome, rather on the large scale [and her] features . . . as with most dark women . . .

light up extremely well before the lamps . . . an eye of fire and expression . . . graceful and impressive."[54] Brichta's husband would form his own opera company years later.

Stephen Ferrero had arrived with his wife Adelaide, a singer and dancer, and their one year old son Edward, born in Malaga when his parents were on tour. Stephen Ferrero operated a dancing academy at 21 Howard Street from 1835 to 1850. By 1859, Edward managed the academy and became both a dance instructor at West Point and a major-general in the Civil War.[55]

Ferrero has a fascinating connection with Giuseppe Garibaldi (July 4, 1807–June 2, 1882), the Great Liberator. When Garibaldi arrived in America in 1850 during his exile from Italy, he recuperated at the home of Stephen Ferrero on Valley Street in Hastings-on-Hudson, New York. Both Ferrero and Maestro Antonio Bagioli had bought property there. Another Garibaldi opera connection involves the impresario, Max Maretzek (1821–1897), manager of the New York Italian Opera Company, which was in production during the time of Garibaldi's stay in New York. Maretzek rented his summer home on Staten Island to Antonio Santi Giuseppe Meucci (1808–1889), the inventor of the telephone, with whom Garibaldi lived from 1850 to 1851. Maretzek visited one day to find Meucci, Garibaldi and Lorenzo Salvi, a tenor from the Havana Opera Company in New York, up to their elbows in tallow from making candles.[56] Antonio Meucci had been a scene designer in Italy and at the Tacon Theatre in Havana, Cuba, where his wife also worked as a costume designer. In 1850, the Meuccis made their way to New York. Salvi first appeared in New York in 1850 with the Havana Italian Opera Company of the Tacon Theatre, where Salvi and Meucci had known each other.

The Montresor opera season of 1832–1833 was not a financial success. The Richmond Hill Theatre was small, "a miserable shell" and not located in an ideal section of the city. Nevertheless, Italian Grand Opera had psychologically taken hold of the city, and Da Ponte made his next move. On November 10, 1832, during the Montresor run, Da Ponte organized the affluent and influential gentry of the city into forming an Italian Opera Association for the purpose of raising funds for what would be the first Italian Opera House constructed in New York City. Their prospectus, dated November 19, 1832, called for purchasing six lots of land at the northwest corner of Church Street and Leonard Street, an area that was "disreputable and unsafe[57] at that time. The Articles of Association were legally incorporated February 15, 1833 and the fund raising began. One of the names on the Board was a the Italian American Oroondates Mauran (1796–1846), whose father Joseph Carlo Mauran from Providence, Rhode Island had been a naval commander during the Revolutionary War.[58] The Italian Opera House was constructed in time for the next opera season at a cost of between $100,000 and $150,000.

This theatre was the first in the United States with a tier composed exclusively of boxes, known as the second balcony. The parterre was entered from the first balcony. The seats in the first balcony and in the parterre were mahogany chairs upholstered in blue damask. The box fronts had a white ground, with emblematical medallions and octagonal panels of crimson, blue, and gold. Blue silk curtains were tied with gilt cords and tassels. The floors were carpeted. The price of the boxes was $6,000 each. A chandelier of great splendor threw light into a dome enriched with pictures of the Muses, painted, as were the interior and the scenery, by Italian artists specially brought from Europe.[59] These artists were Bragaldi, Albi and Guidicini.[60] Bragaldi's curtains and scenery designs were called "magnificent . . . beautiful beyond all precedent." These men, with Allegri, the portrait painter, and with Monachesi, the muralist, later painted scenes for other theatres, including the Astor Place Opera House in 1847.

Under the joint management of Da Ponte and the Milanese impresario, Cavaliere Rivafinoli (aka Chevalier di Rivafinoli), who were assisted by their treasurer Signor Sacchi, the Italian Opera Company opened on November 18, 1833 for a run that lasted until July 21, 1834. The opera chosen for the opening was Rossini's *La Gazza Ladra*. The political exile, Piero Maroncelli (1795–1846), whom historian Giovanni Schiavo called the "great martyr of Austrian oppression," was the chorus director and Michele Rapetti was the orchestra leader. In 1842, Maroncelli helped establish the Philharmonic Society of New York. The cast featured Amalia Schneider Maroncelli, Lorenza Marozzi, Clementina Fanti, Stephen Ferrero, Signor Fabj, Signor Porto, Antonio de Rosa, Francesco Sapignoli, Giuliano Placci and Richaud.[61] The rest of the season's repertoire offered: Rossini's *Il Barbiere di Siviglia*, *La Donna del Lago*, *Il Turco in Italia*, *La Cenerentola* and *Matilda di Shabran*, Giovanni Pacini's (1767– 1837) *Gli Arabi nelli Gallie*, Cimarosa's *Il Matrimonio Segreto*. On March 22, 1834 the first Italo-American opera, *La Casa da Vendere* composed by Maestro Carlo Salvioni, made its premiere in New York City. Other company performers were Bordogni, Ravaglia, Ernesto Orlandi and Rosina Fanti.[62]

Receipts for the season amounted to $51,780, but the expenses of $81,1556 resulted in a loss of $22,500. In fact, at the end of the season, Bordogni refused to sing because the management was behind in her salary. Rivafinoli brought the company to Philadelphia but eventually shifted his energies to North Carolina gold mines.[63] Lorenza Marozzi, Ferrero, Sapignoli, Placci, Mario Bragaldi, Albi, Maestro Carlo Salvioni and Orlandi were familiar names carried over from the Montresor Company. Throughout the season and well beyond, the stars of the Italian opera gave concerts, accompanied by instrumentalists Francesco Sapignoli, Signor Casalani, and Signor Gambati on trumpet.

Notices from September 1, 1834 until November 29, just before the following season opened, report performances taking place at the Euterpean Hall (the former Broadway Theatre) at the corner of Walker Street on lower Broadway; the City Hotel, Niblo's Garden, the Italian Opera House; the New Hall on Anthony Street, and at the Minerva Room, on Broadway between Walker Street and Canal Street. The concerts at the Minerva served as pre-opening teasers for the new opera season. In September 1834, Albina Stella, the "miserable failure" of the 1832 season's *La Cenerentola*, gave singing lessons in the city.[64] In the 1834–1835 season, the Italian Opera Company was again installed at the Italian Opera

House, this time under the co-management of Da Ponte's former treasurer, Sacchi, and the singer A. Porto, who leased the building. The repertoire and company remained essentially the same and began playing on November 10, 1834. Signor Monterasi joined the company and Rosina Fanti was the prima donna. The company was unhappy with Porto's management; so after an unsuccessful season, which closed April 29, 1835, the building was put up for sale by auction but remained unsold. In 1836, Henry Willard and Thomas Flynn became its managers and renamed it the National Theatre. It burned down in 1839.[65]

Coinciding with the 1834–1835 opera season, the regular theatrical season presented other Italians. In November 1834 at the New York Theatre (the former Richmond Hill Theatre), an acrobat, Signor Sciarra and the sixty-five year old Signor Forioso performed an act on the elastic cord and exhibited feats of strength. Sciarra was again in New York in 1835. His act, which included his wife and children, involved his swallowing a thirty-three inch sword in its scabbard and stilt walking, as well as performances on the slack rope. From August 1834 to July 1835 and often thereafter, the juggler and ropedancer Antonio, Il Diavolo, (aka Vivella or Vivalla) and his three sons (two of whom were Lorenzo and Augustus), performed gymnastic exercises on a flying rope at the Park Theatre and at Niblo's Garden, and had a successful run with P. T. Barnum.[66]

The Italian Opera House slumbered throughout the 1835–1836 season, but Italians continued to appear on the stage. Antonio, now billed as Signor Vivella, danced while manipulating cups, balls, rings, bowls and ten plates in motion with bayonets on his nose from November 1835 through April 1836 at the Franklin Theatre and at Peale's Theatre. Years later, he moved to Cuba, became paralyzed, and died on the island. Montresor's Company did not return to New York, but his troupe was engaged for a run from March to May 1836 for the sum of $20,000 by a single individual in New Orleans at the St. Charles Theatre, managed by Mr. Caldwell. Most of the performers and the repertoire were recognizable from the New York opera companies of the previous three seasons. Caldwell claimed that he lost money on the venture.[67]

In 1838, Lorenzo Da Ponte, who had supported and encouraged Italian Opera in the city from its very beginnings, died. Operas, nonetheless, continued to appear in New York. Companies would form and disband, with new impresarios and with familiar names, and would organize and reorganize both the casts and repertoires from defunct companies. The De Rosa, Brichta, Pantanelli, Palmo, Sanquirico, Patti, Maretzek, Franconi, Strakosch, Ullman, Parodi, Cortesi, Pastor were but a few companies to come and go during this transitional period. The Italian costume and scene designers continued to decorate. The Italian opera singers, whether visiting or resident, famous or unsung, plied the circuit from Italy to Havana to the U.S. and back again.

But other new attractions begin to appear at mid-century. The Italian street musicians and organ grinders, often bringing children, arrived. They were called the "little slaves of the harp" that John Zucchi has documented so well. They became the impetus for social activism and legislation initiated by Americans and Italians in America and Italy, partly to prevent the abuses suffered by the children but largely to preserve the quality of life in better neighborhoods.[68] Another novelty appearing at this time was the celebrity Italian language actor. Contracted by American promoters and producers, Italian stars such as Tommaso Salvini, Adelaide Ristori, Giovanni Grasso, Mimi Aguglia, Ermete Novelli, Eleonora Duse, all performed in Italian for New York's American audiences and toured the country. Some, like Aguglia and Salvini's son Alessandro, stayed in New York permanently.

The patterns of Italian musical and theatrical activities continued throughout and beyond the nineteenth century. The acrobats, jugglers, magicians, music teachers, ballet dancers and puppets reveal the variety of itinerant performers who came and soon disappeared because there was no regular audience to sustain a continuous theatrical production.

Theatre in New York City remains consistent with the history of all theatre in that it reflects the society and times that produced it. By the 1860s, there were enough resident Italians in New York City to form a variety of Italian fraternal, benevolent and patriotic associations. These groups organized annual balls and holiday celebrations out of which emerged more New York City homegrown theatrical entertainments, both amateur and professional. The 1870 census counted as many as 4,000 Italian-born residents of New York City. It marked the beginning of the mass migration of Italians to New York and a much more sophisticated and vibrant Italian theatrical presence in the city. [69]

## NOTES

1. 14 September 1746, *Evening-Post,* cited in George C. Odell, *Annals of the New York Stage,* Vol. I (New York: Columbia University Press, 1927), 24.

2. Lawrence Frank Pisani, *The Italians in America: A Social Study and History* (New York: Exposition Press, 1957), 21; Giovanni Schiavo, *Four Centuries of Italian American History* (Staten Island, New York: Center for Migration Studies, 2000), 112–13 and 176.

3. Pasquale De Biasi, "I 50 Anni di Scena di Guglielmo Ricciardi" in *Ricciardiana: Raccolta di Scritti, Racconti, ecc. del veterano attore e scrittore Guglielmo Ricciardi* (New York: Eloquent Press Corp., 1955), 152.; Italo C. Falbo "Figure e Scene del Teatro Popolare Italiano a New York," 3 May 1942, *Il Progresso Italo-Americano,* 5S.

4. Schiavo, 113–16.

5. Schiavo, 120.

6. Arthur Hornblow, *A History of the Theatre in America: From the Beginnings to the Present Time,* Vol. II (New York: Benjamin Blom, 1965), 13; Thomas Clark Pollock, *The Philadelphia Theatre in the Eighteenth Century* (New York: Greenwood Press, 1968).

7. 22 June 1769, *New York Journal,* cited in Odell, Vol. I, 154; 28 April 1768 and 22 June 1769, *New York Journal,* cited in Schiavo, 120

8. Schiavo, 113.

9. Eola Willis, *The Charleston Stage in the XVIII Century: With Social Settings of the Time* (New York: Benjamin Blom), 1968.

10. 7 June 1783 and 2 August 1783, *Gazette,* cited in Odell, Vol. I, 225–26; 9 July 1783, *Rivington's New York Gazetteer,* cited in Odell, Vol. I, 227.

11. 5 May 1774, Rivington's *New York Gazetteer* cited in Odell, Vol. I, 180; Schiavo, 113–117.

12. Ibid; and 19 May, 16 June, and 30 June 1775, Rivington's *New York Gazetteer,* cited in Odell, Vol. I, 180–182; Schiavo, 116–117; and 15 June 1774 and 7 September 1774, *Pennsylvania Journal,* cited in Schiavo, 117.

13. Schiavo, 205–06.

14. 6 January 1791, *The New York Daily Advertiser,* cited in Odell, Vol. I, 289.

15. Thomas Clark Pollock, *The Philadelphia Theatre in the Eighteenth Century* (New York: Greenwood Press Publishers, 1968).

16. Schiavo, 205.

17. 26 June 1787, 22 June 1795, 7 July 1795 and 31 October 1797, *The New York Daily Advertiser,* cited in Odell, Vol. I, 261, 398, and 473–74; 13 June 1787 and 7 June a1795, *The New York Daily Advertiser,* cited in Schiavo, 203–204.

18. Schiavo, 206.

19. Odell, Vol. I, 346.

20. Falbo, loc. cit.

21. 24 February 1795, *Minerva*, cited in Odell, Vol. I, 378–85.

22. 31 January 1798, *The New York Daily Advertiser*, cited in Odell, Vol. II, 6–13; 2 March 1798, *Commercial Advertiser*, cited in Odell, Vol. II, 14–18.

23. Schiavo, 230; Odell, Vol. II, 39.

24. 19 September 1795, 5 May, 26 May, 13 July 1796, *Minerva*, cited in Odell, Vol. I, 399–421; Mary C. Henderson, *The City and the Theatre: New York Playhouses from Bowling Green to Times Square*, (Clifton, New Jersey: James T. White & Company, 1973), 26; Schiavo, 206.

25. *Diary of John Anderson* November 18, 1795 and 21 January 1797 *Gazette*, cited in Odell, Vol. I, 399 and 439.

26. Odell, Vol. II, 68; 8 January 1799, *The New York Daily Advertiser*, cited in Odell, Vol. II, 34.

27. Schiavo, 209.

28. Schiavo, 208; From June 25 through November 25, 1805, the Italian Theatre was, for the first time in New York City, built and located at Broadway and Reade Street.

29. 25 June 1805, *The Morning Chronicle*, cited in Odell, Vol. II, 242.

30. Odell, Vol. II, 242–68.

31. Schiavo, 208.

32. Howard R. Marraro, "Italians in New York During the First Half of the Nineteenth Century," *New York History* (July 1945), 26, 278–306; Schiavo, 200.

33. David Longworth, *Longworth's, American Almanac New York Register and City Directory* (New York: Old Established Directory Office, 1806), 226 and Longworth, 1807, 158; Judith Pearlman, "Lorenzo da Ponte: Ultimate New Yorker." Columbia University Archives-Columbiana Library; Lorenzo Da Ponte, *Memoirs of Lorenzo Da Ponte Mozart's Librettist*. Translated with an introduction by L. A. Sheppard (New York: Houghton Mifflin Company, 1929), 316.

34. Longworth, 1808, 119; Da Ponte, 316; Clement Clark Moore, was the author of "'Twas the Night before Christmas".

35. Da Ponte, 316 and Part IV, Chapter XI; Odell, Vol. II, 223; Longworth, 1810, 156 and 1811, p.72; William Elliot, *Elliot's Improved Double Directory*. (New York: William Elliott at Tontine Coffee House, 1813), xxix.

36. Schiavo, 176–78; Pisani, 36; Odell, Vol. II, 343–44.

37. Schiavo mistakenly dates this in 1819, Schiavo, 205–08; Odell, Vol. II, 548.

38. Paul J. Enea, "Mozart and Italy: A Musical Love Affair." *Italian Tribune News*, Vol. 74, no. 38 (September 23, 2004), 14; Schiavo, 194.

39. Schiavo, 200; Odell, Vol. III, 79.

40. Odell, Vol. III, 79, 328–423.

41. Odell, Vol. III, 411; Vol. IV, 13–89.

42. Schiavo, 230; John S. Kendall, *The Golden Age of the New Orleans Theatre*. (Baton Rouge: Louisiana State University Press, 1952), passim.

43. Odell, Vol. III, 79 and 275–77.

44. Odell, Vol. III, 221 and 369.

45 . Hornblow, Vol. II, 13–14; Falbo, loc. cit.; Joseph Borome, "The Origins of Grand Opera in New York," *New York History*, 27, (July 1945), 169–78; Pisani, 36–37.

46. "New York Theatre Today," *The New York Amusement Gazette*, Vol. III, no. 6; Da Ponte, Chapter XIV.

118     Italian Entertainments in New York City

47. Odell, Vol. III, 268–328.

48. Henderson, 65; 23 August 1828, *New York Mirror* and *Ladies' Literary Gazette*, cited in Schiavo, 230; Odell, Vol. III, 424–538.

49. Da Ponte, Chapter XIV; Odell, Vol. III, 458 and Vol. IV, 106; Schiavo, 200–08.

50. Odell, Vol. III, 592; Schiavo, 179.

51. Schiavo, 197; Odell, Vol. III, 638–93; Hornblow, Vol. II, 102; Borome, loc. cit.

52. Schiavo, 178 and 197; Marraro, loc.cit.; Odell, Vol. III, 637–45.

53. Schiavo, 181–230; Marraro, loc.cit.; Hornblow, Vol. II, 102; Odell, Vol. III, 637–45.

54. Odell, Vol. III, 644.

55. Schiavo, 199–200.

56. Helen Barolini, "Garibaldi in Hastings." Paper delivered at the American Italian Historical Association Conference: "Italian Americans Before Mass Migration: We've Always Been Here," Annapolis 4–6 November 2004.

57. Howard R. Marraro, "Italians in New York in the Eighteen Fifties." Part II. *New York History*, Vol. 30, No. 3 (July 1949), 276–303; James J. Divita, "Antonio Meucci (1809–1889)," in *The Italian American Experience: An Encyclopedia* (Levittown, Pa.: Garland Publishing, 2000), 377; Odell, Vol. III, 645–90.

58. Schiavo, 183–84.

59. Henry Edward Krehbiel, *Chapters of Opera*, cited in Hornblow, 104–05.

60. Schiavo, 230.

61. Schiavo, 183 and 195; Odell, Vol. III, 691–92; Pisani, 37.

62. Schiavo, 183–230; Odell, Vol. II, 104 and Vol. III, 691–95.

63. Pisani, 37; Odell, Vol. III, 695; Schiavo, 183.

64. Odell, Vol. III, 698–99 and Vol. IV, 40–47.

65. Schiavo, 183; Hornblow, Vol. II, 38 and 105; Odell, Vol. IV, 39–41.

66. Schiavo, 203; Odell, Vol. III, 673; Vol. IV, 12–14 and 38–46.

67. Odell, Vol. IV, 70–94; Schiavo, 208.

68. John E. Zucchi, *The Little Slaves of the Harp: Italian Child Street Musicians in Nineteenth Century Paris, London, and New York.* (Buffalo: McGill-Queen's University Press, 1992), *passim.*

69. *The Brooklyn Daily Eagle Almanac: A Book of Information, General of the World, and Special of New York City and Long Island.* (New York: Press of Brooklyn Eagle Book and Job Department, 1908), 153.

# GENOA, WISCONSIN:
## A MID-WESTERN TOWN WITH AN ITALIAN FLAVOR

ERNESTO MILANI
ECOISTITUTO DELLA VALLE DEL TICINO OF CUGGIONO

Genoa, Wisconsin, a small village located on the east bank of the Mississippi River eighteen miles south of La Crosse with a population of approximately 265 people, claims German, Norwegian, Irish, English, American, Italian ancestry. The current Italian American population is approximately 13 percent.[1] Although this tiny settlement is rarely mentioned in state and national histories, the history of Genoa highlights the presence of Swiss-Italian and Northern Italian immigrants who inhabited this town when Wisconsin was admitted to the Union as the thirtieth state on May 29, 1848.[2]

After moving from their native countries to the United States, many of these immigrants first settled in Galena, Illinois, situated on the northwestern part of the state in Jo Daviess County. The first Native Americans were the Sauk and Fox. When others arrived, they mined lead in the vicinity. The town boomed in the 1840s, with its population peaking at 15,000 residents. It has now dwindled to 3,500, with tourism as its main source of economic activity. A recent travel article in the *New York Times* highlighted the city's well-preserved historical center that includes displays on the steamboat era and the Vinegar Hill Lead Mine.[3] In 1840, it was in this frontier town on the east side of the Mississippi River where Father Samuel Mazzuchelli, who died in Benton, Wisconsin in 1864, preached the Gospel in his zealous missionary journeys to convert Native Americans to Roman Catholicism. He wandered all over the frontier area; and through his efforts over twenty-five churches were built, some of which, like St. Michael's, are still standing. His memoir includes his comments on the Black Hawk War. Curiously Ulysses S. Grant and his family had moved to Galena where they operated a leather shop just prior to the start of the Civil War in 1861.[4]

During this period, an adventurous man from Prato in Valle Leventina, Canton Ticino, Switzerland had arrived in Galena. His name was Giuseppe (Joseph) Monti. Born in 1809, he escaped the famine that had plagued Ticino from 1816–1817. He and a large family group left for Baltimore, Maryland in 1832 and traveled to Philadelphia where he met his future wife, Emeline Baron. He worked there as a baker and confectioner. Looking for better opportunities, Monti then moved several times, ending up in New York where, in 1839, his first son, Matthew, was born. However, his destiny led him further west. In 1840, his second child, Josephine, was born in Cincinnati, Ohio. In 1842, he moved to St. Louis, Missouri, and then to Galena, Illinois. Galena had prosperous mining and lumbering industries, but Monti worked in the mines only during slow season because he operated a hotel and bakery.[5]

The 1850 U.S. Census reveals that Galena had a population of about 7,500 people who came primarily from England, Ireland, Germany, and Norway. Italians numbered about twenty; the Monti group consisted of fourteen people. Italian immigrants such as Pietro Morelli (Morrella), Giovanni Pighetti (Pighedddi), Tommaso Guanella (Quinnella), Giovanni Trussoni (Trezoni) hailed from Campodolcino and first migrated from England before settling in Illinois as early as 1837. This group would pre-date the first migration from Valchiavenna by about ten years. Although we have no records on the Pighettis, all the others were present in Genoa.[6]

Galena represented the embarkation point for the ore extracted in the lead mines of Shullburg in Lafayette County, southern Wisconsin. The cargo passed through the small village of Scales Mound, Illinois where the Guscetti brothers from Quinto, Canton Ticino, Switzerland found some work.[7]

Notwithstanding the positive economic outlook of the area, Monti had other plans to make a living. He was commissioned to seek a new area suitable for farming. Going northward along the Mississippi,

Monti arrived at the confluence of the North and South Fork Bad Axe River. An official federal publication describes the area:

> From La Crosse southward for many miles the rocky hills rise abruptly, often almost perpendicularly from the water's edge to a height of several hundred feet . . . Every few miles along the stream are little coves a few acres in extent marking the place where some small tributary creek has cut its way down through the level of the great river into which it flows . . . For this reason many little villages grew up at the mouths of these coves, depending for their existence on the traffic between the back country farmers and woodsmen and the river men.[8]

The Bad Ax area had witnessed one of the most infamous episodes in Wisconsin history. After an 1804 treaty, many Indian tribes were displaced from their homeland: they rarely understood the meaning of the papers they signed. The U.S. government was paving the way for the exploitation of lands that included such riches as prairie grazing land, timber, and a variety of minerals and fertile farmland. The Sauk and the Fox were eventually forced out of Illinois and Wisconsin to Iowa. Dissatisfied with the new environment, Black Hawk, in the spring of 1832, led his tribe of almost one thousand people back to their ancestral lands in Northwestern Illinois to grow corn to feed his starving tribe. His return caused distress among the white settlers. Attempts by Black Hawk to negotiate with the authorities failed, and both state militia and federal troops joined forces to annihilate him. Black Hawk attempted to escape across the central and western part of Wisconsin. He finally surrendered to General Henry Atkinson who had a much larger force. The Native Americans after some minor skirmishes around the Wisconsin River were cornered near the shore of the Bad Ax River. Their attempt to ford the river was foiled by the fire of the artillery of the USS *Warrior* that was patrolling the Mississippi. The attack on August 1 and 2 in 1832 decimated the Native Americans who had no way of escaping. Today this battlefield is the site of Black Hawk Recreational Park.[9]

In 1851, Joseph Monti received 177,44 acres of land from the United States government. The grant went along the Mississippi River past Prairie du Chien, stopping a few miles before Prairie du Crosse. Included in this grant was Hastings's Landing, which Monti thought suitable for many reasons. It had wild pigeons, rolling hills that resembled the Alpine panorama, and a route that led north toward the lumber camps of Wisconsin and Minnesota. Monti made the decision to resettle in this area a few miles north of the Bad Ax River Massacre. In 1854, he laid out the village on section twenty-eight with David Hastings and John Richards and named the area Bad Ax City. The town was named after the unsuccessful Native American attempt to flee the American troops during the Black Hawk uprising. It also sought to celebrate the strange characters found on the many steamboats that plied their trade up and down the Mississippi River.

In 1868, the community changed its name to Genoa to commemorate Columbus' birthplace. This act no doubt enhanced the status of the Italian residents living in the village.[10] While Monti built a hotel made from logs, other immigrants looking to exploit the land for agricultural purposes, slowly moved into Genoa. Among the first settlers in 1860 were William Tibbitts with 160 acres and Elias Shisler with 120 acres. John Ott purchased forty acres in 1853. Gradually other people started to buy land that was relatively cheap and readily available because it needed a lot of work and was not always fertile. In 1855, Joseph Monti convinced a friend from Airolo to join him. His name was Ferdinand Guscetti. He had lived in Scales Mound, Illinois and resettled in Genoa in 1855. He set up his own shop as a wagon master and became the town's first blacksmith.

While Genoa was growing, the political situation in America was becoming quite unstable due to the growing differences between the Southern and Northern States.[11] Although only a few Swiss Italians served in the American Civil War, their history is worth researching. The only Swiss Italian inhabitants of Genoa who volunteered to join the Union forces were the Guscetti brothers: Ferdinand, Jeremiah and Benjamin. Their name was misspelled more than ten different ways. The Guscetti family lived in Quinto, Ticino, Switzerland for centuries. They were *patrizi* and were inhabitants of Ticino in the borough of Deggio before 1700. The family name is probably German and originally might have been Guccio, Arriguccio or Federicuccio. There were so many members of this family, they distinguished themselves by adding Ratt, Ratitt and Orsi to last names. Using a variety of different official documents, many that included misspelled names and incomplete data, original sources had to be collated to match all data.

Ferdinand Guscetti (Goosuth) was born in Quinto, Canton Ticino on March 19, 1824. He married Maria Beffa, a local patrician, in 1849. The economic condition of Ticino had worsened due to the influx of about 20,000 refugees from Lombardy who were escaping Austrian tyranny. Guscetti left his homeland alone in 1853 and made his way to Illinois. The journey took him fifty-two days, and soon he was reunited with his wife Maria and his daughter Giulietta. Guscetti first settled in Scales Mound, Illinois where he worked as a wagon maker and as a maker of snow sleighs, oxen yokes, and coffins. The place was close to the lead mines of Galena and Wisconsin where there was a need for his services. He also opened a store with his brother Benjamin. During this time, two more children were born. In 1858 and 1859, Guscetti purchased 160 acres of timberland. Despite his many economic endeavors, Guscetti could barely make a living. In order to provide for his growing family, the Italian immigrant enlisted in the Union Army during the Civil War. The muster roll of the Wisconsin Volunteers indicates that Ferdinand Guscetti (Gossuth) of La Crosse enlisted on August 30, 1864 as a private. He was a member of Company U, Wisconsin First Heavy Artillery Regiment and honorably discharged on September 21, 1865 in Madison following a period of illness with pneumonia. He returned to Genoa carrying smallpox, which also infected his children. One of the four children born in Genoa, Joseph, died from this disease at the age of three on January 2, 1866. Of his four children, only Matthew, born on September 12, 1862, lived into adulthood, dying in Galesville, Wisconsin on July 3, 1923. Ferdinand continued to live in Genoa, working in both his shop and farm. A member of the Democratic Party, Guscetti died in Genoa on January 8, 1898. His short stint in the Union Army guaranteed him a pension that was eventually collected by his wife Maria Beffa.[12]

Another Italian Guscette from Genoa who enlisted in the Union Army was Geremia, also known as Jeremiah Guscetti or Jeremiah Kussinth. The federal census of 1860 listed him as a bachelor and farm laborer for David Hicook. Enlisting on November 13, 1861 as a private in Company B, Wisconsin Second Cavalry Regiment, Wisconsin, Guscetti was officially mustered out of military service on November 15, 1865. The records also reveal that he was a member of Company E of the Fifth Veteran Reserve Corps. There is no other information available on Geremia. The family believes he probably died during the war as an unknown soldier.[13]

Benjamin Guscetti (Gussette), like his brothers, was also born in Quinto, Canton Ticino, In 1855, at the age of twenty-one, he settled in Scales Mound with his brother Ferdinand. In 1860, he worked as a stonemason. His family consisted of his wife Hanna Blaufuss ( Plaufolz), born in Saxony, and their two children, Louis and Emma, born in Scales Mound in1855 and 1857, respectively. Prior to the Civil War, Guscetti moved north to Wisconsin with his family and became a farmer in Chippewa Falls, just east of Genoa. In September 1864, he enlisted as a private in Company H of the Third Wisconsin Infantry. A bugler, he joined his regiment near Atlanta, taking part in General William T. Sherman's March to the Sea and thereby witnessing the destruction of Atlanta and the forced exodus of all its inhabitants. Sherman's men then proceeded to Savannah, Georgia in December 1864. Benjamin Guscetti was probably already ill and died soon near Savannah on January 4, 1865. President Lincoln wrote a letter of condolence that was eventually given to a local historical center; little consolation for the efforts made by this unknown Swiss Italian bugler.[14]

Like many of his Italian Swiss compatriots, Frederick Guscetti migrated and remained in New York City. Interestingly, he was born in Egypt, either in 1832 or 1842. The circumstances of his birth and the lack of adequate documentation have created a mysterious aura around him. Unlike many Italian soldiers in the Union ranks, Guscetti was not connected with Spinola's Empire Brigade or the Garibaldi Guard that attempted to recruit his fellow countrymen by such leaders as Colonel Frederick D'Utassy, Lieutenant Colonel Alessandro Repetti and Major George Waring, Jr. Guscetti was probably unaware that Repetti was a Genoese typographer and naturalized Swiss Italian from Lugano who returned to Switzerland during the war after facing a court martial. Guscetti also seemed to be unfamiliar with another famous Lombard man at arms, Luigi Tinelli. Frederick Guscetti's service records show that he enlisted as a sergeant on December 6, 1861 at age twenty in Company B, Enfants Perdus Regiment of New York and mustered into the U.S. service on April 18, 1862. On January 30, 1864, his regiment, commanded by Colonel Simon Levy, was consolidated with the First New York Engineers and the Forty-seventh and Forty-eighth New York Infantries. He was then transferred to Company A of the Forty-seventh Infantry Regiment of New York. This regiment fought several battles at Morris Island and at Fort Gregg, South Carolina from July 12, 1863 to November 28, 1863. He was then part of the Florida expedition that ended with the battle of Olustee. Guscetti was taken prisoner and confined at the infamous prisoner camp of Andersonville, Georgia on March 28, 1864. Because he could speak at least seven languages, he interpreted for the numerous foreigners at the hospital. He was finally discharged in Norfolk, Virginia with distinguished service from this company on June 22, 1865. After the war, this Guscetti became a teacher. In 1881, he was in England as a "major USA director of the Society for the Italian inland steam navigation" with his wife Annie Brown and his infant baby Daisy, who was born in Munich, Prussia. His wife Annie, while living in Italy, eventually filed with the U.S. government to collect her husband's military pension.[15]

The gravestone of John Buzzetti, born in Isola, Sondrio, Italy in 1830 acknowledges his presence in the Civil War. He was a private in Company F of the Cazadores Espanoles, Louisiana Militia. His wife Mary Jambois was born in Assumption, Louisiana in 1847 and might have been related to Florence Jambois of Genoa.[16]

The biographies of these men fighting for the Union are limited. It is interesting to note, however, how these newcomers embraced the role of soldiers after only a brief stay in New York or in the uncharted wild frontier of Illinois and Wisconsin. Other people from Genoa—such Edward Cox, Charles Brown, William Pulham, John Carpenter J.E.W. Clayson, William Stevenson, William S. Riley, Albert F. Kuehn—served in the Civil War. But in the Catholic cemetery, only the tombstones of Ferdinand Guscetti, John Buzzetti and Florence Jambois are marked as Civil War veterans. There is a contemporary account of how their native-born neighbors felt about these Italian Swiss Civil War veterans. Apparently, there were few or any surviving letters or journals with friends and family in Switzerland. As for the Italians, there are no viable old records of letters about Wisconsin. The published correspondence of the Valchiavennaschi in Australia, South America and the United States never acknowledge the presence of a large group in this state.[17]

Following their service in the Union Army, some Italian veterans returned to Genoa, Wisconsin. Other compatriots soon followed. The construction of the Catholic Church represented one of the first accomplishments for the increasing number of German and Italian migrants. The first stone church dedicated to St. Charles Borromeo, Archbishop of Milan, was erected in 1864. Its records tell the history of the community along with the gravestones in the cemetery that overlooks the Mississippi River from a steep hill. In 1901, a stone church replaced the old one with new additions, such as the rectory and the school, which thrives today. St. Charles Parish is very active in serving the needs of the community.[18]

Many others followed the first inroads made by Joseph Monti, Ferdinand Guscetti, and Bartholomew Sterlocchi. The arrival of additional immigrants by 1870 had already given Genoa its distinctive Italian flavor. At a time when Italians preferred to remain in and around New York, these people claimed land that in the old country was so hard to acquire. At the end of the Civil War, life returned to normal for Genoa and immigration from Italy continued. Crops changed according to the different needs. Wheat, which was cultivated year after year on the same soil, became unproductive and so that by 1875 many farmers resorted to animal breeding. The census of 1870 depicts Genoa as a mid-western city with an Italian accent. Its Main Street contained the Monti Hotel, Zaboglio Hardware Store, and the Latimer and Red River Inns, all owned by Italians. Records also highlight the presence of Italians. On May 1, 1872, for example, Margaret Rosalie Morelli was baptized in the local Catholic Church. The first wedding saw the marriage of Anthony Levi and Angela Zabolio (Zaboglio) in July 1872. The first burial at Genoa's cemetery was that of Sylvester Pedretti in 1875. The seal of Canton Ticino and Valchiavenna marked the birth of this new parish. Census data reveal various Swiss-Italian families in Genoa, among them the Monti, Lupi, Franzini, Guscetti, Beffa, Pedretti, Morelli. Those from the Campodolcino area in Valchiavenna included Zaboglio (Jabolio), Sterlocchi (Starlocki), Levi, Gadola, Gianoli (Gianolo), Barilani (Bariloni), Vener (Venner, Verner), Paggi (Page, Pagge), Gianera. The family of the deceased Benjamin Guscetti had left Chippewa Falls and resettled in Genoa.[19]

However, a movement of people that seems so straightly connected with a single destination, Genoa, was well diversified, which often happens. In fact, the 1870 records of Illinois and Minnesota birth rates prompt a deeper analysis. While Illinois was a starting point for many Italians, why was Minnesota also inviting to these immigrants? What was the connection between Minnesota and Genoa? Was this presence created by seasonal work from the Genoese or elsewhere?[20] The results of this analysis are fascinating. An undated obituary scrapbook exemplifies similar migration stories among these states. For example, Mary Ursula Trussoni Levi died in St. Henry, Cleveland Township, Minnesota, on April 10, 1902. She was born in Campodolcino on February 20, 1804 and married Lorenzo Levi. They had seven children. After her husband Lorenzo died in 1849, she migrated with her family to Wisconsin, stopping briefly in Genoa where some members of her family lived. However, the 1860 census states that Anthony, Mary's son, now the head of the family, was working as a raft man at the lumber mill in Stillwater, Minnesota. In 1868, she moved to Amery, Polk County, Wisconsin and remained there until 1878 when she moved back to Minnesota to be near her sons Lawrence and Thomas. This new community had a large concentration of Swiss from Canton Grisons (Graubunden) who spoke Romansch. All of Mary's children remained in the area except Anthony, who returned to Genoa and married Angeline Zaboglio, the widow of Silvio Buzzetti. He died there on June 11, 1883. He bequeathed a large sum to the Don Guanella Institute of Pianello del Lario, province of Como, Italy.

Another Trussoni crossed these same lines. Joseph Trussoni married Mary Muggli widow of Gion De Gonda in Stillwater. They never had any children together, but he helped her raise hers. When Mary died, Joseph returned to Chiavenna where he died on March 5, 1895.[21] Stillwater was a work destination or a transitory location for many Italians. The naturalization records in Washington County, Minnesota, indicate a number of Swiss-Italians never found in Genoa, like the Simonetti (Simonette), now Simons; Cappellazzi (Caplazi), Bertossi (Bertopsa), Giossi, Casanova (Cassinova), and Italians like De Stefani ( De Steffaney or De Staffney). Other Italians present in Genoa are Curti (Cuti), Della Bella, Levi, Trussoni (Trucciani), and Paggi (Paggio or Page). As early as 1857, these immigrants had already petitioned to obtain American passports. Before 1861 the Italians were listed as Austrians or subjects of Joseph I, King of Lombardy. Later the reference was made to Vittorio Emanuele II.[22]

Meanwhile, Genoa was evolving. Genoa had its own post office, and Main Street was still the center for business. Zabolio's (Zaboglio) hardware store, Latimer's grocery and hardware store, Monti's hotel and Red River Inn continued to thrive. Ferdinand and Albert Guscetti operated their wagon shop while Fred Morelli and Albert Schubert were the town's blacksmiths. The Chicago, Burlington and Northern Railroad connected Genoa to La Crosse in 1884 and offered some local jobs as section men, jobs that increased their farming income. In the early 1900s the button companies that used clamshells from the Mississippi River as source material offered other employment. We may assume from the various sources that people supplemented their income with seasonal work in the lumber mills.[23]

By the 1880s, Genoa continued to have a distinctive Italian character. Early settlers had large families and more moved into the town. Among the families that just missed the census were the Berras and the Garavaglias. These families were originally from Cuggiono, province of Milan, Italy. By 1882, they represented the vanguard of the thousands of people from the area that left for Detroit; Joliet, Illinois; St. Louis; Herrin, Illinois, and some small areas across the Unites States and South America. The first records show them aboard different ships from Le Havre to New York between 1879 and 1881.

Not many families left directly for Genoa. Besides the Berra and Garavaglia families, there were the Zoia, Calcaterra, Spezia and Garagiola who eventually found jobs elsewhere. The economy in Italy was quite bad. Francis Berra was sixty-six years old and his wife Theresa Garagiola sixty-two when they crossed the Atlantic Ocean in 1881. He lived with his son Anthony for a while and then left for Florence, Wisconsin where he worked as a miner and lumberman. He died there in 1894. Other bands of transient workers from Cuggiono were toiling in the St. Croix and Stillwater lumber mill areas more or less at the same time. Their petitions for American citizenship began in November 1881 when almost twenty migrants filed the necessary documents. They were either unaware of the implications of a new citizenship or had simply decided en masse to start a new life. The long list of misspelled names of people who had participated in the so-called mass migration had just started.[24]

The historical importance of these people is minimal. We see no detailed histories or letter collections. However, they have represented one of the most important agricultural accomplishments by the Italians in the United States. Some farms owned by the Barilani of Genoa and the Fanetti in Bloomer have remained in the same family over 100 years. The most comprehensive analysis about Genoa was performed by the Immigration Commission and presented by William Paul Dillingham on June 15, 1910, by Alexander Cance who was probably of Irish descent and had a scarce knowledge of Italy. He identified the Italians of Genoa as "Piedmontese on the Mississippi," although the first migrants were either Italians from Northern Lombardy or Swiss Italians.

In 1905, Genoa, Wisconsin, fifty Italians, including the Ticinese, out of a population of over 200 in the village and 200 families in the township, chose to clear the land they had bought as homesteaders for five to ten dollars and acre. The main production consisted of barley, corn, potatoes, clover seed, hay, tobacco and hay. Dairy farming generated milk and butter. Unfortunately, the harsh climate prevented these Italians from growing grapes. A close analysis confirms that Ticinese and other Italians preferred to buy their own land, especially since the terms were favorable. This was in large part because their farms were covered with trees. As a result, they often times worked at odd jobs, such as wood choppers, in the sawmills or as section hands on the railroad until, little by little, they could cultivate their cleared lands. This soil was quite productive because it had never been tilled. The main income derived from hay, tobacco, oats and dairy products also depending on the ability of the farmer. All in all the community had managed to prosper and improve. The fast acculturation of the Ticinese and the Italians followed by frequent intermarriages with Germans prompted Alexander Cance to declare the community as non- Italian: "Most of them speak Good English, and converse intelligently and frankly, without suspicion, on agriculture, politics, or topics of current interest . . . The Italians (Still considered as such) attend strictly to their farming. They are honest, peaceful and industrious. Contrasted with the New Jersey colonies, they show more intelligence, initiative, and independent self-reliance than the eastern group."

A century after its founding, Genoa still has an Italian flavor. There are no more Guscetti in Genoa. All have gone somewhere else. But many are still there on the steep hillside cemetery overlooking the familiar steeple of St. Charles Borromeo Church, the Hills of Minnesota in the horizon beyond the majestic Mississippi River.

From time to time various articles have appeared in the local press either to retell the story of the birth of the village or to display old pictures. Frequent articles about the St. Charles Church and its school tell of the sense of community that the church has generated. In 1948, a local newspaper article report told of the farming skills of the three Trussoni sisters. New people have come and others have gone to pursue their occupations. Now hunters roam the woods and the countryside in search of wild turkeys and patient fishermen stand by the shore of the Mississippi and its backwaters for bass, sauger, walleye. My friendship of over twenty-five years with Sister Loretta Penchi from Genoa testifies that our Italian heritage remains.[25]

## NOTES

1. Genoa, Wisconsin, Detailed Profile, http://www.city-data.com/city/Genoa/Wisconsin. htm; Ethnic Groups in Wisconsin: Historical Background, http://www.wiscinfo.dolt.wisc. edu/mklibray/ethn-his.html.

2. Austin H. Russell, *The Wisconsin Story: The Building of a Vanguard State* (Milwaukee: Journal, 1957); Robert C. Nesbit, *Wisconsin: A History* (Madison: University of Wisconsin Press, 1973), *passim.*

3. Galena, Illinois Detailed Profile, http://www.villageprofile.com/Illinois/galena/galena1. html; Jo Daviess County Fact Sheet, http://www.sos.state.il.us/departments/archives/irad/ township-maps/jodaviess, map.html; Martha Jane Pender," In Galena, Illinois" 22 August 2004, *New York Times.*

4. Samuel Mazzuchelli, *Memoirs Historical and Edifying of a Missionary Apostolic of the Order Saint Dominic among Various Indian Tribes and Among the Catholics and Protestants in the United States of America. With an Introduction of the Most Reverend John Ireland, DD Archbishop of St.* Paul (Chicago: W.F. Hall Printing, 1915): "The warlike tribes of the Sacs [sic] and Fox, with their stubborn war (Black Hawk War) against the United States government in 1832 spread confusion for many months throughout the southern and western part of the Wisconsin Territory. There, some of the citizens had been barbarously murdered, but their deaths were avenged later by the united forces of the settlers, who, pursuing the hostile and rebellious tribes, after different bloody encounters, drove the wretched savages to the necessity of swimming across the vast river Mississippi, near Prairie du Chien. How great the slaughter among the Indians it will not be easy to recount because, forced after useless resistance to save life by getting across the river, many perished in that difficult passage. Not provided with a sufficient number of horses, each of these carried more than one rider and so their flight was slow and perilous. The white man ceased not pursuing the fugitives by force of arms, killing them in the very act of leaving the bank. Not a few women and children perished in the current, victims of the cruelty of some citizens, or of their inability to cling to the horses during their dangerous and headlong passage to the river," 1860 *United States Federal Census.* M653, 1416 rolls, 619. National Archives, Washington, D.C.; Father Samuel Mazzuchelli was the founder of the Sinsinawa Dominicans congregation in Wisconsin. He was also responsible for

building several churches. See http://www.sinsinawa.org/AboutUs/History/Mazzuchelli/
Churches.html.

5. Raffaello Ceschi, "L'Età delle Emigrazioni Transoceaniche e delle Ferrovie" in Ceschi,
ed., *Storia del Canton Ticino*, 1998; Michael H. Tepper , ed., *Baltimore Port. Passenger
Arrivals at the Port of Baltimore 1820–1834, from Customs Passengers Lists* (Baltimore:
Genealogical Press, 1982), 465; *1850 United States Federal Census*, M432, 1009 rolls.
National Archives, Washington, D.C.; E.M. Rogers, ed., *History of Vernon County,
Wisconsin*, 1884; *Memoirs of Vernon County* (Springfield, Illinois: Union Publishing
Company, 1884) http://www.leventinaturismo.ch/WEB/airolo/htm.

6. *1850 United States Federal Census*, M432, 1009 rolls, National Archives, Washington, D.C.

7. Shullsburg, Wisconsin Detailed Profile, http://www.city-data.com/city/Shullsburg-
Wisconsin.html; see Rogers, *History of Vernon County*, 530–539.

8. William Paul Dillingham, U.S. Senate, *Reports of the Immigration Commission,
Immigrants in Industries. Recent Immigrants in Agriculture*, 15 June 1910 (Government
Printing Office, Washington, D.C., 1910), 389–409.

9. Peter Shrake, "The Battle of Bad Axe," *Sauk County Historical Society Newsletter*
(Baraboo, Wisconsin: 2001; James Lewis, *The Black Hawk War of 1832*, http://www.
lincoln.lib.niu.edu/blackhawk/page2c.html.

10. *History of St. Charles Borromeo's Parish, Genoa, Wisconsin*, 1967, n.p and n.d.; Chet
Bente,"Hasting's Landing was Genoa's Original Name" July 1964 *La Crosse Tribune*;
Nancy K. Jambois, *Genoa History*; Luciano Iorizzo "The Padrone and Immigrant
Distribution" in Sylvano M. Tomasi and Madeline H. Enger, ed., *The Italian Experience in
the United States*, (Staten Island, New York: Center for Migration Studies, 1970), 63.

11. See Rogers, *History of Vernon County, Wisconsin*, 529–30.

12. *First Regiment Heavy Artillery Regiments, Lists of Recruits not on Company Rolls,
Roster Wisconsin Volunteers*, Wisconsin Historical Society, Madison, 2003, http://www.
wisconsinhistory.org/roster. The surname Guscetti has been found misspelled several
times: Goosuth, Gossuth, Gussette, Guscette,Guesette Gusatti,Guzcette, Guccetti,
Kossuth, Kussinth. This practice was common because migrants were often illiterate
and the transcription was based on the sounds heard. I have seen the evolution of many
Italian names both involuntary and voluntary, but the transformation of Guscetti is
quite remarkable; Rogers, *History of Vernon County, Wisconsin*; Charles E. Estabrook,
ed., *Records and Sketches of Military Organizations*, Madison, 1914; Cheda Giorgio,
*L'Emigrazione Ticinese in California*, Armando Dadò Editore, Locarno, 1981.; Gheda
Giorgio, *L'Emigrazione Ticinese in Australia*, Armando Dadò Editore, Locarno, 1976.;
Gian Pietro Pawlowski, *Bibliografia dell'Emigrazione Ticinese 1850–1950*, Archivio
Storico di Bellinzona, unpublished, Losone, 18 September 1882.; *Military Records of
Individual Civil War Soldiers*. (database) Provo Ancestry.com, 1999; data compiled by
Historical Data Systems of Kingston, Massachusettes in 1997, 1998, 1999, and 2000;
*1860 United States Federal Population Census*, M653, 1438 Rolls, National Archives,
Washington, D.C.; United States Bureau of Land Management, *Wisconsin Land Records*.
(database) Provo, Utah: 1997–Original Electronic data from: United States. Bureau of
Land Management. *Wisconsin Pre-1905 & Cash Entry Patent and Cadastral Survey Plat
Index*. General Land Office Automated Records Project, National Archives, Washington,
D.C.; *Civil War Pension Index* (database) Provo, Utah, Ancestry.com.; Historical Data
Systems; Tony Guscetti to Author, 10 September 2004; Sister Loretta Penchi to Author,
5 August 2004.

13. *Civil War Compiled Military Service Records* (database), Provo, Utah, Ancestry.com,
1999; *2nd Regiment Wisconsin Cavalry Records, Roster Wisconsin Volunteers*, Wisconsin
Historical Society, Madison, 2003, http://www.wisconsinhistory.org/roster.html; *1860
United States Federal Census, Wheatland, Bad Ax, Wisconsin*; M653, 1438 rolls, National

Archives, Washington, D.C.

14. *American Civil War Regiments*. (database), Provo, Utah,: Ancestry.com, Data compiled by Historical data Systems. Third Infantry Regiment, Company H, Roster Wisconsin Volunteers, Wisconsin Historical Society, Madison, 2003; Tony Guscetti to Author, 10 September 2004; Rogers, *History of Vernon County, Wisconsin*, 529–530; Death Records, St. Charles Catholic Church, Genoa, Wisconsin, translated from Latin, compiled and contributed by Sister Loretta Penchi.

15. *Military Records of Individual Civil War Soldiers*. (database), Provo, Utah;Ancestry. com, 1999, Data compiled by Historical Data Systems of Kingston, MA from the following list of works. Copyright 1997,1998,1999,2000, Historical Data Systems Inc, Kingston, MA 02364; American *Civil War Regiments*. (database), Ibid. *American Civil War Battle Summaries.*(database), Ibid. *1870 United States Federal Census* (database), Provo, Utah,: MyFamily.com, indexed by Ancestry.com from microfilmed schedules of the 1870 United States Federal Decennial Census. *1870 United States Federal Census*. (database), Provo, Utah.: MyFamily.com, 2003. Original data. Data in National Archives 1870 Federal Population Census, M593, 1,761 rolls; Minnesota T132; Historical Data Systems, Comp. American *Civil War Battle Summaries*. (database), Provo, Utah,: 1999–. Data compiled by Historical Data Systems, *1870 United States Federal Census*, Albany Ward 10, Albany, New York, M593, 900 rolls, National Archives, Washington, D.C.; Raphael Rues to Author 20 September 2004; Cornelia Schrader-Muggenthaler, *The Swiss Emigration Book*, Vol. 1 (Apollo, Pennsylvania: Closson Press, 1993), 46; William B. Martin, "Battle of Olustee," http:extlab1.entnem.ufl.edu/olustee/capsule.html; Gail Jarvis, "Federal POW Propaganda," http://www.lewrockwell.com/jarvis46.html. This article depicts the despicable situation at the camps the consequence of the refusal by the Union to exchange prisoners. Major Henry Wirz, a German-Swiss immigrant, forbade prisoners to build shelters, thus forcing them to dig holes in the ground for protection. Prisoners were brutalized and denied adequate food and medical care. The death of 13,000 prisoners during their forced stay at Andersonville speaks for itself. For Italian Americans in the Civil War see Henry Steele Commager, ed., *The Blue and the Gray (*New York: Fairfax Press, 1950); Francis A. Lord, *They Fought for the Union* (Harrisburg, Pennsylvania: Telegraph Press, 1960), Associazione Italiani d'America, "Dossier Garibaldi, Ricordi di Italianità http://difgilander.libero. it/fiammecremisi/approfondimenti/ricordi.htm; Marco Sioli. "Nella Terra della Libertà. in *I Tinelli:Storia di una Famiglia (Secoli XVI-XX)*, a cura di Marina Cavallera, 83–86, Franco Angeli, Milano, 2003; Frank Alduino and David J. Coles, The Garibaldi Guard and Italian American Service in the Civil War, *Italian American, Winter 2004; Civil War Pension Index*. (database) Provo.Utah,: Ancestry.com, 2000, data indexed and imaged from National Archives; *General Index to Pension Files, 1861–193,*.T288, 544 rolls, National Archives. There is information concerning Frederick Guscetti in the Forty-seventh New York Infantry records. There is a list of deserters, among them an Italian named Camillo Giustini, see www.spinola.org/47NY/original/roster/namesg.htm; Ships in Port in London & Middlesex, 1881, Part 3, http://www.angelfire.com/de/BobSanders/London81-3.html, "Picture History, Mrs. Frederick Guscetti." The website displays *a carte de visite* photograph of Frederick Guscetti and one of an alleged Margaret Josephine McPherson (1852–1885) with a short narration of her life. She was married in 1871 to Frederick who enlisted in the Civil War in the Forty-seventh regiment and was interned at Andersonville. My interest in the photographs taken in Pennsylvania unveiled a mistake. The picture company confused this Frederick Guscetti with another, Frederick Antonio Guscetti, born in Quinto, Canton Ticino, Switzerland on 30 July 1848 who migrated with his father Severino to Australia in 1855. He married Margaret Josephine Guscetti, who died on 28 January 1885. Frederick survived until 23 April 1912. He could not collect any pension as specified in the Civil War Pension Index simply because he and his wife had never lived in the United States. Who is the lady on the picture, then? Annie B. Guscetti was born in Wells, Somerset, United Kingdom

around 1856, and she might be the lady shown as Margaret McPherson. However, this case of namesake increases the interest about the importance of early Swiss Italian migration to the United States. "Picture History" has admitted their mistake and will hopefully amend the caption. At this point we have another Guscetti to research, http;//www.picturehistory. com/find/p/21589/mcms.html; Picture History Research to Author, 4 October 2004; Gale Research. *Passenger and Immigration Lists Index, 1500–1900s* (database), Provo, Utah: Myfamily.com., 2003.Original Data : Filby, P. William, ed., *Passenger and Immigration Lists Index, 1500–1900s* (Farmington Hills, MI: Gale Research, 2003); Giorgio Cheda, *Ticinesi in Australia*, 147,148, 240; Posters of the Garibaldi Guard and Spinola's Empire Brigade (author's personal archive); G. Martinola, *La Guerra di Secessione degli Stati Uniti d'America Nei Rapporti del Col. Augusto Fogliardi*, Lugano, 1966, 121 (extract from "Rivista Militare della Svizzera Italiana", 1965). Repetti fought briefly in the Civil War and returned ill to Switzerland, followed by the controversy about the alleged harsh discipline of the Italian and other soldiers under his command. He then accompanied Fogliardi in his military mission where they met President Lincoln on June 23, 1863.

16. Ibid.

17. Death Records, St. Charles Catholic Church, Genoa, Wisconsin; Rogers, *History of Vernon County*, Ibid; Giorgio Cheda, *L'Emigrazione Ticinese in California,*. Epistolario: lettere n. 203 e 513,: Paolo Via e Giordano Sterlocchi , *Vengo Caramente a Salutarvi, Lettere di Emigranti Valchiavennaschi in America, 1853–1946*. Biblioteca della Valchiavenna, 1983.

18. Rogers, *History of Vernon County*, 528; *History of St. Charles Borromeo Parish, Genoa*, n.p.

19. Death Records, St. Charles Catholic Church, Monti Joseph (Prato Leventina, Canton Ticino, Switzerland in 1809—died in Genoa, Wisconsin 30 January 1876), Ferdinand Guscetti (Airolo, Canton Ticino, Switzerland 19 March 1824, died in Genoa 9 January 1898); Robert and Maryo Gard, *My Land, My Home, My Wisconsin*, (Milwaukee: The Milwaukee Journal, 1978); Bureau of Land Management, *Wisconsin Land Records*. (database) Provo, Utah, Ancestry.com 1997; Bureau of Land Management, *Wisconsin Pre-1908 Homestead & Cash Entry Patent and Cadastral Survey Plat Index*. General Land Office Automated Records Project, 199x. Under the Treaty of April 12, 1820, Ferdinand Guscetti bought 40 acres on August 1, 1858,and his wife Maria Guscetti bought 40 acres on August 1, 1858 and July 1, 1859, respectively; Maria Zaboglio bought 40 acres on July 1, 1860 and Joseph Monti the same acreage on June 1, 1860; Ancestry.com, *1870 United States Federal Census*. (database) Provo, Utah, MyFamily.com Inc., 2003, Indexed by Ancestry.com from microfilmed schedule of the 1870 U.S. Federal Decennial Census. *1870 United States Federal Census*.(database online), Provo, Utah,: MyFamily.com., 2003. Original data: Data Imaged National Archives, *1870 Federal Census*. M593, 1,761 rolls; part of Minnesota T132, 13 rolls. National Archives; *History of St. Charles Borromeo Church*.21Sister Loretta Penchi, *The Family and Descendants of Anthony Levi, 1819–1889 and Angela Masera, 1829–1885*, La Crosse, WI, 1983; Amanda Freiberg, *Levi Family History*, Omaha, Nebraska, January 14 1987; St. Henry Catholic Church Gravestones, La Sueur County, Minnesota; Washington County Courthouse Records, Stillwater, Minnesota; La Sueur County Courthouse Records, Le Center, Minnesota; Tamborini Alessandro, *Don Luigi Guanella*, Edizioni Paoline, Bari 1957. Don Guanella recalls thinking of his aunt (Ursula Levi) who had died in Genoa (City) at 98 and the cousin benefactor Antonio who had left a significant sum for his religious institution. He remembers the cousins Francesco and Agostino Zaboglio and all his efforts to send a priest to Genoa through Don Giovanni Bosco. (Father Momo was a resident Pastor from early 1875 to 1883); Amanda Freiberg, *A Visit to the St. Henry Colony*. Omaha, Nebraska, May 1986.

20. *United States Federal Census,*1870, Ibid.

21. Sister Loretta Penchi, *The Family and Descendants of Anthony Levi, 1819-1889 and*

*Angela Masera, 1829-1885*, La Crosse, WI, 1983; Amanda Freiberg, *Levi Family History*, Omaha, Nebraska, January 14 1987; St. Henry Catholic Church Gravestones, La Sueur County, Minnesota; Washington County Courthouse Records, Stillwater, Minnesota; La Sueur County Courthouse Records, Le Center, Minnesota; Tamborini Alessandro, *Don Luigi Guanella*, Edizioni Paoline, Bari 1957. Don Guanella recalls thinking of his aunt (Ursula Levi) who had died in Genoa (City) at 98 and the cousin benefactor Antonio who had left a significant sum for his religious institution. He remembers the cousins Francesco and Agostino Zaboglio and all his efforts to send a priest to Genoa through Don Giovanni Bosco. (Father Momo was a resident Pastor from early 1875 to 1883); Amanda Freiberg, *A Visit to the St. Henry Colony*, Omaha, Nebraska, May 1986.

22. Minnesota Naturalization Records, SAM; 49, Roll #1 18520–1868.

23. Jambois, *History of Genoa*, Ibid.

24. The Berra Family Reunion, 21 June 1987; 16 March 2004, Father Charles Nobwana to Author. Private collection of files: Francis Berra, Theresa Garagiola (Careggiola), Maria and Jacob (Giacomo) Garavaglia, Anthony Berra, Sr., and Mary Baroli; Minnesota Naturalization Records, Ibid.

25. *Argus*, Vol. XVIII, No. 25 "View Along River a Joy to Tourists," Plats of Genoa Township 1896, 1896 and 1930; Robert C. Gehl, "Time Changes, Little Italy," 7 May 1967, *The La Crosse Sunday Tribune*; Gerald Doucet, "History of St. Charles Parish, Genoa, Noted; List Developments, *La Crosse Dioceses Times Review*, 1945.; Donald Doucet, "Three Trussoni Sisters Handle All Work on Farm at Genoa" *La Crosse Tribune*, 1948.; Chet Bente " Hastings Landing was Genoa's Original name; Settled in 1852 "*The La Crosse Tribune,*1960.; Chet Bente, " Sunny Genoa was one Known as 'Little Italy'. *The La Crosse Tribune*, 1964.; Genoa Township tax rates 1976–77.; *The La Crosse Tribune*, "The Way it was*"*, October 9, 1977.; Eileen Schoville,"Zabolio hardware store being sold". *The La Crosse Tribune*, December 15, 1979; Marian O'Keeffe, "Eloda Penchi, Mother of Nine Finds Time for Teaching, Parish Work. *Times Review*. June 25, 1981; Marian O'Keeffe, "Small School is Surviving, thank you." *Times Review*, 25 June, 1981; The Big River Inn, Hunting and Fishing Paradise, http://www. thebigriverinn.com; miscellaneous correspondences, Sister Loretta Penchi to Author, 1986–2004.

# PART II

# LITERATURE AND ETHNIC IDENTITY

# Celebrating Helen Barolini and *Umbertina*

## Mary Jo Bona
### Stony Brook University

We celebrate an important milestone in our literary history: *Umbertina* has come of age. Fully an adult, *Umbertina* at twenty five is permanently in print and has been rewarded by exciting and useful secondary criticism, written by such scholars as Anthony J. Tamburri, Mary Ann Mannino, Edvige Giunta, Fred L. Gardaphé, Robert Viscusi, and Maria Kotsaftis, to name just a few. In its initial state of innocence, Italian American literature was in fact unfettered by what Robert Scholes has called "protocols of reading," especially since a secondary order of reflections on this literature was lacking for many years. Seeking help from ethnic and feminist criticism in the 1980s, I felt free to create a way to read *Umbertina*, aware of the mosaic that we call American literature. After all, if Helen Barolini was not deterred by the burial of writers' voices from Italian America, I could make my own path by proclaiming through literary scholarship that adult considerations such as canonization take place when books are reprinted, taught, and questioned. Such proclamations are coming to fruition for Italian American writers.

Devoted to words, their origins, the weight of their history, Barolini herself pays homage to the transformative power of language itself. Like many minority writers before her, Barolini initially felt that she had no context out of which to write. Ironically liberated from narrow definitions of the kind of writer she should be, Barolini became the writer she could be, donning many linguistic hats, and blurring boundaries between genres. Not only has Barolini written historical fiction with the publication of her first novel, *Umbertina*, in 1979, but she later published a combination memoir/

cookbook—*Festa: Recipes and Recollections of Italian Holidays* (1988) and essays that chronicle her writing life in Italy and America, *Chiaroscuro: Essays of Identity* (1997). In her struggle to honor the word, to speak the truth of the writer, Helen Barolini recognizes that "Writing does risk everything. Being an artist, a writer of novels, means wrestling family or national loyalty to the ground to overcome restraints to the truth" (*Chiaroscuro*, 126).

When doing research in 1991 at the Immigration History Research Center in St. Paul, Minnesota, I located the original outline of Barolini's first novel, then called *The Last Abstraction*, and a review of an earlier version of the book. The focus was on the second part of the novel, in which the protagonist, Marguerite (then called Anna-Marie) decides to leave her Italian husband. Then I also found notes explaining that Barolini first envisioned the novel as a trilogy. Combining the separate manuscripts *The Last Abstraction* and *Umbertina*, Barolini adhered to an editor's suggestion, thus compelling, as she later said in an interview, "a complete rewriting . . . I see it more as a novel of development— the three main female characters must develop in new ways in order to survive ("Interview: Helen Barolini," 47).

Barolini's *Umbertina* does important work: it weds Italian and American characters, themes, and topographies. A good portion of the novel is set in Italy with Italian American and Italian characters, extending the national trend of earlier Anglo Americans and their fascination with locating their ingenues in Italy. Within the novel, references and recursions to the immigrant migration are replaced by a fully detailed historical narrative of life in Castagna (Calabria). When one reads Part I of *Umbertina*, the documentary film comes to mind, with its emphasis on historical veracity, detail, and vivid archaic footage. Of her own writing, Barolini states, "I am not a linguistic stylist first and foremost. It is not the words per se, that engage me, but the ideas and human feelings they represent" ("Interview: Helen Barolini," 47). Clearly the style of Part One is that of the history writer, with emphasis, Barolini herself explains, on change through time: "I thought of showing transcultural and transgenerational change, and the losses and gains that each change implies." ("Interview," 47).

Just as Barolini details change through time by focusing on three distinctive female characters, she also changes genres in each Part of *Umbertina* to meet the varying needs of those three characters. It must be emphasized that Barolini refuses to reduce the plights of each female character solely to their roles as women in patriarchal culture. Nonetheless, Barolini orients her novel—both structurally and thematically—around the complicated lives of each woman, attending carefully to their positions as women who must cope with the contingencies distinct to their generation and social backgrounds. William Boelhower's ordering principles of ethnic trilogies in his seminal article "The Ethnic Trilogy: A Poetics of Cultural Passage," with its emphasis on generations, offers a structurally sound method by which to read Barolini's novel, originally conceived of as a trilogy. Thus a generic reading of *Umbertina* can be mapped out.

In Part One of the novel, aptly titled *Umbertina*, Barolini develops a narrative voice and style that is most closely aligned to Italian storytelling traditions, that of the *cantastorie*. The titular character is and remains illiterate in her village dialect, and, not surprisingly, in English later in America. Unlike the unlettered storyteller Rosa Cassettari, whose storytelling prowess translated quite successfully on the written page through her conversations with Marie Hall Ets, a social worker at The Chicago Commons Settlement House, Umbertina's story needs to be told by a third-person narrator. While both the historical Rosa and the fictional Umbertina have intimate knowledge of Italian folk customs and village lore, Barolini's choice to narrate Umbertina's story in third person supports the idea that peasant women of the mid-to-late nineteenth century did not commonly have permission to speak their minds. More tellingly, perhaps, is Barolini's awareness of the linguistic estrangement a peasant woman like Umbertina must have experienced in coming to America. Local dialects in Italy already marginalized the village folk, separated as they were geographically and linguistically from the standard Italian of Tuscany. Coming to America may have increased Umbertina's opportunities for upward mobility, but her silence is a literal manifestation of her alienation from the English language.

Helen Barolini, therefore, functions as the narrative voice not only for the goat girl, Umbertina, but also for the way of life, the village history of Calabria and, later, turn-of-the-century America. Umbertina finds a way to ensure herself a better life because she has the ability to suppress her desire for the charcoal maker and to adhere to her father's will by marrying the older Serafino, who has migrated before to America, representing "something new in her life" (43). Serafino does represent something new, accepting Umbertina as his wife without the customary dowry, living seven years in Calabria before migrating to America. Thus, Barolini undertakes the role of the *cantastorie*, and becomes, as Gardaphé has explained, the history singer, who was the guardian of local tradition ("From Oral Tradition to Written Word," 299).

Barolini's narrator is just that history singer of the village town of Castagna, and of Cosenza, "a provincial capital in the heart of Calabria" (Umbertina, 52). Along with Domenica Sacca, the socialist shoemaker, the *cantastorie* Barolini offers a more detailed and thorough a history of southern Italy during the *Risorgimento* than any literary writer before her. Included within that history from the outset is a poor, disenfranchised woman's point of view: the goat girl from the hills above Castagna. Barolini's song of the *Risorgimento* through the migration and adjustment to America spans eighty years, two centuries, two continents, two histories, and one woman's mixed victory. Towards the end of her life, Umbertina ponders, "She had won, but who could she tell the story to?" (145). That Barolini uses the definite article—"the" rather than the possessive pronoun "her" in the line "who could she tell the story to?" suggests that Umbertina recognizes that her story forms part of a larger, spectacular narrative about migration, which includes painful loss and material gain. Unable to speak the language of her grandchildren, Umbertina's status as an outsider is magnified by the end of her life as she silently sits sequestered under a tree at the ritual picnic, "like an old Indian squaw" (141). Umbertina's sacrifice in coming to America allows her forbears to develop the badges of status that will permit them entrance into realms of knowledge closed to her, including learning

English fluently and reading books. The history singer, Helen Barolini, third-generation writer, nonetheless embraces the vital importance of her grandmother's oral traditions by dedicating the novel to her mother, "the storyteller," who made the creation of *Umbertina* possible.

In her desire to feminize the immigrant experience, Barolini fleshes out the lives of nineteenth-century women in Italy and America. Within Part One of *Umbertina*, Barolini offers us a vivid history lesson, which refuses to focus solely on the traditional migration narrative of male experience abroad. An abbreviated list of topics follows in an effort to reinforce the prolific richness of Barolini's dual history of the nineteenth-century *Risorgimento* (and the subsequent exodus it produced), and Umbertina's experiences as a woman and mother: Dispassionate clergy, invasions of foreign tribes, natural disasters, steep taxation, thieving land barons, absentee landlords, inequality between genders, arranged marriages but no means for the necessary *dote* (dowry), Garibaldi and his 1000 Redshirts, northern oppression of landless southerners, birds of passage, midwives, multiple pregnancies and miscarriages, the uprooting, *lo strappo*, Castle Garden, steerage, seasickness, diapers, menstrual napkins, thieving *padroni*, Mott Street, tenement quarters, Little Italy, *campanilismo, feste*, lost children, lost *coperta* (matrimonial bedspread), secondary migration, Guinea Gulch, loss of language, eating well, upward mobility, S. Longobardi & Sons importing food business, influenza epidemic, weak children, loss of *benessere*.

As in all ethnic trilogies, Barolini's *Umbertina* traces the immigrant self, moving into the modern world, reacting to uprootedness and fragmentation. Focusing on the women's experience, however, compels Barolini to place that self in relation to her original family and the one she is expected to conceive. Governed by what William Boelhower calls a foundational project, immigrant ancestors—men and women—begin life over again, concentrating on the activities of founding, building, and establishing. Umbertina achieves her ideal habitat, but the cost might very well be as great as the loss of her matrimonial bedspread, symbolizing her sacrificial entry to a better life in upstate, New York ("The Ethnic Trilogy," 12).

If one literally numbers generations from the point of immigration into the United States, then Barolini glosses over the second generational story which features Carla, one of Umbertina's girl children. But as Werner Sollors has explained in his well-known cultural study, *Beyond Ethnicity: Consent and Descent in American Culture*, generations are just as much cultural constructs as they are orientation devices. Carla's daughter, Marguerite of Part II of *Umbertina*, is just as much marked by the middle-class aspirations of her Italian American parents as she is by the dominant culture's loathing of Italians in America. Not coincidentally, Marguerite does not learn the homeland language from her parents; she, like her grandmother Umbertina, is estranged from her linguistic heritage. Unlike her grandmother, however, Marguerite is the beneficiary of her family's upward mobility, initiated by first-generation immigrant, *Umbertina*. Marguerite's adult confusions may be complex and multiple, but she clearly suffers the consequences of her parents' shame of ethnicity and concomitant refusal to transmit the local dialect to their children. Marguerite's story is Helen's story. Part Two of Umbertina, like many early narratives by Italian Americans, is fictional autobiography. In 1988, Helen Barolini sent me a letter with her article "A Circular Journey," in which she explains that this piece was the seminal essay from which Umbertina was born. Other works such as "Going to Sicily," "The Finer Things in Life," "Neruda vs. Sartre at the Sea," and "Another Convent Story," many of which are included in *Chiaroscuro* also flesh out the author's life in Italy and America, from growing up in Syracuse, New York, to marrying an Italian poet.

*Chiaroscuro*, Barolini's autobiographical essays, is a testimonial to a life lived deeply immersed in the magic of words, and provides many insights into reading Part Two of *Umbertina*. A case in point: Barolini's seemingly fruitless search for a wick for the antique oil lamp she purchases in Rome proves serendipitous nonetheless, for she discovers the trade name on the base of the lamp that triggers memories of her own mother's devotion to "the finer things in life." Just as her mother's search for fine articles in house sales of the elite in Syracuse, New York, revealed a "passionate search for a past," Barolini's own travels abroad and at home, in literature and in library stacks, helped her reconstruct the history that her "possessionless" immigrant grandparents tried to forget after coming to America (41). Barolini's essays of identity pay tribute to her development as a writer, her educational experiences, and her analysis of Italian American literary culture. These works teach us how Helen managed not to fall victim to the perceived limitations of her gender or generation as her character Marguerite does.

Learning in adulthood the standard Italian language, Helen Barolini eventually married a northern Italian poet from Veneto, and became a translator and a mother. Her childhood ambivalence toward Italy and things Italian gave way to embracing her identities—as an Italian American living in Italy and raising children, who are Italian American and native Italian; as a Sicilian-Calabrian American married to a northern Italian; and as an Italian American woman of the World War II generation, who aspired to be a writer. For Barolini, the visible symbol of her double consciousness is the view of Lake Como, its two arms spreading east and west: "It was emblematic: a pattern of life and work was made strikingly clear as I saw in the lakes both the main body of who I am, American, on the one side, and the Italian tributary. From these two confluences am I and my writing formed. My straddling position could be none other than that of the Italian American" (*Chiaroscuro*, 128).

Barolini is a wordsmith. The term *chiaroscuro* is not obfuscated for Helen by the dark as it is for her fictional counterpart, Marguerite, whose desire to capture historical memory through photography is hampered by her lack of clarity in *Umbertina*. Also part of a feminist reappraisal of post World War II children of immigrant parents or grandparents, *Umbertina* exemplifies the autobiographical imperative to "communicate the truth of unique individuality and the feminist concern with representative and intersubjective elements of women's experience" (Felski, "On Confession," 84).

Marguerite succumbs to the very desires—manifested in sexual love—that would have prevented her grandmother from achieving the goal of migration had she not suppressed her romantic feelings for the charcoal maker.

Unable to cope with the difficulty of working as an artist unto herself and unsupported by a well-meaning but clearly old-fashioned husband, Marguerite resorts to an iron-clad habit not uncommon to many women: supporting a man's needs over her own. As transgressive as Marguerite's affair with a younger married man may seem to be—and oddly fulfilling her grandmother's unrequited love—her focus on his writerly ambitions obliterates her own artistic needs. Pregnant with her lover's child, abortion dangerous and illegal in Italy, Marguerite's death in a car crash driving over the mountains in Italy is less accident than suicide. In Marguerite's life, as in many women's, especially before second-wave feminism, the fallen woman dies and her "favorite escape-hatch" of self-punishment is less choice than a pattern reinforced by Marguerite's gendered position (4).

The paradigm of reconstruction evident in ethnic trilogies allows Barolini to recover the optimism of first-generation ancestors and conclude her novel with a satisfying narrative and feminist resolution. Part Three, Tina, generically might be called a kunstlerroman, the development of a female artist as a scholar. Tina, like Helen Barolini herself, is a lover of language, and uses it to save her life. Learning from her mother's diaries, Tina rewrites Marguerite's life by asserting her right to a self divorced from conventional roles of motherhood and a commitment instead to her life as a Dantean scholar. The privileged child of an Italian poet and an American mother, Tina's choice to study Dante attests to her fluency as a native speaker of the language of the *signori*, not the subaltern language of her great-grandmother's dialect. Moreover, Tina's bi-cultural status allows her to cross borders geographically and linguistically, unselfconsciously.

Tina's devotion to her work nonetheless compels her to run away from the love of her life because her commitment to her own artistry must be assured before she commits to him. Only when she has completed her dissertation project, does Tina meet up with Jason, appropriately at a Central Park Shakespeare play. Barolini weds Anglo and Italian identities by referencing the English bard, the Anglo equivalent to Dante. Barolini signals the imminent success of Tina's forthcoming union with Jason by having her complete the lines that Jason began of the first quatrain of Shakespeare's sonnet #116: "Love is not love/which alters when it alteration finds" (414).

Equally at home in Italian and English, Tina will not have to suppress her desire for artistic knowledge or for romantic love. She is becoming the late twentieth-century version of Umbertina's dream: "you find your place, you work, and like planting seeds, everything grows" (139). That Tina plants rosemary—the symbol of remembrance and of Umbertina herself, who planted rosemary in her garden—suggests her ongoing desire to stay connected to her maternal peasant heritage. In addition, while she does not know of its original owner, Tina's attraction to her great-grandmother's matrimonial bedspread she sees hanging at the Museum of Immigration at Ellis Island signifies her determination to understand the complex pieces of her ancestral past.

Tina's future as an artist/scholar is a threshold experience: she is just beginning her life as an artist by the conclusion of *Umbertina*. As we celebrate the twenty-fifth anniversary of *Umbertina* let us celebrate the full-fledged storyteller in Helen Barolini, whose artistic daring produced one of the most important big books of Italian America.

WORKS CITED

Barolini, Helen. Chiaroscuro: *Essays of Identity*. Madison: U of Wisconsin P, 1999.
_____. *Festa: Recipes and Recollections of Italian Holidays*. New York: Harcourt, 1988.
_____. Interview. By Carol Bonomo Ahearn. *Fra Noi*. Sept. 1986: 47.
_____. Letter to the author. 28 June 1988.
_____. Papers. Immigration History Research Center. University of Minnesota.
_____. *Umbertina*. 1979. New York: Feminist P, 1999.
Boelhower, William. "The Ethnic Trilogy: A Poetics of Cultural Passage." *MELUS* 12.4
    (1985): 7–23.

Ets, Marie Hall. Rosa: *The Life of an Italian Immigrant.* 1970. Madison: U of Wisconsin P, 1999.

Felski, Rita. "On Confession." *Women, Autobiography, Theory: A Reader.* Eds. Sidonie Smith and Julia Watson. Madison: U of Wisconsin P, 1998. 83–95.

Gardaphé, Fred. L. "From Oral Tradition to Written Word: Toward an Ethnographically Based Literary Criticism." *From the Margin: Writings in Italian Americana.* Eds. Anthony J. Tamburri, Paolo Giordano, and Fred L. Gardaphé. West Lafayette, IN: Purdue UP, 1991. 294–306.

Scholes, Robert. *Protocols of Reading.* New Haven: Yale UP, 1989.

Sollors, Werner. *Beyond Ethnicity: Consent and Descent in American Culture.* New York: Oxford UP, 1986.

# Why Helen Barolini's *Umbertina* Is Still New

## Josephine Gattuso Hendin
## New York University

In *The Promised Land* Mary Antin wrote: "To be alive in America . . . is to ride on the central current of the river of modern life; and to have a conscious purpose is to hold the rudder that steers the ship of fate" (356).

Helen Barolini's *Umbertina* charts currents of modern life as they surge through nearly a century of the lives of women. Italian and Italian American women come alive as figures for modernity itself. They struggle against a future-denying fatalism associated with Southern Italy as well as their own divided identities as they strive to find and implement what Antin called a "conscious purpose" to defeat poverty and submission to any fated role.

Barolini confronts Italy and America as points on a journey from past to future in which women are the bridge to change. From the prologue in which Marguerite Morosini discusses her desire to divorce her prominent husband and set out on her own, through Barolini's powerful narrative of Grandmother Umbertina's courage in leaving Calabria and strength in making a new life in America, Barolini creates purgatorial trials that show how difficult it is for a woman to seize control her of life, reject fatalism, and, as Antin put it, "hold the rudder that steers the ship of fate."

Barolini manages to be faithful to both the social facts and inner lives of each generation of women she creates. It is largely social facts that dictate the need to have a husband for Umbertina's generation of women to emigrate from Italy. As Friedman-Kasaba notes, women had "more difficulty gaining entrance to the US than men." In the words of Edward Corsi, director of Ellis Island at the time:

> A woman, if she came alone, was asked a number of
> special questions: how much money she had; if she were
> going outside of New York: whether her passage had
> been paid by herself or by some charitable institution.
> If she had come to join her husband in New York or
> Brooklyn, we could not let her loose on the streets of
> a strange city looking for her husband . . . Sometimes
> . . . the man could not be located . . . Sometimes these
> women were placed in the care of a social agency . .
> . If the missing husband or fiancé still could not be
> traced, the poor alien, despite all her tears, had to be
> returned to her native country (103).

What Barolini brings to these social facts is a deeper understanding of the emotional truths bound up in immigrant marriages.

Yeats's belief that out of the struggle with others we make politics; but out of the struggle with ourselves we create poetry is realized in Barolini's grasp of how social conflicts enter those recesses of feeling and consciousness that resist ideology. Her portraits of Umbertina's generation are celebrations of individuals and families who survive and prevail in a climate of harsh necessity. Political ideologues—whether Socialists or Fascists or even Garibali republicans—have failed to change women's lives; only individual purpose and intelligence liberate them from the past.

One of the great strengths of the book is Barolini's ability to celebrate both individualism and the liberation of women. Her feminism is unscarred by formulaic ideologies that locate all oppression in male domination. While Barolini celebrates the strength and intelligence of women, she never descends into creating stereotypes of men as oppressors who face no obstacles themselves and are responsible for all of the obstacles women face.

For example, Umbertina's husband, Serafino Longobardo, is a kindly, loyal patriarch. Marriage to him was essential to escape Calabria and enter the United States. He is, however, submissive and ineffectual for Umbertina's larger goal of financial security and success in America. It is her business sense that keeps the family moving upward, but she accepts his limitations, recognizes his fine qualities, and regards Serafino as both a beloved companion and a necessary figurehead. Without him she would not have left Italy and escaped a long heritage of poverty and fatalism.

Barolini poses the most sophisticated issues of women's lives through Umbertina's granddaughter Marguerite, who embodies the troubles we make for ourselves by our own fears, hesitations, and insecurities. From the opening scene of a session of Marguerite's psychoanalysis, Barolini pays tribute to the complexities of human feeling and need and never succumbs to simplistic answers.

Through Marguerite, the dilemma of women is played out through Barolini's sophisticated use of both the instruments of emancipation and the seductive retrogressions of desire. On the one hand, there is Marguerite's American education and feminist aspirations for a writing career of her own. On the other there is her marriage to an Italian intellectual who seems to offer a life of art she too will create. The clash of cultures is complicated by the instant gratifications of being the wife of a prominent writer, a position that gives her the social experience of the life of a successful writer but not the release of actually writing herself. She longs to forge an identity apart from her marriage. Here too Barolini avoids simplifications. Marguerite's husband, Morosini, is protective, egotistical, but infatuated with her and no villain. Just as Serafino, opens opportunities for Umbertina, Morosini creates possibilities and entrées, but cannot fulfill his wife's dream of abundance. For Umbertina, abundance meant family and economic success; for Marguerite, who inherits stabilities of community and American comfort, that means a secure identity as an artist.

Times have changed. Umbertina was content to lead the family while Serafino the patriarch and figurehead got public credit. Marguerite's intelligence is a large, enabling factor for Morosini, but it is, after all, the author's name on the book binding that counts, not any acknowledgment of loving help. There is no transfer in intellectual capital in the same way that there is for economic success that everyone shares. The river of modernity has run on, and individual fortune must have its own signature and recognition.

Barolini is unique in posing the relationship between female insecurity and cultural legitimacy as an issue of Italian and Italian

American interaction. This is a complex subject, focused partly on the acquisition of high Italian culture denied Umbertina by her peasant heritage, but enabled by Marguerite's American prosperity and education. That success is complicated and inhibited by the sexual roles and codes inscribed in both Italian and Italian American culture of the time. But again Barolini places Marguerite in a complicated position. She reveals how profoundly the Italian intellectual world is dominated by men, but also suggests that it too is changing. For example, one flamboyant young Italian woman writer has successfully propelled her career forward by strategic affairs with men who can help her. She is a new kind of female predator who can use her sexuality for profit. Marguerite disapproves of this route, but finds no way of her own to succeed.

Marguerite's longing for legitimate success, traditional values, and desire for a different future find no effective solutions. Instead they dictate the terms of her cultural anxiety. She can neither accept her subordinate role nor practice new forms of ambition, nor accept responsibility for not writing.

Marguerite's American education and parental financial success have enabled her comfort with elite Italian intellectuals Grandmother Umbertina could not have addressed.

Yet she cannot feel like a full member of that intellectual world. Marguerite blames Morosini for letting her succumb to demands of childrearing and caring for his needs. She rebels in a dysfunctional way that further reflects her cultural anxiety. She seeks fulfillment in another man, using her position as Morosini's wife to support her lover for a literary prize. Barolini does not minimize the pain of an attempt at identity that is destined to fail again.

The Italian fatalism Umbertina outmaneuvered is inscribed in Marguerite's failed efforts at self-creation. She escaped from her own parent's Italian American ambition and pragmatism by moving to Italy and marrying an Italian writer. That brings her a taste of Italian *belleza*, but undermines her American urges for individualistic success. Marguerite was impressed by Morosini's promise that they will together pursue the life of letters and art.

She sees the failure of her career as a failure of the marriage. She blames the destructive effects of her husband's unconditional love for her. His making no demands on her for a career emerges as a seduction into the sweetness of doing nothing. Ironically her rebellion involves taking a lover who also needs her to work on behalf of his career and who makes her pregnant even as she uses her position as Morosini's wife to promote his career. That continues the cycle of fated failure Barolini sensitively portrays.

Barolini's novel remains fresh and powerful because it gives full weight to how women experience the losses involved with the great gains of our ancestors. Her women are saved from poverty by the Italian ancestors like Umbertina who created the conditions for education and hope that saved them from fatalism and enabled a sense of individual purpose. Yet ironically Marguerite's abandonment of America and embrace of Italian high culture drives her back into the cycle of fatalism and failure. Barolini sketches a reconciliation of that problem through Marguerite's daughter, Tina. Her career plans, completion of an American doctorate in Italian literature, and marriage to a Yankee Italophile hold the promise of breaking that cycle, through a predominately American future. But the novel raises more possibilities.

How can the distance between Italy as past and America as future be negotiated? The practice of art itself provides a superb evocation of reconciliation between Italian and American values in the practice of art itself. How can the practice of art be reconciled with the claims on a woman's life? Barolini embeds an existential truth in one of the novel's recurring symbols—a beautifully crafted bedspread that was the treasure of Umbertina's marriage linens and is now preserved in an American museum. The meaning of the matrimonial bed and this bedspread decorated with an archaic designs of grapes, figs, leaves and flowers is at the novel's symbolic core. It serves metaphorically to connect the matrimonial bed to nature, sexuality and, most of all, to the art that must find an anchor in human relationships. This is the art that unifies and surmounts the binaries of the life of ambition and the life of warmth and desire.

The marriage bed as a form of art is intriguing, but more is meant here. Marguerite cannot achieve a reconciliation between desire and art, but Barolini weaves insights out of Marguerite's attempts. How art itself can spring from primary relationships of sexuality and marriage speaks directly to the cultural anxiety at the core of this book and to the situation of Italian American women artists and writers. The embroidered bedspread is a female form of art. The organic whole of art and sexuality are symbolized in the archaic Italian images of abundance. Those grapes, figs, leaves and flowers on the spread are embraced and enshrined in America's Ellis Island museum and in Barolini's faith in women as the weavers and custodians of an Italian future in America. That art embodies a rich relation between mythic abundance and modern ambition. Fine literature like *Umbertina* uses that relation to hold us in the grip of its ambivalences, its mysteries, and its many, many truths.

## WORKS CITED

Antin, Mary. *The Promised Land.* Boston: Houghton Mifflin, 1955.
Friedman-Kasaba, Kathie. *Memories of Migration: Gender, Ethnicity, and Work in the Lives of Jewish and Italian Women in New York, 1870–1924.* SUNY series on Women and Work. Joan Smith, Editor. Albany: SUNY Press. 1996.

# SEEING ETHNIC SUCCESSION IN LITTLE AND BIG ITALY

JEROME KRASE
MURRAY KOPPELMAN AND EMERITUS PROFESSOR
BROOKLYN COLLEGE
CITY UNIVERSITY OF NEW YORK

## Introduction

This essay on urban neighborhoods in the United States and Italy is the latest in a long series based on research which I have conducted about how the meanings of neighborhood spaces are changed by the agency of even the least of their inhabitants. It attempts to demonstrate how Italian American neighborhoods in United States, specifically New York City, are similar to Italian neighborhoods in Italy, specifically Rome, in the way that they have been changed by the invasion of new and different ethnic groups. The spatial and semiotic logic of diasporic/transnational processes is presented here in the form of descriptions; especially of changing commercial vernacular landscapes. In the Italian American case this process of what the classic urban ecologists called "ethnic succession" is analogous to the aphorism of fish swallowing other fish. For more than a century Italian immigrants to the United States have been changing the meanings of central city spaces. Most stereotypically they created Italian colonies and Little Italies in one form or another. They accomplished this not merely by the power of superior numbers of local inhabitants, but by the momentum of spatial semiotics, i.e. changing the appearances of spaces and places and thereby changing their meanings as well. By the 1970s, the demography as well as the meanings of many of those Italian American ethnicized spaces was being challenged by the influx of new groups. Today some of the best known of these Little Italies remain as little more than what I have called "Italian

American Ethnic Theme Parks," places which are virtually Italian in name only. Back in the country of origin, although Italy has for centuries been a major source of emigrants it has only been since the 1980s that it has been the recipient of large numbers of foreigners seeking more than temporary residence. Even more recently, the demography of quintessentially Italian cities has been changing in response to immigrants. As we can consider how American urban spaces became Italianized and subsequently became less so, we should be able to consider how Italian spaces lose their own, indigenous *Italianità* in response to immigrant settlements and local commercial practices.

In order to demonstrate how Italian central cities have become as American ones cities, an idea once rejected as almost absurd, both old and new approaches are needed. The old is represented by Robert Ezra Park and Ernest Burgess' classical ecological theory of invasion and succession of urban neighborhoods. The new is represented theoretically by Spatial Semiotics and methodologically by Visual Sociology. After briefly discussing these theories and methods we will turn to a consideration of the changing meanings, illustrated by descriptions of ethnically contested spaces in New York City and Rome. The New York City selections are from my recent studies of historical Little Italies, and in Central Rome, of the changing Esquilino neighborhood. The Esquilino is one of the areas that I observed and photographed while at the University of Rome in 1998 to study "New Immigrants to Rome." I returned in 2003 and re-photographed most of the same streetscapes. Here I will focus on the commercial landscape, store windows and shop signs which are interpreted by ordinary people as ethnic markers. It is interesting to note that the strongest semiotic parallel exists with the invasion of both these Little and Big Italy neighborhoods by Asians, especially Chinese. There is also a great irony in these parallels in that during the period of mass migration Americans saw Italians as an integral part of an invading unwashed horde as do contemporary Italians visualize a much smaller influx of documented and undocumented Asian and other aliens.

*Italianità*

Mine is not the only work that emphasizes the importance of understanding the essential semiotic/symbolic character of *Italianità*. Italian Americanist, Fred L.Gardaphe refers to signs indicating qualities such as *omerta* and *bella figura*. (20) My own work identified the spatial and visible components of the complex, as yet undeconstructed, notion of *Italianità* such as how notions of both *omerta* and *bella figura* are visually available as social performance and in vernacular architecture. (1993). As Mike Davis argued for *Latinidad*, I would submit that *Italianiatà* "is *practice* rather than representation." (15) In a related vein, Roland Barthes once wrote that he had watched on television what he thought was "a very French film" "Why "very French"? he asked.

> We see a young woman take her dresses out of the closet and stuff them in her suitcase: she is leaving the conjugal bed and board—situation, adultery, crisis. Well, then it is a good dramatic film. Here is what makes it French: the actors seem to spend their time in a café or at family meals. Here the strange stereotype is nationalized: it belongs to the setting, not to history: hence it has a meaning, not a function. (103)

It is agency which transforms mere representation into practice. I use a simple formula for this process; members of ethnic groups by going about their daily existence present themselves; the observer re-presents their performances in description; which in turn becomes a representation. Roland Barthes and Mike Davis clearly indicate the necessity of exploring the role played by space and place in ethnicity and ethnic identity of all self or otherwise identified social groups. It might be useful for us to think for a moment of immigrant neighborhoods as "Third Spaces" or interstitial places where things such as ethnic identity are being created and then negotiated, demonstrating in this way the agency of ordinary people. (Gutiérrez, 1999) Whereas much of Third Space discourse concerns the negotiation of identities of persons within real and imagined spaces, my own special interest is on how those identities change the meaning of the space in which ethnicity is acted out or practiced. Consequently one can also consider how the newly defined space affects the identities of the people within it. I would argue that by doing *Italianità,* Italian immigrants to America socially created Little Italies. In the same way then, we can argue that new immigrants by displaying their own cultural and social practices are undoing *Italianità* in both Little Italy and for want of a better euphemism—"Big Italy."

## Ethnic Succession

University of Chicago sociologists Robert Park and Ernest Burgess developed an elaborate notion, more of a general descriptive formula than a theory, of city growth and development. (1925) It supposes that cities were like natural environments and as such were influenced by forces that also affected natural ecosystems. The most important of these forces was competition which was expressed in the struggle for scarce resources such as living space and jobs. They argued that competition resulted in "natural areas" dominated by people with shared social and economic characteristics. City-wide competition for the most desirable residential or commercial spaces would be expressed in the form of concentric zones as seen in their famous diagram. Their model was not static, and movement from one zone to the other was termed "succession." For our purposes here this logic was demonstrated by less able migrants strangely "dominating" the least desirable residential sections in urban centers. The classic pattern in American central cities during periods of high immigration had been the development of immigrant enclaves in "Zones of Transition" such as Little Sicily and Chinatown in Chicago located near the Central Business Districts. Rome's Zone of Transition might well be found around the Central Station in the Esquilino. With few other exceptions, the oldest of Rome's central areas have been the most protected from radical change. In recent decades much has subtly changed, and today even working-class run-down areas are being gentrified. Since the 1990s what were the least desirable areas for residence and commerce, near the

central station, have also been "in transition."
Ethnic Succession results from the competition between
new and established groups and is often facilitated by the out-
migration of the more advantaged group. Compared to the United
States residential mobility in Italy is slow. Therefore opportunities
for housing are limited. In contrast to places like New York City
for example, most Roman neighborhoods are not transformed in
a matter of a decade. This history-in-the-making can nevertheless
be easily compared to the centuries old processes of invasion and
succession which have characterized major cities in the United
States. Cities like New York have long been the destination of
immigrants and ecologically understandable spatial patterns had
already been established. Large scale immigration, legal and
otherwise, is relatively new to Italy, where an interest in American
urban sociology has been increasing in recent decades. With few
exceptions, most European sociologists thought of American cities
as of a different species from their own. My work points to greater
similarities than previously assumed. In much the same way that
the appearance of Italian American central city neighborhoods
has changed in response late 20th century documented and
undocumented immigration, so are Italy's vernacular urban
landscapes changing today.

### Spatial Semiotics and Visual Sociology

The question for pre and post-modern urbanologists has not
been "Who or what is where in the city?" but "How and why" they
got there. Researchers look at the same objects but the meanings
of those objects seem to vary by the ideology of the viewer. The
purely descriptive models of Classical Urban Ecology come from a
biological analogy. In the city, equilibrium is expressed through the
interaction of human nature with geographical and spatial factors
producing "natural" areas. Political economists on the contrary see
these natural areas, and ecological zones as the result of "uneven
development", and perhaps even planned cycles of decay and
renewal. Globalization and the movement of labor have changed
the meaning of spaces in both Italian America and in Italy.

The landscapes of both Italian America and Italy are affected by "natural" and migration-driven demographic forces, as well as the powerful processes of globalization, de-industrialization, and privatization. As I have argued elsewhere (Krase, 2004, 17), "Contemporary urban sociologists appear to be suffering from parallax vision. One eye sees the "natural" spatial form and function of the city as a biological analogy as did Park and Burgess. The other eye sees these same urban places and spaces as the reproductions of power, and circuits of capital *a la Castells* (1977), Harvey (1989), and Lefebvre (1991)." I must emphasize that my research into ethnicity and space has not been merely a theoretical exercise. It has important practical applications to the present and future problems of Italian cities which are unprepared to deal with the rapidity of ethnic and racial change engendered by globalization and the development of a European Union (Krase, 1997).

For most, a visual approach in the Humanities and Social Sciences is taking or showing pictures as an adjunct to the "regular" process of research. Visual Sociology is much more than that. In my own work it is both a theoretical and methodological practice for " . . . producing and decoding images which can be used to empirically investigate social organization, cultural meaning and psychological processes." (14). I focus upon what John Brinkerhoff Jackson calls vernacular landscapes which are part of the life of communities which are governed by custom and held together by personal relationship. (1984, 6) Italian administrators and planners of multiethnic cities could benefit greatly from an understanding of immigrant and ethnic vernacular urban landscapes, which is according to Dolores Hayden, " . . . an account of both inclusion and exclusion."(7)

In a related vein, Harvey argued that: "Different classes construct their sense of territory and community in radically different ways. This elemental fact is often overlooked by those theorists who presume *a priori* that there is some ideal-typical and universal tendency for all human beings to construct a human community of roughly similar sort, no matter what the political or economic circumstances." (1989, 265) Visual Sociology and Vernacular

Landscapes are connected via Spatial Semiotics. Mark Gottdiener writes that "the study of culture which links symbols to objects is called semeiotics" and "spatial semeiotics studies the metropolis as a meaningful environment." (1994, 15–16) "Seeing" the uses and/or meanings of space require sensitivity and understanding of the particular culture which creates, maintains, and uses the re-signified space. In other words, even the most powerless of urban dwellers is a social "agent" and therefore participates in the local reproduction of regional, national, and global societal relations.

According to Gottdiener (1994), the most basic concept for urban studies study is the settlement space which is both constructed and organized. "It is built by people who have followed some meaningful plan for the purposes of containing economic, political, and cultural activities. Within it people organize their daily actions according to meaningful aspects of the constructed space."(16) As part of national and global systems, neighborhoods are affected by a wide range of supply-side forces. The connection made between Italian and Italian American vernacular landscape shows that ordinary people can affect their environment, even though they are ultimately at the mercy of larger societal forces. Attention to Vernacular Landscapes in the inner city allows us to see conflict, competition, and dominance at a level noticed only by local residents.

### New York City's Little Italies

In "White Ethnic Neighborhoods and Assimilation" Alba, Crowder, and Logan looked at white ethnic neighborhoods to see the degree of assimilation of Germans, Irish, and Italians in the Greater New York region in 1980 and 1990. (1997) Italians, they found, still had many and large neighborhoods. However, from the 1980s, most of those located in central cities, were declining due to the invasion and succession of minorities in inner-city neighborhoods. Most of these newcomers were new, non-European, immigrant groups for whom the doors were opened wider by the 1965 and subsequent immigration laws. In addition to these regularized groups was a large influx of undocumented aliens.

Racial incidents such as those in Italian American Bensonhurst reminded the authors that Italian Americans vigorously defend their turf, even though at the same time Manhattan's famous Little Italy became home to primarily Chinese. I note here that in the first decade of the 21st Century Brooklyn's Bensonhurst area is being transformed by the influx of Chinese, other Asians, as well as Russian immigrants. Bensonhurst's major commercial street 18th Avenue still carries the title *Cristoforo Columbo* Boulevard. In The Bronx, Belmont, is home to many Albanians and Latinos. In all cases, these areas are still referred to as "Little Italies."

Little Italy is a product and source of both social and cultural capital. Although ordinary people in the neighborhood are ultimately at the mercy of distant structural forces, in their naiveté they continue to create and modify the local spaces allocated to them, and inevitably become part of the urban landscape. Thusly people and spaces become symbols and as a result, they come to merely represent themselves and thereby lose their autonomy. The enclave comes to symbolize its imagined inhabitants and stands for them independent of their residence in it. Localized reproductions of cultural spaces can also be easily commodified and presented as spectacle for visitors such as tourists.

No model or stereotype can ever adequately represent the multiple realities of Italian, or any other, ethnic-America. There is too much in the way of permutations of generations, continuity, and change. But for many novelists, script writers, as well as Social Scientists, Little Italy represents the idea of Italian America. I have suggested that idealized ethnic urban spaces, both "Representations of Spaces" as well as "Spaces of Representation", can be summarized as follows: Oblivion, Ruination, Ethnic Theme Parks, Immigration Museums, and Anthropological Gardens.

1. Oblivion. Oblivion means "the state of being forgotten" and here we find ethnic enclaves erased by Urban Renewal, Highways, bridges, and other construction.

2. Ruins are the rubble of neighborhoods often abandoned in anticipation of "renewal", or cleared of misnamed "slums," which await new uses. These "liminal" zones of "in-betweenness" are on

their way toward Oblivion.
3. Ethnic Theme Parks such as Little Italies are preserved as spectacles for the appreciation of tourists. (Krase, 1997)

The primary focus in this paper are Little Italies and Italian cities as Theme Parks, or Spectacles for tourists. What they have in common is that they are visible commodified cultural representations. David Harvey explains that the "organization of spectacles" can be part of "the production of an urban image" which is an "important facet of interurban competition" as "urban strategies to capture consumer dollars." (233) Although he is primarily concerned with the modern or post modern version of "display of the commodity" (271) under the constraints of "flexible accumulation," he notes that since the ancient Roman "Bread and Festivals" spectacles have existed as a means of social control. (270) In short, the creation and maintenance of Spectacle is associated with a highly fragile patterning of urban investment as well as increasing social and spatial polarization of urban class antagonisms. (273)

## Rome, Italy

It is beyond the scope of this paper to speculate as to the degree that the reality and or the image of Italy will change in response to immigration. Until to the present, the scale of immigration is far less than an even a slow year for places late New York City. It does argue, however that the ecological and semiotic processes of ethnic succession are quite similar. As might be expected there are also similarities between Italian and Italian American attitudes towards "invaders." As noted by Giuseppe Sciortino and Asher Colombo (2004) there is a pattern to the spatial distribution of immigrants to Italian regions which can be explained by work opportunities, geographical proximity, national and local policies and, not least, family and work networks. In Rome for example, the Chinese have established themselves in the restaurant business. I would argue that for all immigrant groups this same logic percolates downward to specific cities within regions, and then to specific areas in cities themselves.

Russell King and Jacqueline Andall's observations, as they were contemporaneous with my research in Rome, are also of value here. Commenting on increasing xenophobia towards, and political posturing about, non-EU foreigners they noted that:

> In very recent years the media frenzy has created powerful yet badly distorted images associating immigrants with widespread violence and crime. National stereotypes are repeated almost daily on television screens and in newspapers: crude associations between North Africans and drugs, Albanians and racketeering; black African women and prostitution. While some immigrants are undoubtedly engaged in criminal activities, the degree of association is vastly exaggerated, and much less prominence is given to Italians' engagement in crime, including that against immigrants. With barely 2.5 per cent of the population in Italy of immigrant origin, much less than in most other European countries, the "crisis in immigration" is truly a crisis of (mis) representation. (155)

Rome had the third highest percentage of immigrants (5.5%), the largest absolute number (211,200), and the greatest diversity of immigrant nationalities, of any province in Italy and might therefore be referred to "as the capital of immigration." They also noted changes in composition of immigrants from 1975 to 1997 and that the most rapid increases were in Asians and those from north and sub-Saharan African. North Africans increased from 1.9% to 17.7%, Asians from 3.8% to 15.7% and sub-Sahara Africans from 2.8% to 10.3%. For Romans, as for New Yorkers, immigration and changing neighborhoods are local as well as national political issues. Caritas reports on a survey of attitudes of Italians towards immigrants in 2002. In it they found that 72 percent of Italians expressed negative attitudes towards their new neighbors, and that there was a direct relationship level of education and hostility toward immigrants. (2003, 72)

My proposal in the early 1990s to come to Italy to lecture and research on how European urban landscapes might change in response to migration by using the American model of ethnic succession was met with amusement by my Italian social science colleagues. At that time the working assumption was that immigrant populations in Italy were temporary migrants not permanent residents. This attitude changed quickly because of regional and world events which were in turn further accelerated by European Union expansion. Now we shall turn to the contemporary Italian urban scene where there is a related problem of visual transformation of the vernacular landscape. Here our focus will be on people as well as buildings. An important aspect of the city scene is the people in the picture. People become part of the space by simply being in it. Tourism is a major international industry and the sales image of Italy is derived in large part from foreigners' mental images of the Public Realms, spaces accessible to all, (Lofland, 1998) of Italians cities and towns. These spaces contain both monumental and vernacular landscapes. We might say that, for tourists at least, Italy itself is one huge multifaceted Ethnic Theme Park. Millions of visitors flock to places like Rome every year with expectations about what the "real" Italy and "real" Italians look like. They come expecting to view an Italy which conforms to their stereotypical expectations.

Luckily for those who market the traditional images of Rome, few visitors travel outside the more ancient and historical center. Perhaps they pass thorough the central station and a few may occasionally ride on public transportation. During their sojourn they will see ethnically diverse crowds of tourists, but not much of the local population. While eating out they seldom will look beyond the dining room into restaurant kitchens. While making purchases at local stores they will not peek into the rear of shops to see the workers toiling there. In short, they see only a small proportion of the Public Realm and the people who live in the city of Rome.

According to the Census (*Censis*) of October, 1991, the population of Rome was 2,775,250, and the percentage of foreigners with permission was 3.9 percent. By 1998 the population grew to 2,812,473, and registered foreigners were 4.8 percent of the population. Multiethnic Rome has residents from 167 different nations. Caritas estimated that in 1998 legal and illegal, temporary and permanent immigrants together were 6.2 percent of the Roman population. There were 134,578 foreign residents in Rome and an estimated 40,000 more who were unregistered. In contrast, since 1900 the New York City has averaged a foreign born population of at least 30 percent. Further information provided by Caritas Roma on school children indicated that the immigrant populations were not randomly dispersed. As one might also anticipate this concentration mirrors the census data which finds the highest concentration of immigrants in the center. Immigrants seem to be connected by major public transportation routes out from center to the northeast, north, northwest, and west.

Those who study immigration in Italy well understand that the published estimates of resident foreigners, as well as information about their origins, are not very reliable. The biggest problem is underestimation of the size of the population because of growing numbers of undocumented aliens (*clandestini*). This is further complicated in places like Rome by the large number of tourists and other foreign visitors. This makes visual sociological research of even greater value for the understanding of multiethnic Italian spaces where foreign populations are more visibly evident on the streets than would be anticipated by official statistics.

I quickly discovered that visual indications of immigrant concentration were not merely residential but in particular kinds of urban territory. After identifying those areas in which I expected to find immigrants I traveled to them by foot, bus and subway. This is important to note because most immigrants, when not walking, regularly use public transportation. My first findings were made in transit. Immigrants make up a larger than expected proportion of those using public transportation, especially on certain routes. Their over-representation is enhanced by the fact that Italians carry on their romance with their cars and scooters by driving to work. Once I arrived at a designated "immigrant" zone I spent hours walking the streets, some of which I revisited some several times.

Of all the districts which I observed, and photographed, the most "visibly ethnic" was near the central station especially the western side and then southward. There, residence, work, shopping, and public transportation are concentrated. It is interesting to note that in general the center of the city with its pedestrian shopping areas and thousands of tourists is multi-ethnic, but not necessarily residentially mixed. Also, in the residences near the station there was a significant undercount of immigrants (probably *clandestini*), who share apartments with registered aliens and who may be sleeping in the same buildings in which they work. My street-level observations, as well as looking into private spaces behind normally closed doors, reveal a much larger immigrant world. Another problem for ethnographic researchers is that Italian residential spaces are difficult to access because they are usually set off from public spaces. Looking for indications of new immigrants around the central station in 1998 I observed a Little Africa, a growing Chinatown, and a flourishing Bengali jewelry trade. Both Chinatown and the jewelry markets seemed to also be light production centers; which would be consistent with undocumented alien workers in sweatshops. Local stores also displayed and sold ethnic foods, as well as other culturally appropriate services, provisions, and clothing. On my return in 2003 there seemed to be fewer Chinese but signs of the south Asian population had significantly increased and a Moslem Middle Eastern (ex.: Palestinian), presence was also more in evidence. There were contradictory signs of upscale gentrification as well as struggling immigrant populations. Ethnic changes, such as "Halal" meat were evidenced in the local indoor public food market, but the outdoor market had disappeared. Clearly the Esquilino is part of Rome's Zone of Transition.

In previous papers I have identified the following situations, places, and activities in which ethnic differences were most visibly notable during my 1998 research in Rome: Public Transportation Centers, Major Urban Automobile Routes, and Centers of Telecommunication such as public telephone banks or long distance telephone service outlets. In 2003 this remained the case. At that time, as well as in 2003, other than the Asian and African section (Esquilino) near the central station few areas in the city were widely recognized, or publicized, as having a distinctly ethnic identity in the sense that Americans speak of ethnic neighborhoods.

## Summary

It can be said with confidence that immigrants (first and second generations) have been symbolically transforming the public spaces of Rome. As had their Italian immigrant counterparts to cities in the United States, immigrants to Rome have been gradually changing the vernacular landscapes by their own, merely physical, appearances as well as their activities in the spaces they use. Their presence and their "difference" also change the value of the space. As have nonwhite migrants to American city neighborhoods, in some cases they have also stigmatized places by their presence. (Krase, 1977). It is interesting to note in this regard that some better off Romans are beginning to flee the least desirable of the central zones citing classic urban dissatisfactions with changing inner city neighborhoods such as "noise," "dirt", and "crime". In contrast, at the same time that some residents move out, in other central Roman areas property values are soaring and what American urbanists would regard as "gentrification' is taking place. This urban development paradox is not inconsistent with observations of David Harvey on "circuits of capital" (1989).

In my first reports on my research in Rome I had asked the rhetorical question of when will the contribution of immigrants to the city's vernacular landscape be represented in tourist books and city guides. I have yet to see directions to Chinatown in Rome or bi-lingual Italian Chinese street signs similar to those found in more established Chinatowns found in London, Paris, and New York. There are, however, other indications of the change such as in the following *New York Times* Travel Section article which for the first time incorporates the ethnic changes in Rome as part of the scene and scenery. The author, Michael Mewshaw, comments on many of the same spaces which I have observed on my many visits and photographic researches: "But even in this quintessential Italian setting, I couldn't help noticing the presence of *extracomunitari*, as the immigrants are called. Every Sunday evening, *Chiesa della Natività di Gesù* throbs with the chants and clapping of Congolese Catholics. Two blocks away at *Chiesa di San Tommaso Apostolo*, Coptic Christians from Ethiopia and Eritrea fill the Via di Parione, with women in flowing robes and the sounds of drums and reed pipes, all of which provokes bafflement in early morning drinkers at the nearby Abbey Theater Pub."

"As I emerged from San Silvestro, it occurred to me that a trek through Roman churches these days constitutes more than a promenade across the grand breadth and glorious length of city. It has become a microcosmic pilgrimage around the globe. Adding the Jewish *Tempio Maggiore*, the Islamic *Moschea di Roma* and the Rome Buddhist *Vihara* to the mix, anyone with energy and curiosity can now touch base with many of the world's major religions and races in a long day's walk." (2004)

Another source of new multicultural meaning can be found here in a description of the Esquilino at an internet home exchange service (Homexchange.com) in July, 2004:

### Rome, Italy Home ID# 35807

"The house is located in the lively, multiethnic, and safe neighbourhood of Esquilino. The Coliseum, S. Giovanni, S. Maria Maggiore are all within easy walking distance (15 minutes or less), and metro, bus and tram stops are all within 100ft of the front door. 10 minutes' walk or two metro stops will take you to the central railway station"

"The modern neighbourhood of Esquilino was built in the 1800's to accommodate the new administration officials for the Italian government after the military defeat of the Pope. It has now become the center of multiethnic Rome, with shops, restaurants, and services geared to serve a mixed clientele. As immigration to Italy is a fairly recent phenomenon, all foreign cultures retain the authenticity of their origins."

Slowly but surely, the meanings of Rome's spaces are changing because of the changed appearance of its vernacular landscapes. One might ask when will "Chinatown," "Little India," or "Little Africa" become part of the tourist landscape and even more critically when will the meaning of "Italian" include, to Italians as well as non-Italians, the racial and national diversity which is growing before their eyes? Such questions require much further discussion and certainly greater research efforts but they can be speculated upon here. What is clear is that ecological and semiotic processes lead to the social construction of real and imagined ethnic spaces and places.

*Acknowledgement is made here to Rector's Committee for Scientific Research, and the Department of Sociology, University of Rome, La Sapienza for support of my photographic research on the "New Immigrants to Rome," in 1998 and The Center for Italian Studies at State University of New York at Stony Brook for follow up study in 2003.

## WORKS CITED

Alba, Richard D., Kyle Crowder, and John R. Logan. "White Ethnic Neighborhoods and Assimilation: The Greater New York Region, 1980–1990." *Social Forces* 75, 3 (1997): 883–909.

Barthes, Roland. "Day by Day with Roland Barthes," in Marshall Blonsky, ed, *On Signs.* Baltimore: Johns Hopkins Press, 1985.

Bourdieu, Pierre. *Outline of a Theory of Practice.* New York: Cambridge University Press: 1977.

Bourdieu, Pierre. *Distinction: A Social Critique of the Judgement of Taste.* Andover: Routledge and Kegan Paul, 1984.

Castells, Manuel. *The Informational City.* Oxford: Blackwell Publishers, 1989.

Colombo, Asher and Giuseppe Sciortino. "Italian immigration: the origins, nature and evolution of Italy's migratory systems," *Journal of Modern Italian Studies* 9, 1 (2004): 49–70.

Davis, Mike. *Magical Urbanism: Latinos Reinvent the U.S. City.* London: Verso, 2001. *"Gli Studenti Stranieri nell'Area Romana" Forum per l'intercultura Promosso dalla Caritas Diocesana di Roma, Centro Studi & Documentazione.* April, 1998.

Giddens, Anthony. *The Constitution of Society: Outline of the Theory of Structuration.* Cambridge: Polity, 1984.

Gottdiener, Mark. *The Social Production of Urban Space.* (2nd Ed.) Austin: University of Texas Press, 1994.

Grady, John. "The Scope of Visual Sociology." *Visual Sociology.* 11, 2 (Winter 1996): 10–24.

Gutiérrez, David G. "Migration, Emergent Ethnicity, and the "Third Space": The Shifting Politics of Nationalism in Greater Mexico." *Rethinking History and the Nation State: Mexico and the United States.* Special issue of the Journal of American History, 86, 2 (1999): 481–517,

Harper, Douglas. "Visual Sociology: Expanding Sociological Vision." *American Sociologist* 19, 10 (1988): 54–70.

Harvey, David. *The Urban Experience.* Baltimore: Johns Hopkins University Press, 1989.

"Italy: Amnesty for Enforcement Assistance?" *Migration News,* 3, 10 (October 1996). http://migration.ucdavis.edu/mn

Jackson, John Brinkerhoff. *Discovering the Vernacular Landscape.* New Haven: Yale

University Press, 1984.

King, Russell and Jacqueline Andall. "The Geography and Economic Sociology of Recent Immigration to Italy." *Modern Italy* 4, 2 (1999): 135–58.

Krase, Jerome. "Reactions to the Stigmata of Inner City Living." *Journal of Sociology and Social Welfare* 4, 7 (September 1977): 997-1011.

Krase, Jerome. "Traces of Home." *Places: A Quarterly Journal of Environmental Design* 8, 4, (1993): 46–55.

Krase, Jerome. "Navigating Ethnic Vernacular Landscapes Then and Now." *Journal of Architecture and Planning Research* 19, 4 (Winter 2002): 274–281.

Krase, Jerome. "Italian American Urban Landscapes: Images of Social and Cultural Capital." *Italian Americana* 22, 1, (Winter 2003): 17–44.

Lebrvre, Henri. *The Production of Space.* Oxford: Blackwell, 1991.

Lofland, Lyn. *The Public Realm: Exploring the City's Quintessential Social Territory.* New York: Aldine de Gruyter, 1998.

Mewshaw, Michael. "In Churches, A Mosaic of Cultures," *The New York Times,* June 27, 2004, Travel Section.

Park, Robert E. , Ernest W. Burgess and Roderick D. McKensie. *The City.* Chicago: University of Chicago Press, 1925.

*Rome, Italy Home ID# 35807,* www.Homeexchange.com (accessed July, 2004)

Sciortino, Giuseppe and Asher Colombo. "Italian immigration: the origins, nature and evolution of Italy's migratory systems." *Journal of Modern Italian Studies* 9.1 (2004): 49–70.

# Psychoanalytic Themes in Robert Viscusi's *Astoria*

ELISABETTA MARINO
UNIVERSITY OF ROME "TOR VERGATA"

*Astoria,* the 1996 American Book Award-winning volume
by poet, critic, university professor Robert Viscusi, has been
the subject of several essays since its first publication in 1995.
Two of them explore some themes that prove to be particularly
remarkable for the present analysis: a 1999 article by Peter
Carravetta[1], and a 2001 contribution by George Guida[2]. Carravetta
focuses his attention on the particular nature of Viscusi's text,
which cannot be "labelled" simply as a novel (if not for merely
editorial reasons), since it is able to display a perfect *fusion* of all
the different literary *genres* (an essay, an autobiography, a memoir,
a "biographia literaria", a "metanovel", a poem, and revisionist
historical fiction, just to mention a few). George Guida, on the
other hand, points out how Viscusi's *Astoria* enables the Italian
American male identity to be finally released from the shackles of
the stereotypical representation to be seen in many of Coppola's
and Scorsese's movies: the "Mafioso," trapped in his code of
silence and honor. In Viscusi's volume, in fact, the narrator is
primarily a "speaking subject" (3) and, thus quoting the title of
one of Viscusi's seminal essays, he "breaks the silence."

   This paper aims at showing that Carravetta's intuition of
the author's *urge* to *combine* what is commonly *disjoint,* and
the importance attached by Viscusi to speaking, as shown by
Guida, can be successfully reinterpreted through the writer's
deep interest in psychoanalysis, which permeates the whole
volume, as the author himself points out by defining it as his
"contribution to psychiatric literature" (15). This paper sets out
to demonstrate that the *language* (through *speaking*—as a kind

of Freudian "talking cure"—and therefore *writing*) becomes the means through which Viscusi manages to heal and recompose his and many Italian Americans' "fragmented self" (a condition typical of schizophrenia), scattered by a personal and a collective trauma: respectively, the death of his Italian mother (signifying the tangible loss of his—up to that moment—never fully acquired Italian identity) and the harsh experiences of isolation, silence and paralysis shared by many first generation Italian immigrants to America, often leading to the *amnesia* of one's past in order to blend in. In this paper, therefore, I will also try to show how in his volume Viscusi seems to aim at joining together the two halves of the psychoanalytic process which are commonly *disjoint,* by acting, at the same time, as a "patient", unfolding his own repressed memories through his reasoning, free associations and dreams (of which the narrative is rich), and as an "analyst," trying to remove mental blocks in his patient (himself and many first generation Italian Americans), thus re-establishing a flow of thoughts, as the volume itself seems to testify by employing the "stream of consciousness" technique, which refuses to accept any chronological order and binary logic of mutual exclusion, an example of which may be "the American vs. the Italian identity."

Although it is almost impossible to outline the plot of such a rich and multi-layered volume, it can be said that *Astoria* explores the *recherche* of the writer who, on the second anniversary of his mother's death, in 1986, while he is lecturing at the University of Paris, visits the tomb of Napoleon in the church of *Les Invalides* only to discover that his mother *is* Napoleon (7). A whole series of parallelisms and metaphors stems from this apparently paradoxical assertion: *The Terror* (title of the second section of the volume, after the first one, entitled *Les Invalides*), that is the gloomy phase after the first outburst of the French Revolution, seems to be the mirror of the displacement, fear and anxiety felt by many immigrants in the new American context. *The Revolution,* the title of the final part of the book set in Italy, appears to be an ironic reference to a "revolution" that has never taken place in Italy and, at the same time, to the radical transformation undergone by so many families (including Viscusi's) that in different times tried to escape what he calls "the ferocity of Italian poverty" (100), by leaving their country of origin to pursue the American dream. What "triggers" all these personal and collective memories is Viscusi's bumping into a Parisian sweater shop, called "La Storia", immediately linked in the mind of the writer with the Italian neighborhood in Queens (New York) where his mother spent her childhood and which gives its title to the volume: Astoria. By employing the "free association of ideas", that is one of the main "psychoanalytic engines" of this narrative, Astoria (the place) is often connected by the writer with "la Storia" (the history) and with "l'A-storia" (the absence of history), defined as "the archeology of removals and rearrangements" (36) as an amnesiac void which overwhelms the author thus stirring a feeling of dizziness, imbalance and loss of one's identity which is signified by the "fragmentation" of the pronoun "I", up until the very last pages of his *recherche,* in which "I" eventually reappears (throughout the rest of the text, in fact, "I" is scattered into a "he"/ a "you"/ a "we"/ a "they," and sometimes into the entire paradigm of possibilities, as if the author was unable to perceive the *self* as a whole). This imbalanced, mental condition is identified in the *Prologue* by Viscusi himself—the "patient" and the "analyst" in his volume—as "the Stendhal Syndrome" of which he claims he had discovered a *variation* by writing *Astoria*: as psychoanalyst Graziella Magherini (the one who first theorized its existence) points out, the syndrome is provoked in tourists by the overwhelming *presence* of history in cities of art, whereas in Viscusi's case it is generated by the overwhelming *absence, removal* of history (A-storia).

In order to proceed in healing his divided self with his Freudian "talking cure" (which, it is necessary to remember, implies the patient's investigation of his/her *past*), Viscusi has to fill in the gap in his *personal history* and in the *collective history* of many Italian Americans and, as Freudian and Lacanian psychoanalysis has explained it happens, the writer succeeds in doing so, through a complex system of metaphors, of "displacements" and "transferences" to use the correct psychoanalytic terminology.

Only when he is in Paris, in fact, he can reproduce, repeat and then understand the same situation of total estrangement faced, at first, by his own mother and by many Italian immigrants, grappling with a new language and a totally unknown context. Only in Paris, which is neither the US nor Italy, he can overcome the scission of the Italian American self and look at himself as if in a mirror (71). Only in Paris, the city of his meaningful "Enlightenment," the "talking cure" can therefore start, since in Viscusi's words "the *omertà* was at last broken" (142), thus reinterpreting in a psychoanalytic way the above-mentioned idea expressed by critic George Guida, in whose opinion *Astoria* is a volume in which the stereotype of the Italian as a "Mafioso" is eventually overcome. Only when he looks at Napoleon's exaggerated red stone tomb (99) Viscusi can come to terms with his mother's death, and understand both her and many Italian Americans who had managed to make a successful living in the US: they were the Corsican leader Napoleon (presented by Viscusi as an "Italian immigrant"–70); they *were* his *history* because, just like him, they were "*parvenu,* [ . . . ] *noveau riche* willing to do anything to get ahead" (114). As the writer remarks, Napoleon:

> was us, Italian to the exact degree he had escaped being Italian, Italy because he had succeeded in escaping Italy, his great originality nothing other than the completeness of his recapitulation of the whole story, the outsider in Italy, become an outsider from Italy become a general and a republican become his own successor become an exile become an exaggeration in red stone (99).

This seems to be the true origin of the woman's necessity to mentally "block" her Italian past (since "one only succeeds in America by forgetting"–70), and of her firm intentions not to teach her son (young Bob Viscusi) the Italian language, and not to communicate anything to him of her past struggle, which turns into a blank space in "la storia", into an unutterable secret, as Viscusi remarks by making reference to his childhood:

Conversation in l'Astoria was, as I see it now, almost
entirely a textile of avoidances, every single scrap of
perfected ritual designed to assuage fears and doubts
that almost never had any chance to surface directly
[ . . . ]; the secrets [ . . . ] were doubly closed to [us
children's] finding out, because we did not know, and
never learnt, how to speak Italian (173).

This description is strikingly close to the one of schizophrenia
offered by psychologist Anna Oliverio Ferraris in her 1996 volume
entitled *Psicologia, i motivi del comportamento umano*, which can
be paraphrased as such: schizophrenics do not wish to be exposed
any longer to the traumas of life and therefore, as a defensive
attitude, they do not communicate with the others, because this
could upset their precarious balance; moreover, they often tend to
be still, thus avoiding movements for as long as they can (307–08).
Be it said incidentally, Viscusi's mother is profusely described in
the section meaningfully entitled "Les Invalides", when she lies
*motionless* in hospital, almost as a victim of a particular kind of
schizophrenic, paralyzing plague affecting a large part of the first
Italian America.

After uncovering, exploring and understanding the collective
trauma of the Italian immigrants to America, after filling the blank
space in history—thus subverting the very concept of *A*-storia—
Viscusi, the "analyst" and the "patient", can address the dilemma of
*his own* "divided", "double" self, in the last section of his volume.

Once having accepted the idea of his mother's physical death,
the writer's relationship with her seems to be *transferred* to his
relationship with his "*mother*"-tongue (Italian), and with his
"*mother*"-country, Italy, where the final part of the narration is
set. As the reader gathers from the volume, Viscusi starts to learn
Italian as an adult, thus *unveiling* the secrets of his childhood and
beginning to piece together his identity as an Italian American.
The Freudian "talking cure" through *speaking* and *writing* Viscusi
has so far employed to unravel the traumas of first generation
immigrants, turns into an effective means of processing the loss
of his mother, of mourning her without lapsing into *melancholia*:

"while my mother was dying I was writing, and after she died I completed successfully a paper about the *body* of Italy"³ (212). The writer's stream of consciousness pushes him as far as to say that "[he] thought that Italy was the *body* of [his] mother and [his] grandmother and that [he] would come back from there [ ... ] *whole again*" (217). Through these words it is possible to understand the connotation Viscusi attaches to his own Italian "Risorgimento", meaning with this expression a concept well beyond the mere historical phenomenon but a "rebirth, a resurrection" (241). He, I, we, they, the paradigm of Viscusi's scattered identity at the beginning of his *recherche*, are therefore replaced by an "I" who has been healed, whose Italy has become part of such a well-rounded, such an organic "self"—defying any binary logic of reciprocal exclusion—that even words lose their national "labels" and freely flow together, in a vitalizing stream:

> I could hear Italy now because it was inside me talking,
> and slowly enough that I could understand the words,
> which seemed to have no language of preference, but
> would come seeping into the dream in Latin, or French
> or Italian or Spanish or English or Greek or German.
> (262)

The writer's psychoanalytic pilgrimage (278) is therefore completed: a new Robert Viscusi and a new Italian America are born after his/our travel through l'Astoria.

## NOTES

1. Compare Peter Carravetta, "Figuras of Cultural Recognition: A Reading of Robert Viscusi's *Astoria*", in *Melus*, Fall 1999.

2. Compare George Guida, "Novel Paesans: the Reconstruction of Italian American Male Identity in Anthony Valerio's *Conversation with Johnny* and Robert Viscusi's *Astoria*", in *Melus*, Summer 2001.

## BIBLIOGRAPHY

Carravetta, Peter, "Figuras of Cultural Recognition: A Reading of Robert Viscusi's *Astoria*", in Melus, Fall 1999.

Freud, Sigmund, *On Metapsychology—The Theory of Psychoanalysis: "Beyond the Pleasure Principle", "Ego and the Id" and Other Works*, Penguin, London, 1991.

Guida, George, "Novel Paesans: the Reconstruction of Italian American Male Identity in Anthony Valerio's *Conversation with Johnny* and Robert Viscusi's *Astoria*, in *Melus*, Summer 2001.

Magherini, Graziella, *La sindrome di Stendhal, il malessere del viaggiatore di fronte alla grandezza dell'arte*, Ponte alle Grazie, Milano, 2003.

Olivierio Ferraris, Anna, Olivierio Alberto, *Psicologia, i motivi del comportamento umano*, Zanichelli, Bologna, 1996.

Viscusi, Robert, "Breaking the Silence: Strategic Imperatives for Italian American Culture", in *VIA. Voices in Italian Americana*, 1.1, 1990.

Viscusi, Robert, *Astoria*, Guernica, Toronto, 1996.

# LA TRIBUNA ITALIANA: A CELEBRATION OF ITALIAN IDENTITY

## MICHAEL T. WARD
## TRINITY UNIVERSITY

In the following pages, I will discuss a publication that was of great significance to the Italian American residents of Texas and surrounding states: *La Tribuna Italiana*. Throughout the twenty-six years of its existence, this weekly was a mainstay of a group that, while assimilating to a new environment, maintained close contacts with their native country. Its pages reveal both a continuing love of this homeland and a deep-rooted attachment to America—as well as the attainment of an equilibrium between these tendencies. Because of the wealth of information the paper presents, and limitations of space, I will only sketch major features of this important journal.[1]

The founder of the *Tribuna* bore the Americanized name of Charles Saverio Papa. He was born on June 13, 1888, in Cefalù, Sicily, and was apprenticed there as a barber, but left the island in 1904 (or 1905), traveling to New York City. Despite his lack of knowledge of English, he took up the profession in which he had been trained, working in the city's East Side. Shortly thereafter he moved to Baltimore and then to Richmond, Virginia, where he entered into partnership with a fellow *Cefaludese*, Salvatore Presti. Nostalgic for his place of origin, he returned for a visit, but then discovered that he preferred life in America. Subsequent to his departure from Italy he moved to Dallas, arriving on May 28, 1908, in the midst of a great flood; his impression was that this city must be the New World version of Venice. In Texas he again opened a barbershop, and then several more such businesses. Papa decided to try his hand at importing, and brought over one shipment of olive oil from his native city. This enterprise, however, was not successful, and he returned to the tonsorial trade, establishing an impressive upscale salon.[2]

His drive to be of service to fellow Italian Americans moved Papa to found *La Tribuna Italiana*. It began with only an idea: the fledgling editor lacked a printing press, could rely on no staff, and benefited from few financial resources. He borrowed office space, bought a desk for fifty cents, located an Austrian printer, and went to work on the first issue. Although the journal was always said to have originated in 1913, the first number actually saw the light on June 20, 1914. Papa functioned as solicitor for advertising, business manager, editor, assistant printer, and even janitor. During the *Tribuna*'s early period, its founder worked only part-time at the paper, continuing his barber practice in order to pay the debts he accrued. For the first two years the publication more often showed a monetary loss rather than a profit. At one point funds were very close to exhaustion, and a shoemaker named Joe Musso lent Papa sufficient cash to print an issue whose existence was in grave doubt.[3]

In January 1916, Louis Adin arrived in Dallas from El Paso, Texas. He was already a printer of some experience, having worked for ten years at the daily *La Prensa* in Buenos Aires and later at the *Dallas Times Herald*. Papa and Adin soon became partners. The new arrival was highly accomplished in Italian composition and could prepare excellent editorials, in addition to writing effective news stories. He was also very skilled on the linotype, and was capable of translating or writing original text while simultaneously setting type. Because the *Tribuna* only had access to the required machinery two nights a week, much of the copy had to pass from English to Italian, and then into print format, in one process. By 1920, the paper had a circulation of approximately 7,000, and was widely read in Texas, Oklahoma, and Louisiana.[4] *La Tribuna Italiana* had always maintained close ties to the native country of its public, but such relationship waned as Italy began its imperial expansion in the 1930s.[5] When the Fascists declared war against the Allies in 1940, the journal changed its name to *The Texas Tribune* and began to be published entirely in English. Louis Adin had frequently commented that he was fluent in five languages with English his weakest tongue, and he retired at this time. Charles Papa died in an automobile accident on November 21, 1947, but the weekly continued production until 1962—first under the direction of Bob Langley and, beginning in 1951, Langley and Joe Genaro.[6] Although not the first Italian-language newspaper in Texas—anteceded by others in Galveston, San Antonio, and Houston—the *Tribuna* survived much longer than its predecessors.[7]

In an effort adequately to assess the *Tribuna* over its lengthy time of publication, I examined in detail sample numbers from a twenty-year period beginning in 1918. I chose three dates spaced evenly in the years considered, and analyzed the particular issues that came out closest to them: February 12, June 12, and October 12. I reasoned that this last day—the anniversary of Columbus' discovery of America—would be particularly fertile ground for meditations both on Italy and on experiences in the adoptive land. The selection of February and June responded to my attempt to investigate what might be called "normal" versions of the paper, in contrast to those celebrating holidays, which might often contain little news and an abundance of festive material. I also took particular note of three editions from June 1940: that of the 8th, that of the 15th—in which the change of name and language of publication is announced—and that of the 22nd, at which time the English paper had become known as *The Texas Tribune*.

While scattered copies of *La Tribuna Italiana* can be found in a handful of libraries, the sole reasonably complete set of weekly editions exists only on microfilm, available exclusively at the Center for Research Libraries in Chicago. In addition to lacking random numbers throughout the twenty-six years of its run, the extant duplication is missing the first three years. The quality of this medium is on occasion quite poor, making consultation of it somewhat problematic.

The structure of the journal, which came out on Saturday, did not change substantially through the years, being modified chiefly via expansion of its contents. Beginning as a four-page publication, it grew to eight in 1922. In 1918, its subheading is "The Italian Tribune of Dallas"; in 1922 this becomes "The Only

Italian Publication in the State of Texas" (with 'Newspaper' replacing 'Publication' by 1926). In 1930, this preliminary material was flanked by a box at the left declaring the weekly to be "An American Newspaper Printed in Italian" and one at the right stating the paper's motto: *"Frangar non Flectar."*[8] By 1934, this finds its counterpart in another front-page aphorism, *"Pro Patria Semper."*

The journal always consisted in large measure of articles borrowed, and often translated, from other publications. Such pieces eventually came to be included under a heading which—with some fluctuation through the decades—is *"Spigolando da Giornali e da Riviste."* There also appear on a regular basis—again, with slight variations in titles—what are termed *"Notizie di Cronaca Locale,"* giving mostly social news concerning the Italian community in Papa's city. It was later accompanied by a similar section in English called "Dallas Doings." A rubric first entitled *"Notizie dall'Italia"* was later expanded into *"Notizie ed Avvenimenti d'Oltremare."* The column labeled *"Nostre Corrispondenze delle Città del Texas"* offered material of local character, and was followed—in the paper's most well-developed phase—by selections in English dedicated principally to civic and cultural functions in specific locales, as indicated by such headings as "Beaumont Babble," "Bryan Boomings," "Flashes from Fort Worth," "Galveston Gossips," "Houston Happenings," and "Port Arthur Personals."

During this period of greatest expansion, the *Tribuna* began to make use of contributions from journalists in Italy, with the first such pieces coming—perhaps not surprisingly—from Papa's native territory. These eventually included sections with such names as *"Dalla Sicilia," "Dalla Calabria,"* and *"Dalla Toscana,"* as well as *"Dalle Colonie Italiane"*—the last of which focused mainly on events in Ethiopia. Other regular, syndicated columns in English begin to appear toward the middle of the 1930s, but these came and went as the years passed. To name a representative few from the issue of June 9, 1934, we have "News Review of Current Events the World Over" by Edward W. Pickard, Arthur Brisbane's "This Week"; William Bruckart's "Washington Digest";

Ed Howe's "Howe About: *[sic]*," and "Seen and Heard around the National Capital" by Carter Field. In addition there appeared advice columns concerning etiquette and medical matters. At around the same time we begin to see comic strips and captioned photographs, all in English. By 1938 there is a front-page editorial column called "Weekly Review of Current Events" by L. E. Adin, Junior, which subsequently is moved to page two, its place having been taken by a section discussing events of *"La Guerra."* Typical of our journalists' circumspection, this last component is preceded by a caution that—because its contents have been translated from other papers—the editors are not responsible for the exactness of the original source. A perennial constituent of *La Tribuna Italiana*—that lasted even after the transition to a virtually all-English publication—consisted of serialized extracts from Italian novels, located always on the last page. Especially popular are the works of Carolina Invernizio, famous for her Gothic compositions; offered in Papa and Adin's weekly are, for example, portions of *L'Atroce Visione*, *La Donna Fatale*, *Dora: La Figlia dell'Assassino*, and *La Resurrezione di un Angelo*.[9]

Every issue of the *Tribuna* that I consulted contains a wealth of advertisements, exclusively in Italian during the early phase, but with some in English in later years. Besides those pieces clearly identified as of a commercial nature—usually found on the left and right of the page—there appear certain endorsements disguised as news stories. Although many of the products and institutions touted presumably would have been popular among any residents of the Southwest, there are some clearly thought of as ideal for the *Tribuna*'s readership.[10] In a 1922 issue, for example, Dallas County State [Bank] claims itself to be *"una buona banca per gli italiani,"* adding that Europeans changing money are assured of good rates (11 Feb. 1922). Another number from that same year—two years into Prohibition—contains an ad for Blue Ribbon Malt Extract, described as being excellent for *"cucina," "focaccie,"* and *"bevande casalinghe a base di malt* [sic]" (10 June 1922). A later, full-page announcement addressed to "Mr. Advertiser" emphasizes the effectiveness of communications in Italian when dealing with the area's immigrant population (13 Feb. 1926), and political publicity frequently speaks directly to those sharing in the cultural patrimony of Italy (e.g., 9 June 1934). A major supporter of the *Tribuna* through the years was the National Macaroni Company of Dallas (e.g., 9 Oct. 1926a) Two blurbs from the February 12, 1938 issue of the *Tribuna* catch the reader's attention: one urges Italian store-owners to stock Dr Pepper (perhaps sales declined after the repeal of the Eighteenth Amendment),[11] and another—for Old Gold cigarettes—begins with the suggestive exhortation, "*Ascoltate, O Popolo!*"[12]

Such advertisements are particularly abundant in the annual Columbus Day editions of the paper. In 1926, 1934, and 1938, *La Tribuna Italiana* put out multiple separate issues commemorating the discovery of America, usually one general number and others dedicated to the immigrant populations of different cities. That these were not distributed solely to the localities mentioned may be indicated by the curious fact that there is no overlap in the contents of the individual editions.[13] Most all commercial announcements included here begin with variants of the phrase, "*In Omaggio al Sommo Navigatore Italiano Cristoforo Colombo Che Scoperse Questo Grande Continente 434 Anni Orsono,*" and end with "*Colle Congratulazioni ai Lettori della Tribuna Italiana*" (e.g., 9 Oct. 1926c, 13 Oct. 1934a) There is frequently an attempt to link Columbus' achievement with the particular item in question. To return to Dr Pepper—a quintessentially Texan product at the time— one advertisement in Italian notes that America advanced as best it could until this soft drink was "discovered" in 1887 (13 Oct. 1934a), while another in English expresses regret that the Genovese explorer arrived too early to 'discover' the beverage (8 Oct. 1938b).[14]

There stands out a commercial piece that seems particularly significant in the context of *La Tribuna Italiana*'s balance between support for the mother country and allegiance to the United States. Present in an edition from October 9, 1926, is a recommendation to purchase *Il Carroccio* (whose name alludes to an ancient Italian war wagon symbolic of liberty),[15] a publication here characterized as a "*Rivista nazional-fascista*" ideal for all those "*difensori della causa italiana in America*" (Oct. 9, 1926d). Indeed, virtually from the outset, the contents of this newspaper showed it to embrace the policies espoused by the new arrivals' native land, an overt adherence that ended only at the declaration of war on England and France. Issues from the crucial year 1918 and from 1922 offer pieces critical of Italy's treatment by her allies (e.g., Feb. 9, 1918, Oct. 14, 1922). In a 1926 number (June 12, 1926), the translation and rephrasing of an article on Fascism puts a positive spin on this movement, even though the original author's outlook was clearly skeptical.

During the subsequent period, the *Tribuna*'s own perspective becomes even clearer. We find, for example, a summary of a pro-Fascist speech (Oct. 9, 1926c) and borrowed pieces expressing approval of Mussolini's consolidation of power and financial strategies—as well as admiration for improvement in the behavior of Italian youth attributable to Fascism's new spiritual atmosphere (Feb. 10, 1934). There appears an article stressing Il Duce's role as mediator between Germany and nations that fear her (June 9, 1934), followed by one that praises the Italian government's farmland reclamation (Oct. 13, 1934a) and the *"nuova atmosfera economica e sociale creata dal Regime"* (Oct. 13, 1934b). A section claiming that Mussolini has eliminated *"la questione del Mezzogiorno"* (Oct. 13, 1934b) precedes a citation of the leader's declaration that Italy must be a warrior nation like Sparta (Oct. 13, 1934c).

Favorable remarks are particularly intense in 1938. Pieces offered in the *Tribuna* that year praise the doctrine of *autarchia* or "economic independence"—one of the foundations of Fascism (Feb. 12, 1938; cf. June 8, 1940),[16] assert that Hitler and Mussolini have become *"gli apostoli di pace"* (Feb. 12, 1938), and laud Italy's progressively increasing reconstruction (June 11, 1938). Other articles trace a glowing history of Fascism (June 11, 1938), present a human-interest story centering on a young girl who worships the Italian dictator (Oct. 8, 1938a), give positive details on "How Mussolini Works" (Oct. 8, 1938a), and cover the construction of a new peace shrine in Rome (Oct. 8, 1938c). Stories similar in nature are found even in 1940, by which time a large proportion of the notices from abroad concern the motherland, the progress she has made, and her relations with other countries. An editorial from that year declares optimistically that Italy will only engage in war if provoked (Feb. 10, 1940).

We find as well in the journal a wealth of local information sent in from across the Peninsula by what are called "*i nostri corrispondenti.*" Such items are often of a sensational character, lacking in what might be termed real news value. One story, for example, touches on "*Una Palermitana alle Prese con la Vicina di Casa,*" another describes a "*Sanguinosa Rissa tra Due Messinesi per Ragione di Gelosia,*" while a third narrates how "*Una Donna di Palermo Cade e Si Rompe un Braccio*" (June 8, 1940).[17] Beginning in the late 1930s, the paper regularly published a schedule for the shortwave radio station 2RO from Prato Smeraldo (near Rome), which broadcasted in a large number of languages (e.g., Feb. 12, 1938, June 8, 1940).[18]

While sympathetic to Italian interests, the editors of *La Tribuna Italiana* make clear their staunch allegiance to the new homeland and its policies. To return to the publication's earliest period, we find constant promotions for U.S. War Savings Stamps, both in advertisements and articles (e.g. Feb. 9, 1918, June 8, 1918, Oct. 12, 1918). An issue from the early 1920s rails against one political candidate described as a member of the "*Capuccioni* [sic] *Bianchi*" (evidently, the Ku Klux Klan), and reproduces calls by President Warren Harding and other national figures to respect the law (June 10, 1922). As the events of World War One fade into the past, news reports concerning the United States tend to be of an objective nature, although there appeared openly patriotic essays from time to time, particularly in those numbers dedicated to Christopher Columbus (e.g., Oct. 13, 1934a). In the same 1938 issue that portrays the Axis leaders as peacemakers, we come across a section recalling the accomplishments of Abraham Lincoln and a note decrying the recent assassination of Georgia's Reverend Charles H. Lee, a strong adversary of the corruption rampant in a local resort area (Feb. 12, 1938; cf. Feb. 10, 1940).[19] One syndicated column ridicules the country's blissful unawareness of the threat of war (June 11, 1938), while another article rejects the menace of a "*quinta colonna*" and speaks of America with measured praise (June 8, 1940). The selection of materials, and editorial comment, regarding United States policy on such matters as morality, Prohibition, free trade, electrification, and federal subsidies, show that Papa and Adin—and, one might assume, their readers—espouse less government control and more personal liberty (e.g., Oct. 12, 1918, Feb. 11, 1922, Oct. 14, 1922, June 14, 1930, Feb. 10, 1940, June 8, 1940). For several years before conversion to *The Texas Tribune*, the Italian paper offered its readers a set of questions and answers in preparation for the citizenship exam.[20]

Perhaps the clearest demonstration of the balance struck between reverence for Italy and appreciation of the adoptive country can be found in a series of editorials published during the *Tribuna*'s last half-year of existence.[21] Among Adin's remarks are repeated calls for all immigrants to become citizens (Jan. 6, 1940), "*il che non impedisce che un buon italiano conservi in cuore un profondo amore ed una incondizionata dedicazione alla sua Patria lontana*"; citizenship is necessary, we read, for being able to work, for practicing business (since licenses are not granted to foreigners), for receiving old-age pensions (even if all workers must contribute to the system, regardless of their residency status), and for ensuring a smooth return from trips to Italy (Jan. 27, 1940). The *cavaliere* criticizes the slowness of the "Americanization" process and suggests it be made easier, especially for the largely unlettered elderly population (Feb. 3, 1940). A later piece, however, praises Princeton students for their faith in Mussolini's capacity as mediator (Feb. 24, 1940), while another issue commemorates April 21—the foundation of Rome—as Fascism's eighteenth "*Festa del Lavoro*."[22] The latter article describes with enthusiasm a revival of the ancient Roman spirit and exhorts all Italians to remember their origins with due pride, combining past glories with present greatness. Italy, says Adin, is at a difficult divide between opposing forces, but the wisdom of Il Duce will settle the question (April 20, 1940). On May 4 of that year we read of the editor's supposition that his homeland will shortly enter the conflict alongside her ally Germany. Despite the superficial influence America has left on him and his compatriots, Adin affirms, they should not forget that they are Italian, nor disregard the injustices committed against the *patria* following the previous war; he adds that the United States has nothing to fear from either Germany or Italy (May 25, 1940). A subsequent editorial commemorates May 24, 1915 (Italy's declaration of hostilities against Austria–Hungary)[23] by reproducing a lively passage written by Mussolini—and, this time, predicts that instead of intervening, Italy will remain neutral *"per senso di alta nobiltà verso gli alleati di ieri"* (May 25, 1940). A commentary published two weeks later, however, makes patent Adin's deep gratitude toward his adoptive land, asserting that empty threats concerning a fifth column have left the great melting pot unscathed: *"regge alla bufera dei tempi collo Zio Samuele a simbolo di giustizia e di generosita"* (June 8, 1940).[24]

The five elements of the Appendix are extracted from the last issue of *La Tribuna* Italiana and the first of *The Texas Tribune,* and—I believe—are representative of the editors' patriotism, as well as their realistic outlook. The "Notice to our Readers and Patrons" stresses allegiance to the United States, explains that the change in language will eliminate any doubt as to what Italian Americans are saying among themselves, and calls for harmony between those of different backgrounds. *"Un Caldo Appello ai Nostri Lettori"* reflects a certain anxiety regarding the proposed change in format. The following lengthy, untitled editorial—impressively rich in content and emotional overtones—emphasizes the *Tribuna*'s function as an instrument of "propaganda *di italianismo*" and a connection between immigrants and their native land, characterizing the adoption exclusively of English as a means of survival under new circumstances.[25] The next two sections—from the newly-constituted journal—highlight, respectively, the significant impact exerted by United States immigration policy, and the patriotism of those arriving from foreign shores. This final piece—"Our Name is Changed . . ." accentuates continuity in spite of modification, confirming the possibility of maintaining affection for both old and new loved ones—an outlook characteristic of the paper through the decades. Mindful of achievements within Italy while benefiting from all America had to offer, Papa and Adin harmonized the best of two worlds. Thus, *La Tribuna Italiana*—well established and highly successful throughout a significant part of the southern United States—never ceased to celebrate the Italian identity of its readers.

#### APPENDIX

*La Tribuna Italiana* (15 June 1940)
*Notice to our Readers and Patrons*

With this number La Tribuna Italiana completes its twenty-sixth year of existence. During these many years, this publication has served its readers, advertisers, and the public at large in an honest and sincere manner, all this accomplished with the aid of subscribers and advertisers to whom the publishers are extremely grateful.

We wish to notify the public at large that beginning next week, June 22, the name "La Tribuna Italiana" will be changed to "The Texas Tribune." On this, the beginning of the twenty-seventh year of publication, we sincerely hope that we may serve all those whom we have served in the past, and in the same sincere and honest manner.

It shall be in the future as it has been in the past. We shall continue to uphold the principles upon which our adopted nation was founded: Life, Liberty and the Pursuit of Happiness. Let no man doubt us in this hour of international conflict. Our interests and our homes and our patriotism are in this country. We Americans of Italian extraction are in truth Americans.

Likewise beginning next week, all reading matter and advertisements in this publication will be in the English language, with the exception of a continued story which will be completed. Our purpose is to render available to all people the communications which take place between Americans of Italian derivation, in order that all may know where our sympathies lie, a thing which becomes evident upon examination of our way of life. Our sympathies lie with the Allies and the democratic powers which are fighting for the civilization that we know—the American Way of Life.

The publishers close with the hope that within the United States of America, the great melting pot of the New World, there will be no strife between peoples which have been derived from different Old World nations. There is no intelligent place for this. We have a job to do together, Americans all.

*La Tribuna Italiana.*

## *La Tribuna Italiana* (15 June 1940)
### *Un Caldo Appello ai Nostri Lettori*

Il giornale che vi ha serviti fedelmente per oltre un quarto di secolo, col prossimo numero entra in una nuova fase della sua vita, più difficile, più ostacolato di quanto lo sia stato mai durante la sua lunga esistenza. Preghiamo i lettori che non risiedono nello Stato Texas *[sic]* di mettersi al corrente col loro abbonamento. Quelli che sono in arretrato di parecchi anni potranno mandare solo $2.00 per un anno di abbonamento, se non possono fare uno sforzo maggiore.

Ci è doloroso di dichiarare che coloro che non avranno ottemperato a questa richiesta per il primo del prossimo Luglio, verranno tolti dalla lista.

I lettori del Texas, se vorranno mantenere in vita il giornale dovranno fare al più presto la rimessa dell'abbonamento.

## *La Tribuna Italiana* (15 June 1940)

Questo è l'ultimo numero del ventiseiesimo anno di pubblicazione della "Tribuna" ed è anche l'ultimo numero che verrà pubblicato in lingua italiana. Abbiamo servito i nostri lettori con fedeltà, con sincera passione nel compito di propaganda di italianismo che abbiamo sempre creduto fosse un dovere di pubblicisti, poichè i destini della Patria d'origine erano nel nostro cuore, come nel cuore di tutti gli italiani d'origine, nel posto più vitale e più caro.

Ventisei anni di pubblicazione ininterrotta significano uno sforzo non indiffere te *[sic]*, poichè il giornalismo settimanale non è mai stato prospero e perchè la pubblicità su un giornale di lingua straniera non è mai troppo abbondante.

Ma, man mano che gli anni passavano, ed il nostro giornale acquistava quell'anzianità che impone nel campo della pubblicità, sopraggiunse anche un po' di prosperità e fu allora che il suo formato venne ingrandito e venne assicurato il servizio di un corrispondente italiano che cominciò col mandare notiziario della Sicilia, allargandolo poi alla Calabria ed alla Toscana, le provincie d'Italia che danno il maggior contributo di emigrati allo Stato Texas ed al Southwest.

Eravamo orgogliosi della nostra "Tribuna". La confrontavamo spesso con altri giornali che ci pervenivano da colleghi in giornalismo, ed il confronto ci convinceva sempre più che compivamo un lavoro proficuo, mantenendo un continuo contatto i nostri lettori residenti in America, coi loro paesi di origine; convinti che per divenire un buon cittadino del Paese che ci ospita, conviene anche conservare un grande rispetto per quello che ci ha dato i natali.

Abbiamo anche sentito continuamente il dovere di incitare i nostri connazionali ad ottenere la cittadinanza americana ed abbiamo mantenuto costantemente una rubrica di istruzioni per lo studio sufficente [sic] a superare l'esame che è imposto agli applicanti. È stata nostra costante convinzione che l'acquisto della cittadinanza, per coloro che erano stabiliti permanentemente negli Stati Uniti fosse un dovere verso la Nazione che ospita con tanta generosità coloro che vi si stabiliscono coll'intento di lavorare e di progredire. E gli italiani qui emigrati, che hanno compiuto questo dovere possono meglio ancora onorare la loro Patria di origine, perchè si assimilano al popolo americano e compiono una costante penetrazione italiana, attraverso le merci che vendono, attraverso i loro figlioli che frequentano le scuole pubbliche nelle quali quasi invariabilmente si fanno onore.

Sin dall'inizio delle ostilità in Europa ebbimo l'intuizione che su di noi gravava un serio pericolo. Sapevamo che le ingiustizie commesse ai danni dell'Italia col trattato di Varsalia e l'ostilità dimostrata dagli alleati della Guerra Mondiale in occasione della campagna etiopica, colle famigerate sanzioni, avrebbero influito sulla decesione *[sic]* dell'Italia. Ma, data la sua posizione geografica, ebbimo sempre la speranza che sarebbe rimasta neutrale, non per patema d'animo, ma piuttosto perchè come neutrale avrebbe potuto meglio assistere la sua nuova alleata tedesca. Di fatti le quantità di merci che giunsero in Germania attraverso l'Italia devono essere state di una entità considerevole, per causare il blocco inglese.

Colui che decide dei destini d'Italia ha voluto altrimenti e lunedì scorso la guerra alla Francia ed all'Inghilterra è stata dichiarata.

Non vogliamo ripetere qui nemmeno la minima frazione dei commenti che hanno seguito l'ingresso dell'Italia nella guerra: furono salaci, probabilmente suggeriti dall'impulsività di un popolo amico di una delle potenze colpite. Sappiamo solamente che la Stampa Italiana non sarà più gradita in questo paese anglo-sassone per eccellenza ed abbiamo deciso di adattarci alle circostanze: col prossimo numero, che sarà il primo del nostro ventisettesimo anno, la Tribuna Italiana cambierà il suo nome in "Texas Tribune" e la lingua italiana sarà completamente eliminata, ad eccezione del romanzo dell'ultima pagina che continuerà fino alla fine del libro in pubblicazione.

Una decisione così radicale chiede una spiegazione: cerchiamo di rimanere a galla e di conservare il diritto di pubblicazione. Se la guerra avrà una durata relativamente breve ci sarà forse possibile di riprendere le pubblicazioni nella forma che abbiamo conservato per tanti anni; se invece la guerra si prolungherà per molti anni, la lingua italiana si sarà resa così inutile che non verrà mai più ripresa.

In questo grave momento di separazione forzata dalla nostra lingua, sentiamo il dovere di esprimere ai nostri fedeli lettori tutta la nostra gratitudine per averci accompagnati fedelmente nelle venture del giornale. Molti di essi sono stati molto di più che semplici lettori: ne contiamo un numero rilevante di benemeriti della Stampa Italiana, che hanno talvolta sacrificato i propri *[sic]* interessi per darci un appoggio efficace, incondizionato. Di loro serberemo un eterno ricordo, e se mai la vecchia "Tribuna" potrà risorgere sui ruderi di questa guerra micidiale, ci rivolgeremo nuovamente a loro, colla fiducia di trovarli ancora amici e sostenitori.

La riorganizzazione del giornale in una lingua che non è la nostra, non sarà molto facile e per qualche settimana "The Texas Tribune" lascierà alquanto a desiderare: i lettori vorranno essere indulgenti, come noi fiduciosi in un miglior avvenire. Fino ad allora, chi scrive questa colonna vi risparmierà i suoi commenti, non sempre assennati.

*The Texas Tribune* (22 June 1940)

We, the publishers of The Texas Tribune, do not feel that we owe our readers an apology for the change made in our paper. For the last sixteen year [sic] the United States adopted the policy of closed door *[sic]* in regard to immigration; especially for the Latin race. Sixteen years of natural elimination among the old immigrants, composing the blackbone *[sic]* of our paper, had undermined the efficiency of "La Tribuna Italiana" and we had for a long time contemplated the change into the English language, so as better to serve our second generation, overwhelming majority in the Italian families.

Sixteen years without new blood, without a new element, worked more and better toward Americanizing old immigrants, than any propaganda to said effect.

We are confident that The Texas Tribune will now serve better than before the cause of the Italian in the United States, especially so in the State of Texas where their minority is almost amazing.

The policy of The Texas Tribune will not be any different from the one of "La Tribuna Italiana". We realize that the readers of our paper expect us to respect and continue the tradition of the Italian race: we are too jealous of our future to overlook this part of our duty as publishers. And then, as soon as peace is reestablished in the world, if the readers demand it, nothing will keep us from resuming the publishing of a section of the paper in the Italian language.

We received many and many encouragements but we are not deluding ourselves in the conviction that the consent is unanimous. The opposition, so far, is silent: perhaps our first issue will provoke the bulk of protest and we are prepared to stiffen our shoulders.

*The Texas Tribune* (22 June 1940)
*Our Name is Changed:*
*Our Stand the Same—Americanism*

Today is the Texas Tribune's birthday.

With last week's issue of the paper, "La Tribuna Italiana" completed its twenty-sixth year. With this issue, "The Texas Tribune" is born.

We have changed our name, but our policy is the same.

For 26 years the Tribuna has stood for all things American, for freedom, for opportunity, for justice and fair play. Today we stand, strong as always, for these same things, and we ask that Italian Americans give us their support and loyalty, as they at all times, have given their loyalty to America.

Through 26 years, this newspaper has voiced its conviction, has stood for clean government, has supported the institutions that give America its character before the world, has not been afraid to fight men in high places, if, in its judgment, they were not fitted for their responsibilities.

And we shall continue to stand for what, to our minds, is Americanism at its highest.

New World Americans, people from the crowded countries of Europe, love America, not more deeply, perhaps, than native born Americans, but certainly more consciously. We have of our own free choice come to America, seeking here the opportunities for ourselves and for our children that we could not find in our native lands. We have become Americans because we so wished. Here we have conducted our business, here built our homes, here brought up our children.

Loving our mother country, we deplore her mistakes, pity her suffering, but like the girl who leaves father and mother and cleaves to her husband, we are married to our adopted country, America.

The strength of America is the welding into one great country many men of many lands. The essence of Americanism is the ability of rich and poor, men of many creeds and of many racial strains, to live together in peace and good will.

This country has reached out its hospitable arms and taken in peoples from older civilizations that they might find new freedom for themselves, and they, in return, have helped, with their muscle, their brains, and their art, to build America. Italian Americans have so built, faithfully, patiently, and well.

We hope that American citizens, those born here and those who have deliberately become Americans, will continue to realize that in our common aim is our strength; that America in the stress of this critical time needs us all working and working as one man to preserve our noble heritage.

These lines from one of our most beautiful patriotic songs we could sing like a prayer today:

"America, America, God shed his grace on thee;
"And crown they [sic] good with brotherhood, from sea to shining sea."

## NOTES

1. Apart from the observations of Valentine Belfiglio (cited below), *La Tribuna Italiana* has not attracted scholarly attention. Sally Miller, in her survey of foreign-language journalism originating within the United States, remarks that, "[t]he immigrant or ethnic press has received relatively little study"—a neglect that she characterizes as "remarkable" given the significance of such organs to those who did not speak English (xi). Unfortunately, Miller's compilation fails to include any constituents relating to the Italian American population, "because no specialist was sufficiently free of constraints to undertake the assignment" (xiii). While she optimistically cites a forthcoming publication that (we read) will fill this lacuna (xiii), it appears that the projected work was never completed. A good source for data on contemporary ethnic newspapers is Wynar and Wynar, who offer a section on the "Italian Press" (pages 100–108), providing—among other specifications—the date that each journal was established.

2. Belfiglio 71; *Texas Tribune* 24 June 1944: 1+; Dicapua; "Charlie Papa"; *Texas Tribune* 24 June 1961: 1; Davis and Grobe 2: 747.

3. Belfiglio 71; *Texas Tribune* 24 June 1944: 1+; "Charlie Papa"; *Texas Tribune* 24 June 1961: 1.

4. A Columbus Day advertisement for Keen Kola appearing in the mid 1920s congratulates readers of the *Tribuna* in the following towns. Texas: Brownwood, Carthage, Fort Worth, Henderson, Houston, Jacksonville, Kaufman, Lubbock, Nachogdoches [sic], Pittsburg, Ranger, San Antonio, Shiner, Sweetwater, Texas City, and Waxahachie; Oklahoma: Chickasha, Enid, Lawton, Mangum, Oklahoma City, Picher, and Shawnee; Louisiana: Shreveport (9 Oct. 1926a).

5. It should be noted, however, that by 1938 the *Tribuna*'s editor is identified as "Cav. [that is, *Cavaliere*] L. E. Adin," in recognition of his having been honored by the Italian government (12 Feb. 1938). This title disappears in the first edition of *The Texas Tribune*, accompanying the change to an all-English format (22 June 1940).

6. Belfiglio 71; *Texas Tribune* 24 June 1944: 1+; Davis and Grobe 2: 738, 747; "Head-On";

2; Dicapua; "Charlie Papa"; Wharton 167.

7. Belfiglio 68–70. As he observes in these pages, before the turn of the twentieth century urban Italian immigrants in Texas subscribed to papers from Italy, New York, Chicago, San Francisco, or New Orleans. In 1906 there appeared in Galveston Il Messaggiero Italiano—which subsequently moved to San Antonio (1906–1913)—followed by *La Stella del Texas* (1913–1918) and *La Patria degli Italiani* (1925), both also from Galveston. Published only in 1925 was San Antonio's *La Voce Patria*, while Houston had *L'Aurora* (1906, 1911–1923) and *L'America* (1925).

8. 'I will break but I will not bend'—a saying sometimes attributed to Seneca.

9. Also appearing in the issues I examined, for example, are Invernizio's *La Figlia della Portinaia, Le Figlie della Duchessa*, and *Odio di Araba*. For a recent analysis of her sensationalist novels, see Cantelmo. Works by other authors carried serially by the *Tribuna* before the predominance of excerpts from Invernizio include such novels as V. Amanzi's *Il Cenciaiuolo di Parigi*, Raffaele Sabatini's *Lo Sparviero del Mare*, Federico Soulie's *Eulalia Pontois*, and Bruno Sperani's La Fabbrica.

10. The classic 1920s sociological analysis by Park, in a chapter on "Advertising," presents the following affirmations: "Reading some of these foreign papers is like looking through a keyhole into a lighted room. In many cases the advertisements reveal the organization of the immigrant community more fully than does the rest of the paper . . . The advertisements also reveal to what extent an immigrant group has adapted itself to American ways." (113–114).

11. As is well known, this was accomplished officially on December 5, 1933. For an excellent overview of events leading to the inauguration of prohibition, and its demise, see Pegram.

12. The latter, in all probability, was meant to evoke in readers the image of the leader of their native land, who often addressed his citizens with similar energy.

13. In citing these Columbus Day issues, I will use letters, along with the date, to separate those appearing in different communities.

14. An informative and often amusing history of the early years of the Dr Pepper Company—whose chief product was created in 1885—is provided by Ellis.

15. "Naturalmente, per il suo carattere di simbolo, la perdita del carroccio in combattimento era la più grave alla quale si potesse soggiacere." ("Carroccio").

16. "On March 23, 1936, Mussolini officially employed to [sic] term autarchy to define the regime's long-term goal of economic self-sufficiency as a step toward putting Italy on a permanent war footing." (De Grand, 106).

17. Some other pieces from that same issue–all from Sicily–are entitled "Un Trapanese Preso a Pugni dal Padrone di Casa," "Due Bambine Travolte da un Cavallo a Gibellina," "Una Donna di Sancipirrello Cade dalla Scala," "Due Autisti Palermitani Vengono alle Mani," "Tenta di Difendere la Sorella e Viene Accoltellato dal Cognato a Palermo," and "Discordie di una Donna di Monreale con il Marito."

18. For a thorough history of Italian radio, see "Origini," where it is noted that the Prato Smeraldo station began operation in 1930 as the first shortwave transmission directed outside Italy, was sabotaged in 1943 while under German control, and subsequently saw its operations transferred north to avoid capture by the enemy.

19. In spite of the importance this figure must have assumed, I have been unable to discover any information regarding his life or activities.

20. While some of these bilingual queries are what a reader might expect, others seem a bit peculiar—perhaps especially because of the composer's having felt the need to provide appropriate responses: "Q. Are you an anarchist? A. No. / D. Siete voi un anarchico? R. No... Q. Did you ever break any laws of the United States? A. No. / D. Avete mai trasgredito alle leggi degli Stati Uniti? R. No." (10 Feb. 1940).

21. The dichotomy Adin may have experienced might possibly be summed up in the title of a work initially published during the *Tribuna's* formative years, in 1923: Speranza's Race or Nation: A Conflict of Divided Loyalties. Despite the ambiguity such phrases might evince, the text that accompanies them—in an echo of our own editor's patriotic words—expresses an unmistakable call for "conformity to the American spirit, to American life and history, to American ideals and aspirations" (Speranza 263).

22. "Mussolini prohibisce la celebrazione del 1 maggio in Italia e durante il fascismo la festa del lavoro viene spostata al 21 aprile, giorno del cosiddetto Natale di Roma. Tuttavia, negli anni del regime, in molte località italiane i lavoratori antifascisti continuano a commemorare il Primo Maggio in varie forme clandestine" ("Festa").

23. It may be instructive to recall that "[t]he decision to renounce the Triple Alliance which bound Italy to Austria-Hungary and Germany, and enter the war in May 1915 on the side of France and Britain, was itself internally divisive." (Morgan 7).

24. As has been pointed out, while the media in the United States did present a few pieces regarding Mussolini's alleged activities of a subversive nature, "[n]either the American public nor the federal government ever became overtly agitated by the threat of an Italian Fifth Column." (MacDonnell 75).

25. A cynic might suggest that the evolution to a publication entirely in English—and the editors' defense of such a move—are motivated more by desperation than patriotism. A careful consideration of this passage, however, refutes such a view.

## WORKS CITED

Belfiglio, Valentine J. *The Italian Experience in Texas.* Austin, TX: Eakin Press, 1983.

Cantelmo, Andrea. *Carolina Invernizio e il romanzo d'appendice.* Firenze: Firenze Atheneum, 1992.

"Carroccio." Istituto della Enciclopedia Italiana. *Enciclopedia Italiana di Scienze, Lettere ed Arti.* 35 vols. Roma: Istituto della Enciclopedia Italiani, 1949–1950.

"Charlie Papa and the Texas Tribune: 1913." *The Italian Texans.* The University of Texas Institute of Texan Cultures at San Antonio. 2nd edition. [San Antonio]: University of Texas Institute of Texan Cultures at San Antonio, 1994.

Davis, Ellis A. and Edwin H. Grobe. *The Encyclopedia of Texas.* 2 vols. Dallas: Texas Development Bureau, 1920.

De Grand, Alexander. *Italian Fascism: Its Origins and Development.* 3rd ed. Lincoln, NE: University of Nebraska Press, 2000.

Dicapua, Stephanie. "Texas Tidbits: Italians Made Their Way to Texas—and Made Their Mark." Texas Monthly December 2001: 1–4. (<http: www.texasmonthly.com/mag/issues/2001–12–1/tidbits.php?967363370>)

Ellis, Harry E. *Dr Pepper: King of Beverages.* Dallas, TX: Dr Pepper Company, 1979.

"La festa dei lavoratori." (<http://www.webscola.it/jumpNews.asp?idUser=0&idChannel =11&idNews=9915>)

"Head-On Auto Collision Fatal to Italian Leader, Publisher." *Dallas News* 22 Nov. 1947: n.p.

MacDonnell, Francis. *Insidious Foes: The Axis Fifth Column and the American Home Front.* New York: Oxford University Press, 1995.

Miller, Sally M., ed. *The Ethnic Press in the United States: A Historical Analysis and Handbook.* New York: Greenwood Press, 1987.

Morgan, Philip. *Italian Fascism, 1919–1945.* New York: St. Martin's Press, 1995.

Notes. The University of Texas Institute of Texan Cultures at San Antonio.

"Le origini della radiodiffusione in Italia: La vera storia della radiodiffusione in Italia. Cronistoria della radio dal 1923 al 2000: Con il contributo di Annino Vitale." (<http://www.radiomarconi.com/marconi/cronologia.html>)

Park, Robert E. *The Immigrant Press and its Control.* New York: Harper & Brothers Publishers, 1922.

Pegram, Thomas R. *Battling Demon Rum: The Struggle for a Dry America, 1800–1933.* Chicago: Ivan R. Dee, 1998.

Speranza, Gino. R*ace or Nation: A Conflict of Divided Loyalties.* New York: Arno Press, 1979.

*The Texas Tribune* [Dallas]. 1940–1962.

*La Tribuna Italiana* [Dallas]. 1914–1940.

Wharton, Clarence R. History of Texas. Dallas: Turner Company, 1935.

Wynar, Lubomyr R. and Anna T. Wynar. *Encyclopedic Directory of Ethnic Newspapers and Periodicals in the United States.* 2nd ed. Littleton, CO: Libraries Unlimited, Inc., 1976.

# MENTAL WANDERING IN CAROLE MASO'S *GHOST DANCE*

MARIA PAOLA MALVA AND FRANCO MULAS
UNIVERSITY OF SASSANI

Vanessa Turin, the main character in Carole Maso's novel, *Ghost Dance* experiences a meaningful exploration into the deepest dimension of the human mind in search of one's own roots and self. Through this process she tries to find out the reasons of her father and mother's silence about their past. The turmoil of her inner being is revealed to the outer world with compelling questions such as *"Where is my family? Where did Mom go?"*[1] And in order to find an answer to these questions Vanessa has to visit, with a new awareness, the darkest parts of her mind, enlightening them with the power of imagination and the recollections of long passed times. Thus, the loss, meaning the physical and spiritual disorientation which pervades the mind of a being who can't find a sense of belonging, becomes in this novel a quest for a complete identity. The fragmentation that takes place when one's own traditions are repressed, in the attempt to conform to the request of society, leaves an emptiness which causes a feeling of loss and despair.

In this novel, the powerful force of fantasy is represented by the Topaz Bird (*the brilliant bird of imagination*), which will help Vanessa understand the reasons of her mother's suffering and of her father's silence and at the same time to discover her own talent and creativity. She is able to construct a meaningful pattern of events putting together fragmented memories and experiences relying on the power of her mind, free of all constraints, abandoning herself to a world defined not by the rational and often contradictory rules of society, but to the creativity that springs from the essence of a free mind, governed by the natural instincts which control the most hidden stratification of the human soul.

Thus, the author indirectly criticizes the American ideal of progress and modernization, which inevitably leads to the subjugation to a work ethic which deprives man from his natural vitality, dreams and fantasy, transforming him into a small device of a giant mechanical system. Vanessa, the heroin, escapes this crude reality with a flight into imagination, where words charged with a healing power and storytelling becomes a mean to cure the afflicted mind. Thus, she tells the story of the Topaz Bird, gaining from it the strength that will help her face and overcome the aversion caused by a society which leads people to reject their own identity; forcing them to become part of a universal bunch, allowing them no room for diversity. Her own grandfather for instance, in the effort of blending into the American society sacrifices his cultural traditions rejecting them:

> *Did his father announce that there will be no more Italian spoken in his house? No more wine drunk with lunch, as he burned the grapevines? Did he tell his wife there would be no more sad song from the old country? How much she must have wept, hugging her small son to her breast! (74)*

His origins cannot be, however, totally wiped out from his mind and soul, and they will re-emerge at the moment of his death when he pronounces his last words in his native tongue: "The language that he had given up in this country now came steaming back. My grandmother squeezed his hand. She talked back to him." (139)

This particular instance enlightens Vanessa making her ever more aware of the loss of her grandfather, both as a person and as a carrier of Old World values. The fragmentation experienced by the old generation in the process of Americanization emerges from the words of a woman who, only after the death of her husband, is able to break the silence which has caused so much pain to her, finding finally the strength to reveal to her grandchild the reasons which brought her to hide her Italian ancestry:

> Your grandfather never let me speak Italian in the house . . . He never let me cook my own food. I missed that so much,' she said in the loneliest voice I had ever

heard' . . . 'He never let me sing you to sleep with the
sweet songs from Italy I loved so much."(223)

Maso's aim in this novel is to show that when the ancestral ties
are broken, rejected or suppressed, the characters experience a sort
of internal illness that can be cured only through a re-conjunction
with their own origins. Thus, in order to fill the generational
gaps, Maso re-evokes hers with a journey through memory and
imagination. Vanessa, uncertain about her own identity, is in search
of a past which can tell her where she stands in the present. The
title of the novel, *Ghost Dance,* suggests a sense of the abstract
and of the intangible, traits which often distinguish many female
characters of the Italian American novel: a constant motion, a
sense of instability, women who wander in a constant search for
their own place in the world.

The novel begins with an internal, omniscient narrator who,
even though she herself is part of the story, introduces the character
describing abstract and concrete perceptions: "she is waiting for
me . . . she is not anxious at all." (5) In a moment, the narrator
steps into the mind of the main character and the actions described
become abstract: "slowly she clears a wide path for me trough
the snow, and as I step safely, in her mind." (5) The characters
associate reality and imagination mingling the concreteness of the
snowy scenery with the imaginary figure who steps into her mind
acquiring a concrete and a tangible shape as well as a dimension
that gives her a sense of safety and protection. Everything that
takes place in the mind appears to be safe, protected from the
harshness of the outside world. The mind becomes the fantastic
refuge where all sorts of thoughts, desires and wishes can mingle
and develop without constraints. The ghostly figure who wonders
in Vanessa's mind is the memory of her mother as it was the last
time she saw her in the station. Vanessa sees the station, not as a
frenetic place saddened by farewells and goodbyes, but as a place
livened by vitality and hope, representing a place of transition and
motion which identifies the restless character of her mother always
on the move, in a constant race towards some unreachable thing.
Vanessa's mother, thus, personifies the element of restlessness

which characterizes other protagonists of the Italian American female novels such as Marguerite in *Umbertina*, Carmolina in *Paper Fish* and others. In a moment of epiphany in which Vanessa contemplates the snowy scenery, brightened by the glittering sun, she finds the inspiration to conclude her poem. The setting is dominated by the positive attitude of the narrator, who defines herself "dangerously happy." (5) This appears as an happiness which has a positive insight of the world: "The poem is complete: the world is a cathedral of light." (5) This joyful atmosphere is characterized by tones and colors that depict a bright picture of the world such as the whiteness of the snow, an element that stands as s symbol of purity, and the brilliance of the sun, which wipes away the shadows and puts out pleasant warmth. In this text the opposites cold and warm mingle generating a pleasant atmosphere: "The city sparkles like a jewel in the sun." (5) It is in this joyful and luminous atmosphere that Vanessa chooses to re-evoke and bring to life her mother's memory. This positive glare has the purpose of chasing away the negative elements such as the suffering and the pain which are unconsciously related to the tragic destiny which has prematurely ended her mother's life: "On such a day it is possible to believe that sorrow will turn into one great vapour and blow off and be gone forever that the childhood dream of fire will turn out to mean nothing in the end." (5)

The magic of storytelling emerges throughout the novel as an element that brings hope and fills the mind with a positiveness that erases the harshness of reality. Vanessa recalls the stories that her mother used to tell her, feeling the same sensations she used to feel when she was still alive: "We were like lovers drifting off to sleep together, whispering in the dark." (11) Storytelling is represented in this novel, with the symbol of the Topaz Bird: "Only the luckiest people are born with a bird flying over their lives. It's no ordinary bird, mind you . . . " (11) While telling the stories, her mother would ask her to imagine the Topaz Bird: "She was asking me to see the topaz bird with her." (11) This is a clear example of how storytelling brings the narrator and the listener into a single thinking entity, showing that through thought the two can reach a deep soul communion. Vanessa's alienation from reality can be seen in the following: "I feel the warm breath as I descend into sleep and hear her voice long after she has left the room." (11) Through the use of sensorial powers—smell, touch and sight—the mind is able to preserve elements that in real life are bound to disappear. In fact, even when her mother, after telling the story, leaves the room, she still can feel her mother's through sensorial elements such as: the smell of her skin, the touch of her lips, and the sound of her voice. Storytelling appears as an element strictly connected to the female gender, transmitted it from generation to generation. Vanessa's grandmother sees the Topaz Bird for the first time, while she is giving birth to her daughter: the scene is brightened by the brilliant glare of the Topaz Bird, which stands as a symbol of rebirth, winner over death: "In fact my grandmother was entering a new stage as she stood before the Topaz Bird, having brought it back, after so long, with her daughter's birth: it was the beginning of the end of her life." (11)

Abandoning oneself to the powers of imagination and fantasy is considered by the outer world as a sort of illness: "She was mad, they knew, to see things that way, but 'let her be.'" (15) This is what people said about Vanessa's grandmother who, determined to immortalize the imagine of the Topaz Bird on a canvas, collected various types of materials related to the image reproduced in her mind. In the same way, for Vanessa the fantasy and the creativity of the mind becomes an inevitable process, which must be nourished, teaching her own mind to gather details in order to produce the most clear and accurate images: "I learned to halves the distance, then make smaller divisions. I might suddenly smell rain though the day was sunny, feel the texture of her hair . . . " (16) As we can see, in this novel, only female characters are blessed with the power of imagination; Vanessa's father, missing this kind power, is not able to use his imagination thus losing himself in the deepest darkness of his own existence: " . . . my father saw nothing when my mother was away—or what I imagine nothing to be: fields and fields of black or dark green or blue." (19) He can only see the representation of nullity in a dark extension of black and dark green and blue shadows: "His life is down there—in deep blue, in gray, in green in tangled plants, in dim light." (19)

The word tangled in this context is used to express the sense of being trapped in a dark abyss, which prevents him to see any light. In her imagination, Vanessa dives into this pool of darkness in the attempt to free her father from the obscurity that overcomes him, giving him the possibility to see beyond it. In this process of liberation she fights an endless struggle against a mysterious force: "I dive once, twice, hold his head in the air," (19) but she is brought back to reality by the trivial sound of the water running out of the faucet, and by her father's simple and common statement: "how about a movie?" (19) These words, however, give her the temporary illusion of having succeeded, even if only in part, in bringing him out of the dark abyss of his life: "He is back in the air again. I have succeeded in some small way, I think." (19) The expression, I think, leaves, however, a trail of uncertainty over her success. All these quotations are a clear example of how the author of this novel explores the mental process of her characters: Vanessa imagines to free her father from the sea weeds which entrap him under the abyss of his own meaningless life, in so doing she links the water of the ocean (depths of imagination) with that of the water faucet (gloominess of daily life). Because of this she admits to have, only in part, succeeded in her attempt "in some small way." Her father appears as a flat character, mainly interested in banal TV shows-which represent the destructiveness of the American technology that sterilizes the mind preventing any kind of creativity: "Sometimes, to get our father to speak, we would invent home works assignments in which it was necessary for him to answer questions." (28)

In this imaginary context, the past acquires vivid and detailed dimensions, which reveal each particular aspect as if it were real. Fantasy enables Vanessa to paint under a subjective light the memory of her dear ones: "So the dead are even more detailed in appearance than the living . . . " (13)

Verbs such as to imagine, to invent, to recall, to think are very frequent and give the text a sense of unreality and freedom of perception and thoughts. Such constructions are often repeated in the same page: "I have spent hours and hours on trains imagining you, your life." (33) "I often imagine you are waiting for somebody who will never return . . . have invented many lives for you, made up many stories." (33) "If you work hard, if you concentrate. Build, in your imagination, the circumstances in which such an action could take place. You can invent anything you have to, anything you want. You can do it all." (96) This last quotation shows how the power of imagination can break through all codes defining a world of its own, independent from the rules which confine and limit the objective reality. In the mind of the main characters the fundamental function of imagination is translated with the ability to go beyond and achieve a superior status which allows the character to freely shape his own existence without limits of any sort. These mental wanderings gain a phantasmagorical dimension: relationships as well as people are described as if they were apparitions that if not treated with the proper care could easily vanish into nothing. It seems that the author wants to underline the precariousness of the events and of the human relations as well as the fragility of the characters: "If it was an apparition, then he do must nothing to dispel it from his psyche. If I was some wild animal, caught in this room, any sudden movement might frighten me." (34)

The narrator seems to doubt his own presence as a concrete physical being. The constant motion which characterizes her mother is expressed by Vanessa as follows: "something in my mother herself, some early retreat, a pulling back, a stepping away that made me aware that soon she'd be leaving again?" (39) "This is how I remember her best: an extravagant exotic figure, descending stairs or getting into the car, but always saying good-bye." (42) Vanessa unconsciously suffers from the absence of her mother and to preserve her presence she uses both memory and imagination. Storing in her mind her mother's details allows her to recall her image any time she wants, thus overcoming the sense of loneliness which constantly pervades her: "It is one of those moments frozen in my mind forever: the hat, tilted to the side, covers one eye . . . I would keep her with me. I would keep the sparkle in her blue eyes and put it back into the lake . . . " (39)

In this context the lake, represents the mirror which allows the splitting of the image. In fact Vanessa, looking at her reflection in the lake sees her mother as she remembered her: "We looked into the lake at our own reflections." (85)

Vanessa is aware that for her mother as well, memory and imagination were necessary tools to build around herself a utopia in which was possible to live her own life without the limitation imposed by society. With the following sentence Vanessa's mother gives us an idea of how vital it was to alter the world in order to make of it a more habitable and a bearable place: "Often, I knew, she altered or remade the world, revising it, making it a more habitable place, a more bearable one, or sometimes just more complete." (49) It is important to remember the strong relationship that her mother had with another woman, who became the centre of her life. The feelings they shared were characterized by mutual understanding, respect and a deep passion which surpassed all limits which she, however, had to hide from society.

The novel starts with a positive tone that gradually fades into a sort of confusion and restlessness, which reveals the loneliness and the interior paralysis that afflicts the characters. The lack of communication emerges from statements such as: "I have very little contact with anyone else." (66) Outside the ghostly world of her imagination, Vanessa has little contact with people, especially men. Jack the strange man who comes in and out of her life appears as a ghostly figure who represents the brutality of a life driven by primordial impulses that bring man and woman to an animal status. The recurrence of blood in their love-making emphasizes the violence and abuse which deeply contrasts the tenderness and mutual respect that characterizes the relationship with the few female friends she has. The constant search for her mother: "Where did Mom go?" (65) And the failure to find an answer to this question, underlines the painful acceptance of the unknown around her mother: "I have grown accustomed to the silence that collects around the receiver in response to this question." (65)

A relevant aspect in this novel is given by the notion of time that is constantly stressed by elements such as the passing of the seasons and the transformation that the world undergoes during this process. The colours and the smells are associated to memories which come about during each different season recalling, with deep intensity, special particularities of life: "In winter she became lost to me . . . She is back in summer though it is December now." (97) This sort of stream of consciousness shows how the mind of the protagonist shifts from time to time without any logical sequence of events, wandering from past to present driven only by the magical power of nature. In this sort of ecstasy the wandering mind creates fantastic associations: the blooming flowers of springtime are shaped into personification of the dearest people. Vanessa's mother refers to the memory of her child recalling the flowers that she likes the most: "Is that my daffodil? My Lilac? My bluebell? My mimosa?" (97) On the other hand, in Vanessa's mind the memory of her mother is brought back with deep intensity from the changing of the seasons which mark the passing of time: from the cold winter to the fragrance of the blooming flowers in springtime. In the irreversible reality these elements no longer exist, they slowly fade away leaving a sense of loss, which can be fulfilled only by the subjective enlightenment of imagination.

In this novel, the restlessness of the characters parallels the precariousness of the human existence, where all certainties vanish leaving a sense of instability and, in the effort to find strength in human relationship; they move blindly towards the unknown, often falling in the hopeless illusion given by drugs. The illness, which often afflicts the characters in the Italian American novel, is here revealed through the hallucinatory effects of drugs, which for Vanessa can be translated as a further effort to escape the harshness of reality and as a reason to let herself go to a transgressive life in which she can display her attraction for other women. Her relationship with Martha, characterized by tenderness, passion, mutual respect and complicity introduces her to the use of drugs: "There was happiness and peace. When they came back from the trances they told their dreams to others. They had seen the dead." (198) On the other hand, the violent relationship she has with Jack, which often seems a sort of punishment, exhorts her to come out of them. However, the only way out of this state of disorientation Vanessa finds it in the power of imagination which allows her mind to build an imaginary world where she feels protected from the harshness of life: "And hand in hand, on the edge of the sand, they danced by the light of the moon, the moon." (101) The light of the moon seems to suggest a soft and positive familiar element, creating a sense of peace and serenity, which encourages closeness and familiarity with the dear ones, who are no longer alive. They are recalled to her mind in a ghostly dance which takes place on the edge of the sand, thus remarking a place of transition, "the edge," between the sea and the earth. The ghostly figures of the dear ones undergo a sort of metamorphosis from earthly into marine creatures who appear and disappear in the immensity of the ocean: "I could easily touch my mother, but I do not want to frighten her away or make her feel as if she is trapped. I do not want her to misconstrue the situation or to think that I am changing."(225)

Natural elements such as the sand, the moon, the flowers, the rain emerge in this text endowing it with an aesthetic quality which removes the loneliness, the decay and the impossibility to communicate to each other that seems to afflict the characters in the real world. The sensorial dimension is highly evidenced by verbs of movement such as "the wave danced," (101) which match the rhythmical movement of the ghost dance, thus transforming the restlessness of the living characters into a beautiful dance in the imaginary world of fancy. The constant movement of the characters and the ongoing movement of the waves underline a paradox in which emerges the power of the eternal and unrefrainable nature and the futility and fragility of human life bound to get lost in the immensity of the universe: "which is the bliss of solitude." (101) The author seems to be suggesting that man can only find one's better self through the imagination, the memories and the fusion with the surrounding nature: "It's misty; there's a smell of dew, of damp mushrooms, of nuts—chestnuts. They lie in the wet herbs, say nothing, listen to the odd two note whistle of a bird. It's spring." (101) The power of the senses, sight, smell, hearing bring the mind of the protagonist into a different dimension enabling her to recall past situations and to re-establish contacts with her beloved mother. Beside the imagination, Vanessa's creativity is alimented by the beautiful world of the library; for her reading is a way to move in a different world where she finds the missing parts of her puzzled life: "Here is a lover of books, a woman dizzied by them, transformed in some way." (101) This novel stands as an emblem in showing that without the impetus of our memory, the world of storytelling and the power of imagination the world is sterile ground where the events of life go on unmarked without a purpose other than the mere existential needs common to every human being. The creativity of a cultivated mind feeds itself with the colours, the light and the fragrance of imagination and generates a delightful power which transforms apparently meaningless aspects of life into a key to read the most intimate aspect of our being.

## NOTES

1. Carole Maso, *Ghost Dance* ( New Jersey: The Ecco Press, 1995), 65. All references in parenthesis are to this edition.

# PART III

# POETRY

## Fuochi artificiali, 4 luglio 2004

### Maria Famà
#### Translated by Maria Elisa Ciavarelli

Mio fratello, gambe divaricate nell'oscurità
figura sua indistinta
mi rammenta mio padre
or morto già da dieci anni

Mio fratello dà inizio ai fuochi artificiali della festa
in umida aria calda:
abbaglianti scoppi di stelle colorate
alti getti di fiamma e fumo
con striduli suoni assordanti

Penso ai bombardamenti dell'Iraq
l'orrenda distruzion di vite e case
tra raffiche di fuoco e di frastuono

Mio fratello accende piccoli cannoni e minuti portamissili
che carenan su per la strada ed esplodon
tra striduli e tra fiamme

Vi son soldati, insorti, combattenti per la libertà
dall'altro lato del pianeta questo Quattro di Luglio
retti o sbigottiti incerti o intenzionali
combattono con fuoco o con rumore

# FIREWORKS ON JULY 4, 2004

## MARIA FAMÀ

My brother stands legs apart in the dark
his shadowy figure
reminds me of our father
now more than ten years dead

My brother sets off holiday fireworks
in the hot, humid air:
glaring starbursts of color
tall jets of flame and smoke
shrill earsplitting sounds

I think of the bombardment of Iraq
the startling destruction of lives and homes
amidst the blasts of fire and noise

My brother lights up little tanks and tiny missile carriers
that careen up the street and explode
with shrieks and flames

There are soldiers, insurgents, freedom fighters
halfway around the planet this July Fourth
righteous or scared unsure or deliberate
they fight with fire and noise

Quando nostro padre tornò dalla Seconda Guerra Mondiale
ferito sul campo di battaglia
di ventitrè anni di età
con Purple Heart e spalle colme di proiettili shrapnel
andò a vedere i festivi fuochi artificiali
con nostra madre, la di lei sorella e i genitor di lei

Il fuoco e il rumore lo riportò qual lampo
alle terribili battaglie che aveva combattute in Francia
corse, chinò il capo, s'immerse per coprirsi
nostra madre, i genitor di lei, sua sorella gli corser dietro
gridando
"la guerra è finita!"
"Tu sei in patria!"
"Sei salvo!"
"Questi son solo fuochi artificiali!"

Prego che un giorno
tutti i soldati, gl'insorti, i combattenti per la libertà
si fermino a guardare i fuochi artificiali
con figli e persone care al loro lato
come ha fatto eventualmente nostro padre
s'accorgeranno come se n'è accorto lui

che son salvi e in patria

questi son solo fuochi artificiali

la guerra è finita.

When our father returned from the Second World War
   wounded in action
   twenty-three years old
   with a purple heart and a back full of shrapnel
he went to see the holiday fireworks
with our mother, her sister, and her parents

The fire and the noise flashed him back
to the terrible battles he'd fought in France
he ran, ducked, dived for cover
our mother, her parents, her sister ran after him
shouting
"The war is over!"
"You are home!"
"You are safe!"
"These are only fireworks!"

I pray that one day
all soldiers, insurgents, freedom fighters
will stand and watch fireworks
with children and loved ones at their sides
as our father eventually did
they will realize as he finally did

   they are safe and home

   these are only fireworks

   the war is over.

## DIRITTI CIVILI

MARIA FAMÀ
TRANSLATED BY MARIA ELISA CIAVARELLI

Io e la nonna eravamo sedute nel suo salotto del New Jersey
  a guardare il Movimento dei Diritti Civili alla TV
Io ero bambina, lei di mezz'età
lei era venuta negli Stati Uniti dalla Sicilia
dopo la Seconda Guerra Mondiale
non riuscì mai a dominar la saltellante, contorta
lingua dell'inglese e questo l'afflisse

Eravamo sedute e guardavamo animosi bimbi andare a scuola
  circondati da adirata calca
osservammo i marciatori, sit-in di snack bar,
iscrizioni in liste elettorali, sceriffi, cani,
la forza massima di tubi da getto volti sulla gente
sbattuta sul marciapiede

"Perchè?" chiese la nonna. Voleva
  sapere perchè stava succedendo questo
"Vogliono votare, nonna
  Vogliono andare alla scuola o al ristorante che vogliono"
"Perchè non possono? Son nati qua
Io posso andare a qualsiasi posto voglio e non so parlare inglese
Posso votare e non so parlare inglese
Perchè io sì quando non posson farlo loro?
Questo è ingiustizia!"
"La lor gente una volta erano schiavi, nonna"
"E noi fummo sempre mezzadri, quasi schiavi,
del Duca d'Averna

## CIVIL RIGHTS

### MARIA FAMÀ

My grandmother and I sat in her Jersey living room
   watching the Civil Rights Movement on TV
I was a little girl, she middle aged
she'd come to the States from Sicily
after the Second World War
she never mastered the jumpy, twisty
tongue of English and this pained her

We sat and watched brave children walking to school
   surrounded by angry mobs
we watched the marchers, the lunchcounter sit-ins,
the voting registrations, the sheriffs, the dogs,
the full force of fire hoses turned on people
knocked to the sidewalk

"Perche?" my grandmother asked. She wanted to
   know why this was happening
"They want to vote, Nonna
   They want to go to whatever schools and restaurants they want"
"Why can't they? They were born here
I can go anyplace I want and I can't speak English
I can vote and I can't speak English
Why can I when they cannot?
This is injustice!"
"Their people were once slaves, Nonna"
"And we were always sharecroppers, almost slaves,
to the Duke D'Averna

Questi sono i veri americani"
Io ricordo che la nonna non menzionò mai il colore
i cronisti della TV continuavano a dire "negri"
Tutti quelli che vide erano americani
che lavoravano qua
che parlavano inglese

La nonna sapeva che Mussolini aveva arraffato l'Abbissinia
sapeva le parole della canzone "Facetta nera"
sapeva che i siciliani erano andati in Etiopia a lavorare
avevano sposato donne carine di là
conosceva un parente che chiamavano l'africano
che lavorò e amò in Africa
si vantava di quanto fosse meraviglioso là

Ora negli Stati Uniti il suo paese d'adozione
Ora in quella che pensava fosse la terra della libertà
la nonna era sbalordita, inorridita
delle immagini della TV
continuava a dire
"io non son nata qua
non so parlare inglese
eppure posso votare, andare dove voglio
Perchè io posso quando loro no?
Questo è ingiustizia."

These people are the real Americans"
I remember that my grandmother never mentioned color
the TV newspeople kept saying "Negroes"
All she saw were Americans
who worked here
who spoke English

Nonna knew Mussolini had grabbed Abyssinia
she knew the words to the song "Faccetta Nera"
she knew Sicilian men had gone to Ethiopia to work
married the pretty women there
she knew a relative they called LAfricano
who worked and loved in Africa
he bragged how wonderful it was there

Now in the States, her adopted country
Now in what she thought was the land of liberty
my grandmother was astounded, horrified
at the images on TV
she kept saying
"I was not born here
I cannot speak English
yet I can vote, go wherever I want
Why can I when they cannot?
This is injustice."

## IN E FUORI CONTATTO

### ANTOINETTE LIBRO
#### TRANSLATED BY MARIA ELISA CIAVARELLI

Attraversando il fiume Turtle
l'erba delle paludi della Giorgia
brilla nel vento di marzo

un daino come l'ombra
d'un semiricordato
nome sussulta, poi scivola

entro la macchia. Qui
pende il musco
con dimessa eleganza

grigio fosche al crepuscolo
le paludi cavan memorie
dalla punta delle nostre dita.

All'interno di codesta tasca
riposa la tua lettera;
"gli alberi si son schiusi in boccioli

giorni fa"
la risposta si sprende
vuota come luna piena

sicchè più tardi senza un suono
la muschiosa aria si stanca
e ci sprofonda nel sonno

### IN AND OUT OF TOUCH

TONI LIBRO

Crossing Turtle River
the Georgia marsh grass
shines in the March wind

a deer like the shadow
of half-remembered
name startles, then slips

into the wild. Here
the Spanish Moss hangs
in shabby elegance

greyly dull at dusk
the swamplands suck memories
out of our fingertips.

Inside this pocket
rests your letter;
"the trees broke into bud

some days ago"
the reply rises
empty as the full moon

so then without a sound
the musky air tires
and settles us to sleep

ove sogni di giovani alberi
che sboccian lontano
s'accoppiano

col daino che sussulta
e scivola
di nuovo nella macchia.

where dreams of young trees
blossoming far away
are coupled with

deer that startle
and slip
back into the wild.

POSTFAZIONE

ANTOINETTE LIBRO
TRANSLATED BY MARIA ELISA CIAVARELLI

L'unica forma di vincere
è con le parole
eppur il tempo

per vincere
è passato
Accetta invece

l'accelerato battito
del cuore
e mani umide

Dopo tutto
invece di questo malessere
avresti potuto trovar-

ti
con promesse
da mantenere

Qui le promesse
non son fatali
e gli abbracci

non soffocano
Qui le aspettative
giaccion supine

## AFTERWORD

TONI LIBRO

The only way to win
is with words
yet the time

for winning
is past
Accept instead

the quickened beat
of the heart
and damp hands

After all
instead of this malaise
you could have found

yourself
with promises
to keep

Here promises
are not fatal
and embraces

do not smother
Here expectations
lie flat

come terre bagnate
dove si posan
uccelli selvatici

as wetlands
where the wild
birds roost

## Poesia Fratello

### Rachel Guido de Vries
### Translated by Maria Elisa Ciavarelli

Le cellule rimaste io frego contro il petto,
l'enorme tua maglietta Yankees quella in cui or dormo,
sovente, e quelle le notti in cui tu appari
dentro del mio corpo. La stoppia del tuo mento, la tua
gota sulla mia, la tua mano sul mio gomito,
e poi la gota tua di bimbo ch'io ho sfiorato
con tutto l'amor mio. Sì piccino e sempre tenero,
nella tua costituzion che crebbe e si gonfiò
mentre tu celavi il dolor tuo. Ti sento come credo
lo possa fare una madre, sapendo che qualcosa in te
non sarebbe mai esattamente giusto. A volte mi sforzo
di ricordar le tue risate, la tua sporadica risonante gioia,
il ragazzo che tu eri. Ti chiamavo mio.

Io vengo su di me tutta pien di lagrime,
non sognando. Vago attraverso i nostri anni
ricordandoti. T'accolgo cellula a cellula.
Vorrei dirti che sei salvo e che lo son anch'io.
Raggomitola il solitario tuo io e prova solo amore.
Dev'esser bello aver questa sorta di fede,
immaginarti in qualche modo lassù, in questi azzurri cieli,
l'anima tua già liberata. Aspettandomi. Non dolore,
non bisogno e non desio.

                                        Terrena,
stendo le mani per coglier un tantin di pioggia. Conficco
la primaveril vanghetta nella melmosa terra, vedo come

## BROTHER POEM

### RACHEL GUIDO DE VRIES

What cells are left I rub against my chest,
your big Yankees' tee now what I sleep in,
often, and those the nights when you appear
inside my body Stubble of your chin, your
cheek on mine, your hand upon my elbow,
and then your baby cheek I brushed
with all my love. So small and tender always,
inside your frame which grew and swelled
as you withheld your pain. I feel you as I think
a mother might, aware that something in you
never felt quite right. Sometimes I make myself
recall your laughter, its ocasional booming joy,
the boy you were. I called you mine.

I come upon myself all full of tears,
not dreaming. I'm roaming through our years
remembering you. I welcome you, cell to cell.
I'd like to tell you that you're safe, and I am too.
Curl up your lonely self and feel just love.
It must be lovely to hold that kind of faith,
to picture you somehow above, in these blue heavens,
your soul set free. Awaiting me. No sorrow,
no need, and no desire.

                                        Earthbound,
I hold my hands to catch some rain. I dig
the springtime trowel into muddy earth, see how

s'attacca il fango al di sotto delle unghie, come riempie ogni
fessur di palma,
e così ci uniamo. Forse così c'incontriamo, proprio qui,
dove premo le mie labbra sulla terra che riscalda.

dirt clings under nails, fills each crevice on my palms,
and so we join. Perhaps like this we meet, just here,
where I press my lips to warming earth.

## STORIE DEL FUOCO

RACHEL GUIDO DE VRIES
TRANSLATED BY MARIA ELISA CIAVARELLI

1
Sotto esili alti tronchi di fuoco mattutino
brucia una piccola caverna. Persino i più piccini
si meravigliano del fato. Due bambine in abiti
antiquati si abbracciano, appollaiate su
minuto bordo di cenere argentata. Se seguo
l'incavato sentiero fin in fondo dove gli eretti
tronchi lo permettono, nel profondo della più azzurra fiamma,
una madre conforta un piccino addolorato,
che s'affligge per quelle due bambine con coraggio.
Son cadute, trecce ondeggianti, nel calor in cui la loro sponda
è sprofondata.

2
Che potrebbe voler celare il più vecchio tronco,
appiattandosi com'or fa, come se
potesse sprofondare in cenere un istante,
scosta i suoi dolosi possessivi
sogni, e torna ancor, reso
solo più scaltro dal suo incontro colle fiamme.

3
C'è un pugno di desiderio nell'albergo
di ognuno. Lo puoi sentire nel modo in cui le stanze
s'accendon per un minuto quando entri,
un vil fremito di calor ch'esplode
se tu divien gagliardo senz'avvertimento: qualcuno

## STORIES FROM THE FIRE

### RACHEL GUIDO DEVRIES

1
Beneath tall slender logs of morning's fire
burns a small cave. Even smaller people
wonder about fate. Two small girls in old
fashioned dresses hug each other, perched on
a tiny ledge of silver ash. If I follow
the hollowed path as far back as standing
logs allow, deep inside the bluest flame,
a mother comforts a grief-struck child,
who grieves those two brave girls. They
fell, braids swinging, into heat their ledge
gave into.

2
What might the oldest log want so to hide,
skulking down as he does now, as though
he can sink into ashes for a while,
push aside his incendiary dreams
of possession, and still return, only
made wilier by his meeting with flames.

3
There's a fist of desire in everyone's
hotel. You can feel it in the way rooms
charge up for a minute when you enter,
a sneaky thrill of heat that explodes
if you get lusty without warning: someone

con sbiaditi jeans in piedi proprio in modo giusto;
un medico che accende una sigaretta, labbra gonfie
come se stesse per baciar amante; una donna
seduta sola al chiar di luna a Santorini,
orson trent'anni.

4
Poiché siedo sola innanzi a lune
che si dilatan in fuoco, son da esse eccitata
e dal vento tra pioppi e pini.
I pronti richiami delle povere gavie saran
sempre dal dolor menati, or da esso rese insane
o ebbrie potrebbe dirsi, si lisciano frenetiche
qual adolescente, o qual poeta,
innanzi a fiamme.

in faded jeans standing just the right way;
a doctor lighting a cigarette, his full lips
as though about to kiss a lover; a woman
sitting alone in moonlight on Santorini,
thirty years ago.

4
Because I sit alone before the moons
that swell in fire, aroused by them
and by wind through the aspens and pines.
The poor loons' mercurial calls will
always be grief-struck, now insane with it,
or drunk one might say, over-preening
like a teenager, or like a poet,
before the flames.

## I GLADIOLI DI MIO PADRE

ALBERT TACCONELLI
TRANSLATED BY MARIA ELISA CIAVARELLI

Li aravamo sotto i piedi
sparpagliandone i petali, lingue curve,
su terra arata. Or crescon
in giardino legati collo spago
indisturbati nella lor grazia.

Molto tempo fa, ero giovane
era un altro paese

## MY FATHER'S GLADIOLI

### ALBERT TACCONELLI

We used to plow them underfoot
scattering pink petals like curled tongues
over turned earth. Now they grow
in the garden tied with string
undisturbed in their grace.

It was long ago, I was young,
it was another country.

**IL GIORNO CHE M'HAI LASCIATA, MARY ANN MANNINO**

MARY ANN MANNINO
TRANSLATED BY MARIA ELISA CIAVARELLI

Ero lì in piedi prossima al frigo
quel sabato mattina.
La finestra sull'acquaio aperta
Potevo sentire l'aria fresca
d'ottobre tutta mele e zucche.
Sul davanzale la lanterna di zucca
che io e i ragazzi avevamo scolpita
la tua vecchia pipa in bocca.

Tu eri dall'altra parte del tavolo
nell'aperto vano della porta
indossavi quel maglione blu che io avevo comprato
dal Wishbook di Sears il Natale prima.
I ragazzi tra di noi
vengon giù dai fumetti del sabato
coi piatti lordi di colazione tra le mani.

Quel momento di rivoluzione colto prima
Ch'esplodessero le tue parole dalla bocca
"Tu non m'ami," dicesti. "Non mi hai mai amato."

Ed io ero lì.

Gli occhi dei ragazzi qual cervo
colto in fanali d'auto
volti verso di me.

## THE DAY YOU LEFT ME

MARY ANN MANNINO

I was standing by the refrigerator
that Saturday morning.
The window over the sink was open
I could feel the crisp October
air all apples and pumpkins.
On the sill the jack-o-lantern
the kids and I had carved
had your old pipe in his mouth.

You were on the other side of the table
in the open doorway
wearing that blue sweater I had bought
from the Sears Wishbook the Christmas before.

The kids between us
come down from the Saturday cartoons
holding dirty breakfast plates.

That one revolutionary moment caught before
The words exploded from your mouth
"You don't love me," you said. "Never have."

And I stood there.

The children's eyes like deer
caught in a car's head lights
turned toward me.

Io sapevo quel che dovevo fare. Chiedere scusa.
In qualche modo dir ch'io avevo torto per volerlo.
Solo volerlo. Forse guardar le stelle
dalla spiaggia, forse ballar alla
Seconda il Giorno di Capodanno, o forse
far l'amor ad alba già inoltrata.

Ero lì mentre
Tante cose mi sfuggivan dalla mano
casa, figli, presente,
Futuro, il cappel felice che tenevi al
mare, la tua borsa sulla panca
prossima alla porta, il tuo kit per barba in bagno,
Tanti Natali e Pasque, vacanze e
Rappresentazion scolastiche
Tutto quel che potevo fare era restar lì senza parlare.

I knew what I should do. Apologize.
Somehow say I was wrong for wanting.
Just wanting. Maybe to watch the stars
from the beach, maybe to dance on
Two Street New Years Day, or maybe
to make love past dawn.

I stood there while
So many things slipped from reach
the house, the children, the past, the
Future, the happy hat you kept at
the beach, your briefcase on the bench
by the door, your shaving kit in the bathroom,
So many christmasses and Easters, vacations and
School plays
All I could do was stand there wordless.

MEDITAZIONI SUL DIVORZIO E ALTRE PERDITE

MARY ANN MANNINO
TRANSLATED BY MARIA ELISA CIAVARELLI

I

I petali cadono
dagli alberi
          in primavera
Ti piaccia
o non ti piaccia. Non si può
disfare.

Ho pensato magari prendo la colla,
prendo l'Elmer's e una scala
li ricostruisco
con cura, uno ad uno.
Ma, no. I margini
sarebbero tutti bruni,
raggrinziti.

II

I petali in terra
s'adunano qual vetrí frantumati
quando alcun ragazzo sfrenato rompe
la vetrina d'un negozio.
Istantaneo danno
          brutto foro
          spaventoso.

## Meditation on Divorce and Other Losses

Mary Ann Mannino

I

Petals fall
        off trees
                in Spring.
Like it
        or not. It can't
                be undone.

I thought maybe get glue,
get Elmer's and a ladder
put them back
carefully, one by one.
But, no. The edges
would be all brown,
shriveled.

II

Petals on the ground
pool like shattered glass
when some wild boy breaks
a store-front window.
        Instant damage
                ugly hole
                        scary.

III

Non preoccuparti
d'orli raggrinziti,
io li posso stirar
lisci fra la carta cerata,
poi prendo la colla,
salgo sulla scala
con i petali stirati in
un cestino.
Li riattacco.
Bada a prender colla
resistente all'acqua
altrimenti sforzo
sprecato a causa della pioggia.
    Però
Andranno bene,
la stessa apparenza, dico?
Si leveranno al vento
Come prima?

III

Don't care about
shriveled edges
I could iron them
flat between waxed paper.
then get the glue,
climb up the ladder
with the ironed petals in
a basket.
Put them back.
Be sure to get water-
resistant glue or
else wasted
effort because of rain.
    Still
Will they look alright,
the same, I mean?
Will they lift in the wind
Like before?
Or will people point,
stare at a purple tree
mid-September?
"Weird." "Unnatural."
Things are, sometimes,
supposed to fall
apart.

# ABSTRACTS

CAROL BONOMO ALBRIGHT, "JOSEPH ROCCHIETTI'S REFERENCES IN HIS 1835 NOVEL, *LORENZO AND OONALASKA*"

The earliest known Italian American novel, was *Lorenzo and Oonalska*, which was published in the year 1835. This book is replete with both subtle and overt references to the Republican thinkers of the late 18th and early 19th centuries as well as references to the earlier Enlightenment thinkers. In this paper, I suggest and discuss the significance of these important allusions, references, and citations from the text.

EMELISE ALEANDRI, "ITALIAN AMERICAN ENTERTAINMENTS IN NYC BEFORE THE MASS MIGRATION"

While I have already written extensively on the entertainments of Italian Americans after the Mass Migration, which entertainments both were totally informed by and reflected the immigrant experience. The Italian entertainments and practitioners in both music and theatre before the Mass Migration had different and varied reasons for their existence. This paper identifed things Italian in New York pertaining to music and theatre before 1875, among them Lorenzo Da Ponte, Antonio Meucci, early Italian opera, musical concerts and literary events, Italian organizations (i.e. Tiro a Segno) of the early century and their celebrations, as well as visiting Italian performers such as Duse, Grasso and Salvini.

B. AMORE, "A STONE STORY: ONE HUNDRED YEARS, CARRARA–VERMONT, THE LEGACY OF THE 'FIRST EXPEDITION'"

The "First Expedition" of marble carvers from Carrara, Italy arrived in Vermont in 1882. They created a legacy in the marble towns of Proctor and West Rutland, the place which eventually became the home of the Carving Studio and Sculpture Center a little over one hundred years later. The three interconnected worlds of the quarries and studios of Carrara, the early Italian immigrants who brought their expertise to Vermont, and the contemporary sculptors who have profited from their bequest, speak to the force of a tradition spanning geography and generations.

The Apuan Alps in the Versilia region of Tuscany, look as if they have perpetually snow covered peaks, but as one approaches Pietrasanta and Carrara, it becomes evident that the white is all marble. This is the birthplace of many of the carvers who, at the end of the 19th century emigrated to Vermont.

The Romans opened the first quarries in Colonnata, above Carrara, during Caesar's reign using the labor of Sicilian slaves, and they have been quarried continuously ever since. There are still traces of these *Tagliate Romane* on some of the walls of the older quarries (Dolci 43). Michelangelo, the most famous sculptor to utilize Carrara marble, is said to have chosen stone from some of these same quarries.

Among the Carrarese, there are often twenty generations of people in a family who have worked the marble in one form or another for hundreds of years. Some of these men made their way to Vermont in the late 1800s and continued the traditions with which they had been raised.

Carrara, Italy, was the one and only source for the highly skilled carvers that Colonel Redfield Proctor, President of the Vermont Marble Company, needed for the growing demand for marble sculpture. In the spring of 1882, these pioneer immigrants, the "First Expedition," arrived in Sutherland Falls, the home of the Vermont Marble company. In 1884, there was a political revolt in Carrara which resulted in a new wave of immigration to the Proctor quarries and finishing sheds. On February 12, 1894, these first immigrants formed the Societa' di Mutuo Soccorso modeled after the mutual aid society in Carrara which provided social security and insurance. On May 1, 1909, *The Circolo Corale Ricreativo* was formed. The Italian Aid Society is still active today.

The Carrara sculptors at the Vermont Marble Company formed a professional elite among the thousands of men who worked in the quarries and the sheds. Many of the sculptors had studied at the Accademia di Belle Arti in Carrara and were highly skilled in clay modeling, plaster, mold making and all aspects of carving marble. They worked on some of the most important monuments in Washington D.C. including the Jefferson Memorial, the Supreme Court Office Building, and the Tomb of the Unknown Soldier.

TERI ANN BENGIVENO AND LAWRENCE DISTASI, "THE WANING STORY OF THE ITALIAN AMERICAN EXPERIENCE IN HISTORY TEXTBOOKS"

The panel will examine the lack of information regarding the Italian American experience in textbooks grades four through the collegiate level. The Western Regional Chapter (WRC) of American Italian Historical Association hosted a textbook summit in April to begin gathering solid data on the Italian American experience or lack of same, as recorded in history books. Several participants gathered and reported on the texts they analyzed, most of which indicated decreasing levels of attention to the Italian American experience. The WRC is in the process of compiling all of the data. Bengiveno and DiStasi then made brief presentations to the 2004 Curriculum Commission meeting May 20 in Sacramento at the California Department of Education. Contacts were made with publishers and resources were exchanged in an effort to make sure the Italian American experience is not written out of textbooks completely. The fact is that California, Texas and Florida are the states the publishers target due to their size and influence nationwide. Our hope is to address this problem at the state as well as the national level. The panel will report on the actions taken thus far and also examine the future goals of the project. This is a problem of national significance and the participants hope to learn from other scholars and community members as well as to gain support in this effort.

MARY JO BONA, "CELEBRATING HELEN BAROLINI AND *UMBERTINA*"

We celebrate an important milestone in our literary history: *Umbertina* has come of age. Fully an adult, *Umbertina* at twenty five is permanently in print and has been rewarded by exciting and useful secondary criticism, written by such scholars as Anthony J. Tamburri, Mary Ann Mannino, Edvige Giunta, Fred L. Gardaphé, Robert Viscusi, and Maria Kotsaftis, to name just a few. In its initial state of innocence, Italian American literature was in fact unfettered by what Robert Scholes has called "protocols of reading," especially since a secondary order of reflections on this literature was lacking for many years. Seeking help from ethnic and feminist criticism in the 1980s, I felt free to create a way to read *Umbertina*, aware of the mosaic that we call American literature. After all, if Helen Barolini was not deterred by the burial of writers' voices from Italian America, I could make my own path by proclaiming through literary scholarship that adult considerations such as canonization take place when books are reprinted, taught, and questioned. Such proclamations are coming to fruition for Italian American writers.

Devoted to words, their origins, the weight of their history, Barolini herself pays homage to the transformative power of language itself. Like many minority writers before her, Barolini initially felt that she had no context out of which to write. Ironically liberated from narrow definitions of the kind of writer she should be, Barolini became the writer she could be, donning many linguistic hats, and blurring boundaries between genres.

NORMA BOUCHARD, "SCREENING THE SILENT FILM: REGINALD BARKER'S THE ITALIAN AND THE RESURGENCE OF AMERICAN NATIVISM"

Between 1900 and 1914, over three millions Italians arrived in the United States. The representation of the men and women of the "great exodus" has left a significant mark in American silent cinema where dozens of stories of Italian immigrant communities and the individuals in them can be seen. However, it was also in this cinema that the Italian immigrants became coded as either bizarre, odd characters, or dangerous people prone to criminal activities (as is the case of the 1906 film by Porter, "The Black Hand"). When placed against in this context, Reginald Barker's The Italian, produced by Thomas Ince for Paramount in 1915, has been correctly hailed for its objective, serious representation of the difficulties awaiting those who, like Beppo Donzetti (played by George Beeban), had chosen the path of emigration to urban New York City as a means to better their lives (i.e., Brunetta, Cortes, d'Acierno at alt.) Nevertheless, the Italian cannot be exhausted by enthusiastic assessments of its realism. As I will argue in this paper, the film's divisive language, narrative, and spectator address resonate the anxiety of a culture that, by 1915, had embarked on the path of a dramatic reversal of its immigration policy that would eventually lead to the legislation of 1917 and the Immigration Acts of 1921 and 1924. When situated within this context—elucidated, among other historians, by John Higham—the Italian's peculiar mode of realism emerges as a means to fulfill a very precise ideological function at the time of the resurgence of American "nativism" and its hegemonic discourses.

ALESSANDRO BUFFA, "LOCAL CULTURE/METROPOLITAN CONNECTIONS: ITALIAN AMERICAN YOUTHS AND SPACE OF IDENTITY IN NEW YORK, 1957–1963"

In my paper I will look at some spaces created by Italian American youths who come from working class sections of New York at the end of the 1950s and early 1960s. In doing this I will draw on an interview I made with an ex–Doo–Wop singer, Emilio, who grew up in Bensonhurst, Brooklyn during the fifties and sixties; and the novel *The Wanderers* written by Richard Price in 1974 which is about youths from different ethnic backgrounds who live in the Bronx between the end of the 1950s and early 1960s. Specifically, I will consider how Italian American youths occupied multiple hybrid spaces: those of the family and of the Italian diaspora, those of the neighborhood, schools and workplaces, and finally those of a wider metropolitan youth culture. I argue that the local streets of the neighborhoods, the space at home, the candy stores, and other public spaces, represented at the same time a local and a metropolitan space of identity.

For many scholars, Italian American neighborhoods are reproductions of Italian villages in an urban environment. However, even if we can find some of these aspects in the various Italian neighborhoods in the US, it is important to say that in these areas we see a multiple space composed of local, diasporic, and urban/metropolitan elements. Moreover, I suggest that the Italian neighborhoods in the 1950s and 1960s represented a contact zone characterized by encounters, conflicts, and struggles between Italian American youths and for example; African American, Puerto Rican, and Irish youths. The use of space by Italian youths embraced and revisited at the same time the idea of "*Italianita.*" On the one hand it is based on conventional aspects of Italian American culture, historical stereotypes and idealized ideas about Italy. On the other, they organized the everyday life of the neighborhood by drawing on things which were part of a contemporary, hybrid, metropolitan culture which emerged in those years in urban centers.

Finally, my idea is to reconceptualize the city space in late 1950s and early 1960s, looking at it as a kind of borderland. I don't suggest an easy process of hybridization, since contact zones are not pacific spaces. Rather, as Marie Louise Pratt defines them, they are "social spaces where cultures meet, clash, and grapple with each other, often in contexts of highly asymmetrical relations of power." It is in this sense that I propose to revisit the idea of "*Italianita.*"

LAURIE A. BUONANNO AND MICHAEL D. BUONANNO, "THE "FUTURE OF ITALIAN AMERICAN STUDIES AT U.S. UNIVERSITIES"

This paper takes as its starting point a report on the "Future of Italian American Studies at U.S. Universities," as reported in the AIHA Newsletter, Volume 37 (1–2), Spring 2004: 11–14. The newsletter authors write of discussions at the American Historical Association's January 2004 meeting, "The sessions were organized by Dominic Candeloro and figure, we hope, as the beginning of a much longer and sustained discussion on the future of Italian/American studies in US colleges and universities." Distance education provides an opportunity for students to explore the Italian American experience even when their home campuses do not teach courses in Italian American Studies. This paper will report on a pilot project in which two professors, one a member of faculty at a Florida community college and the other on faculty at a SUNY university college, team teach The Italian American Experience. The course is being taught via the SUNY Learning Network (http://sln.suny.edu) in the summer 2004. The Italian American Experience is an upper-division course listed in the department of interdisciplinary studies at SUNY Fredonia.

This paper will report on several aspects of this pilot project, including organization of the course, the team-teaching experience, and student evaluations.

ILARIA BRANCOLI BUSDRAGHI. "THE ITALIAN "STONE-MEN" IN THE GREEN MOUNTAIN STATE: FROM ITALY TO VERMONT, 1880–1915"

Beginning in the 1880s, artists and artisans from the granite and marble districts of Piedmont, Lombardy, and Tuscany migrated to Proctor and Barre, in Vermont. In a period when the stone industry was booming, their centuries-old expertise was sought after; the contribution they made to the growth and quality of the stone industry is a source of pride. This talk will focus on the social, political and economic forces in Italy which led these skilled workers to emigrate to Vermont at the end of the 1800s, and it will also describe how the sense of the value of their skill and their political awareness shaped their experience of assimilation in the United States of America.

LOUISA CALIO, "SHE IS EVERYWHERE PANEL"

My contribution to this new anthology of spiritual feminist writings compiled and inspired by Lucia Chiavola Birnbaum's work, is entitled "Poet as Initiate: Remembering the dark mother within Women's Poetry of the '70's. I will discuss my own personal initiations and the poetry that emerged from a period of traumatic transition at age twenty-eight during the 70s, when personal crisis led to a descent from which I recovered cellular memories of a dark mother who guided me to reshape my life. Her name was given to me: Isis and like Isis, I would travel in Africa to search for lost pieces of myself, my male counterpart, going to the Nubian Niles among other African countries to rediscover the gods living within me that still danced and spoke. I placed my experiences within the context of other poets who seemed to have shared similar experiences at the same time: Daniela Gioseffi, Diana di Prima and Ntozake Shange.

Crisis and soul are often connected. Perhaps for my generation, the 1960s was a decade of crisis, breaking open the acceptance of old ideas of race, gender or war and providing us with an opportunity for change. In some cases, personal crisis opened us to soulful memories and experiences beyond our rational thinking. Unlike priestesses of old who were prepared for initiation by a guide or teacher, we often lived through hellish experiences before reclaiming ourselves. Individual collapse is not unique to poets, but the discovery at the end of the labyrinth, after the dark passage of our divine mother was. For Daniela Gioseffi who named her "The Great Mother" and "Etruscan Priestess" for Diana di Prima who called her "Loba" of the many forms, for Shange a goddess of Egypt, schetia, we all shared the essential found God in ourselves and loved her fiercely!!!

No longer dependent upon outer authority and patriarchy for approval or self definition, these women poets of the 70s began to channel their own messages and images of the divine within and without and a new feminine archetype was born belonging to both genders. She was black or white, old or young and in between, red and sexy or not, animal, plant, mineral and watery; she belonged to all and the Earth, a Mother herself. I will also share the language of soul that developed from these inspired poets who reclaimed a dark mother for all of us whose histories were lost and suppressed by two thousand years of European patriarchy.

NANCY CARNEVALE, "LANGUAGE IN THE RACIAL CONSTRUCTION AND ASSIMILATION OF ITALIAN IMMIGRANTS AND THEIR CHILDREN"

This paper examines the use of language (Italian and the Italian dialects) as a marker of racial difference as well as the central importance of English in the effort to assimilate both the first and second generations. Although scholars have increasingly called attention to the issue of race and color with regard to Italian immigrants and other southern and eastern European newcomers in this period, the way that language served to racially construct Italians has not been sufficiently considered. At the same time that the immigrant language marked Italians racially, the English language assumed a prominent role in the assimilation of Italians and their children. The latter is evident in the pedagogical practices of the New York City public schools and the Americanization campaigns documented in the records of the Bureau of Naturalization. Professor Carnevale's work highlights the centrality of language to then contemporary understandings of the ability of Italian immigrants to assimilate to American culture.

JUDITH PISTACCHIO BESSETTE, "THE CHANGING FACES OF A VILLAGE."

For several years I have been conducting academic research on the village of Lymansville (North Providence), Rhode Island. Integral to the research are two textile mills: the historic Lyman Cotton Manufacturing Company (1809), and the 1885 Lymansville Wool Manufacturing Company.

A second component of my research consists of oral history interviews with family members and former neighbors who worked in the Wool Manufacturing Company. The majority of interviewees were Italian American octogenarians at the time of the interviews in the middle to late 1990s. They were the children of the first generation of Italian immigrants.

FRANK J. CAVAIOLI, "AMERICAN COLONIAL ITALIAN: AMERICAN HISTORIOGRAPHY"

Italian Americans have had an impact on the development of early America. Peter Sammartino (1904–1992), founder of Fairleigh Dickinson University and a strong advocate of Italian American History, advanced this point by stating, "If we take the sum total of the influences of philosophy, of government, and in jurisprudence, discoveries, exploration, the influence on literature, on music, on art, on architecture and on science, then America would not have been the country it is without the contributions of Italians, and this stretches from the thirteen to the nineteenth centuries."

Much of the research of the Italian experience in America has concentrated on the modern era, beginning with the mass immigration of the 1880s to the contemporary period. Clearly, this work has provided a greater understanding of Italian American history; it has also integrated that history in the wider span of American civilization. Indeed, it has become an important part of the growth of ethnic-immigration history. However, the chronicle of colonial Italian American history through the American Revolution has been limited. Work has been done, as this presentation will show, but that work has been minimal, repetitive, and lacking in comparative analysis. Therefore, this study will examine the historiographical record of Italian American history from the beginning of the colonial era through the American Revolution in an attempt to appreciate what has been accomplished and to emphasize what needs to be done.

It is important to state that in the past generation many Italian scholars have been engaged in researching, recording, and teaching Italian American Studies in both countries. They have joined in cooperative ventures with their trans-Atlantic American colleagues. Because of space constraints, however, this study will focus on the work of Italian American scholars.

DAVID COLES AND FRANK ALDUINO, "JOHN GARIBALDI: AN ITALIAN SOLDIER IN THE STONEWALL BRIGADE"

Historians have given little attention to immigrant soldiers who served the Confederacy. At the outbreak of the war, individual Italians enlisted in a variety of military units while groups of Italians served in regiments from Louisiana and Alabama. John Garibaldi, a native of Genoa, came to the United States at the age of twenty and eventually settled in Virginia's Shenandoah Valley. He enlisted in the Twenty-Seventh Virginia Infantry, which became part of the famed Stonewall Brigade, in 1861. Garibaldi took part in the Shenandoah Valley campaign of 1862. Captured at the battle of Kernstown, he was imprisoned for several months before being exchanged. He returned to his unit in time to take part in the fighting at Fredericksburg, Chancellorsville, Second Winchester, Gettysburg, and the Wilderness. Captured for a second time at Spotsylvania, Garibaldi was exchanged in the fall of 1864, but his subsequent military service is unknown. After the war the Garibaldi taught school and farmed before his death in 1914.

It is unfortunate for historians that the Garibaldi letters, apparently the only significant surviving collection of letters from an Italian American Civil War soldier, make virtually no mention of the author's ancestry, or of the problems facing immigrants in the Confederate armies. The very absence of such comments, however, may in itself be revealing. With such a small antebellum Italian population spread throughout the United States, and with only a few cities boasting even a modest concentration of Italians, immigrants like Garibaldi probably accepted the need for quick assimilation into the mainstream population. His letters, full of comments on family, food, living conditions, the progress of the war, the movements of his unit, and combat operations, are similar to those written by many native-born combatants. Just ten years after his immigration to the United States, the native of Genoa seems, at least in his correspondence, to have been comfortably acclimated to the dominant American culture and society.

MARINA CORREGGIA, "THE DEVELOPMENT OF THE ITALIAN CONSULATE IN SAN FRANCISCO: FROM PRE-UNIFIED ITALY TO THE LATE 19TH CENTURY"

Diplomatic relations between the United States of America and pre-unified Italian states were established rather late, in the mid-19th century. In the preceding period, prior to the U.S. Declaration of Independence and shortly thereafter, contacts between Italian states and North America were limited to small communities established across the Atlantic and to high-profile personalities: explorers, politicians, intellectuals and jurists. On the American side, however, diplomatic initiatives with some Italian states began immediately after U.S. independence was declared. Beginning in the late 18th century, American envoys attempted to establish relations of friendship and trade with the grand duchy of Tuscany, the Republics of Genoa and Venice, and the Kingdoms of Sardinia and Naples. Smaller Italian states and the kingdom of Sardinia had representation in the U.S. throughout the first half of the 19th century, but these were limited to the main cities of the East Coast and the South, such as New York, Boston, Philadelphia, New Orleans and Mobile.

The first diplomatic contacts with West Coast states did not begin until the second half of the 19th century, with the Gold Rush. Starting in 1848, this event turned California into a mecca for miners, adventurers and entrepreneurs of all kinds. San Francisco, until then a sparsely inhabited bay, became the Gold Rush capital and one of the most active harbors in the world. News coming city from California spread everywhere in Europe and stimulated the interest of pre-unified Italian states in trading with the region, which led to the first appointments of consuls general and trade envoys.

This paper focuses on the development of diplomatic-consular relations between pre-unified Italian states and the U.S. West Coast in the 19th century. After a brief introduction about the economic situation of California in the second half of the 19th century, we will discuss the opening of the consulate of the kingdom of Sardinia in San Francisco. In particular we will examine the figure of Leonetto Cipriani, the first Sardinian consul in California, and the functions of the consulate in San Francisco, during his tenure. The following chapter will focus on Giovanni Battista Cerruti, the first consul in San Francisco appointed after the unification of Italy, and on his interesting report on the Italians of San Francisco. His report, compiled in 1865 provides a detailed account of consular activities on the West Coast. The last chapter offers a general overview of the development of Italian consular legations in the U.S. in the 19th century, specifically focusing on the development of the San Francisco consulate up to the early 20th century.

GIOVANNA P. DEL NEGRO, "THE PASSEGGIATA IN AN ABRUZZESE TOWN: WALKING, SEEING, AND A UNIQUELY ITALIAN MODERNITY"

Affectionately called the little Paris of the Abruzzo, the hilltop village of Sasso in central Italy is well known for its evening *passeggiata* (promenade). Sassani often point to the town's attractive thoroughfare and popular *passeggiata* as a sign of their *civilita* (civility) and cosmopolitan sensibility. In this paper, I will explore the kinesics and proxemics in the event and illustrate how the process of seeing and being seen is achieved in this sphere of social life. I will specifically deal with posture, clothing, styles of walking, patterned uses of space and techniques of seeing in public. Finally, I will discuss the concepts of *disinvoltura* (poise or ease of manners) and *bella figura* (to cut a fine figure) and show how they bear upon the local ideologies of style and comportment.

BENEDICTE DESCHAMPS, "ENGLISH AS A TROJAN HORSE: *IL PROGRESSO ITALO-AMERICANO*'S EFFORTS TO REACH SECOND-GENERATION IMMIGRANTS IN THE 1930s"

In 1927, Carlo Barsotti, the owner of the New York-based Italian-language daily *Il Progresso* introduced an English column in the pages of his newspaper. Two years later, press magnate Generoso Pope, who took over *Il Progresso* after Barsotti's death, launched the "English Feature Section," a weekly all-American page which was published in the Sunday edition. Professor Deschamps' paper will show how *Il Progresso* used the English language as a "Trojan Horse" to try and capture the readership of second-generation Italian immigrants whose complex relationship with both the Italian language and their Italian heritage had led them to overlook the Italian press and turn increasingly to American periodicals for information. The evolution of *Il Progresso*'s editorial policy, the choice of topics selected for the English Section, the way fascist Italy was presented in the English page, and the ambiguity of the messages directed at the second-generation is carefully examined.

MICHAEL DI VIRGILIO, "THE ITALIAN ELEMENT IN THE NEW SMYRNA COLONY AND ST. AUGUSTINE, FLORIDA, 1768–1800"

In 1768, the Scotsman Dr. Andrew Turnbull established an indigo plantation south of St. Augustine in British-controlled East Florida. Calling the colony "New Smyrna," Turnbull recruited roughly 1400 colonists (indentured servants) from the Mediterranean, primarily from Minorca, but also from Corsica, Greece, and

Italy. Within this group were some 110 Italians, Corsicans, and Greco-Corsicans, the majority of whom were male.

Reacting to the harsh conditions of the colony, the Italian recruits led a failed revolt in the first year. All the colonists endured exceptional hardships and over two thirds of them perished by 1777. After the failure of the colony, the surviving colonists moved to St. Augustine, which returned to Spanish rule in 1773. Through intermarriages, the Italians, Corsicans, and Greco-Corsicans quickly became absorbed in the predominant Minorcan culture and became an integral part of their socio-economic networks, which included small farming, business, and maritime activities.

Although a pan-Italian identity never emerged, the descendants of the Italian element in the New Smyrna colony, known as "Minorcans," nonetheless became important players in both St. Augustine history and Florida history in general. Today, individuals with surnames like Pacetti, Trotti, and De Medici (and their various corruptions) are present not only in the St. Augustine area but throughout the American South. Their history and origins are without a doubt an important, yet under examined chapter of Italian American history.

KATHARINE EMSDEN, "TONTY: ITALIAN LIEUTENANT WITH LA SALLE ON THE MISSISSIPPI"

Midway between the landing of the *Mayflower* and George Washington's early encounter with the French in Appalachia, an Italian in the service of Louis XIV stood by the side of Cavalier de la Salle at the mouth of the Mississippi River. In 1682, their names alone were inscribed on the bottom of a copper kettle below a wooden cross at the delta: Robertus Cavelier cum Domino Tonty. Thus did France claim the vast interior of *l'Amerique Septentrionale*.

Henry de Tonty is also known as a founder of Chicago and of Biloxi. Sadly, the significance of this Gaetan has been overshadowed in recent history by the self-made nobleman who commanded him. Yet it was Tonty who established a chain of forts along 800 leagues of the Mississippi and who, for twenty-five years, defended the frontier from English, Spanish and Iroquois encroachment. His life and writings and the universal praise earned from friend and foe alike, which continued for seventeen years after La Salle's assassination, form the ideology of an era that determined the destiny of our land. Sources about that merit study of the first Italian to arrive since Columbus. Archives from Naples, Paris, Quebec, Chicago, Baton Rouge and Harvard University augment the numerous Jesuit Relations, Tonty's diary (Paris, 1693; London 1695) and works of Pierre Margry, Francis Parkman, and Anka Mulstein.

MICHELE FAZIO, "DUELING HERITAGES: MULTIETHNIC IDENTITIES IN ITALIAN AMERICAN LITERATURE"

Cross-cultural marriages are a predominant theme in literature produced by third generation Italian American writers where, interestingly, the effects of assimilation Italian American immigrant families faced in literature by first and second generation writers are replaced by the inter-ethnic conflict of Italian Americans marrying outside of their ethnic group. Writers such as Don DeLillo, Tina De Rosa, and Carole Maso all create male characters in their first published works who marry a non-Italian woman. The resulting stories create a pattern of (dis)integration that outline the burgeoning relationship and its subsequent collapse. This new wife and mother comes to symbolize the antithesis of the typical Italian American matriarchal figure, which significantly ruptures the continuity of an Italian American ethnicity. The children produced in these marriages—or lack thereof—redefine what it means to be Italian American; in other words, the future of the Italian American family rests upon a multiethnic identity thereby questioning the roles authenticity and hybridity play in framing American society. This paper seeks to explore the impact dueling heritages play on the development of third (and fourth) generation Italian Americans as represented in DeLillo's short story "Take the "A" Train" and Maso's and De Rosa's novels *Ghost Dance* and *Paper Fish.*

GEORGE GUIDA, "ITALIAN AMERICANS: A TRANSLATION AND COMMENTARY ON MARIO SOLDATI'S AMERICA 'PRIMO AMORE'"

Mario Soldati (1906–1999) was one of twentieth-century Italy's most prolific authors, and one of its most successful. His first successful book was an account of his two-year stay in Depression-era America, *America primo amore* (1935), a book that has not heretofore been translated into English. Throughout the narrative, but especially in a single chapter entitled "Italian Americans," Soldati offers us a rare first-hand critique of Italian American society of the era, from an Italian perspective. Arriving in New York in 1929, expecting Italian Americans to be "all rich, all gentlemen, all civilized," the twenty-three year-old Soldati was soon disillusioned by the realities of Italian American society in New York City. Instead of New World gentility, Soldati encountered a society in which many members of the American-born generation were arrogant, ostentatious, and contemptuous of the immigrant parents who had made possible their lives of relative privilege. He discovered that these younger people spoke strange Italian-inflected varieties of English that seemed to him both bizarre and vulgar; that they felt little connection, and often disdain, for Italy and Italian culture; and that they deluded themselves into believing that Protestant America had fully accepted them as just plain "Americans." Soldati's assessment of Italian American life in 1930s New York has no analogue in our literature.

JOSEPHINE GATTUSO HENDIN, "WHY HELEN BAROLINI'S *UMBERTINA* IS STILL NEW"

Helen Barolini's *Umbertina* charts currents of modern life as they surge through nearly a century of the lives of women. Italian and Italian American women come alive as figures for modernity itself. They struggle against a future-denying fatalism associated with Southern Italy as well as their own divided identities as they strive to find and implement what Antin called a "conscious purpose" to defeat poverty and submission to any fated role. Barolini confronts Italy and America as points on a journey from past to future in which women are the bridge to change. From the prologue in which Marguerite Morosini discusses her desire to divorce her prominent husband and set out on her own, through Barolini's powerful narrative of Grandmother Umbertina's courage in leaving Calabria and strength in making a new life in America, Barolini creates purgatorial trials that show how difficult it is for a woman to seize control her of life, reject fatalism, and, as Antin put it, "hold the rudder that steers the ship of fate." She also manages to be faithful to both the social facts and inner lives of each generation of women she creates.

JENNIFER-ANN DIGREGORIO KIGHTLINGER, "'MANGIANDO, RICORDO': ITALIAN AMERICAN WOMEN AND FOOD IN JOSEPHINE GATTUSO HENDIN'S *THE RIGHT THING TO DO* AND TINA DEROSA'S *PAPERFISH*"

Many Italian American scholars have voiced their "anxieties" surrounding food studies; discussions of Italians and food—particularly Italian women and food—may perpetuate stereotypes. Others remind us that "food represents one of the most powerful vehicles by which economically and/or culturally marginalized and oppressed people have celebrated their cultures" (DeSalvo and Giunta, i). Traditionally, Italian American women have been responsible for preparing ethnic foods for the family. In preparing—or choosing not to prepare traditional Italian meals, women have great influence over the passing of ethnic identity. The displaced immigrants' instinctual embrace of ethnicity, family tradition and—an often romanticized—Italian birthplace is often in direct conflict with a desire to Americanize. For many Italian American women novelists, ethnic food plays an integral part in conveying the painful process of negotiating those desires.

In an attempt to forget the old ways, Hendin's Gina Giardello often refuses to eat. If "mangiando, ricordo," Gina seems to believe "*non mangiando, non ricordo.*" While Hendin never explicitly describes Gina's abstinence as an eating disorder, the suggestion is certainly present in the text. Unwilling to digest—metaphorically—her father's traditional prescriptions for Italian American femininity, Gina is unwilling to digest—literally—the food representative of that culture. For Gina's parents and thousands of southern Italian immigrants, an abundance of food is a marker of prosperity and success in their new world and a means of celebrating the ethnic values they believe made prosperity possible. Rejecting food, Gina rejects the foundation of the new Italian American family and abandons the ancestral history her father holds above all else.

William Boelhower, in "'*Pago! Pago!*'" contends Italian American families and neighborhood communities are based on "The Gift Principle," a basic economic principle of exchange. Boelhower discusses food with references to merchants who give food in return for goods (instead of money), or families who exchange homegrown foods. But the implications of the gift principle for Italian American women are much more complex.

Bona's *Claiming a Tradition* notes the Italian American women writer's tradition of equating America with illness and Italy with health. DeRosa's

Paperfish embraces the tradition. Doriana's illness pushes Carmolina out into the Americanized Chicago streets. When she returns, flushed and sick with fever, Grandma and her Italy are Carmolina's sources of wellness. The family's fears and anxieties are only mitigated by the joys and comforts of Grandma's rich ethnic history, food and tradition. DeRosa often (and in seemingly subtle ways) links food to remembering and reclaiming ethnic homeplace. This paper will examine the negotiation of Italian American female identity in Hendin's *The Right Thing to Do* and DeRosa's *Paperfish*, focusing on culinary representations of ethnicity and eating ritual and the ways in which these representations and rituals are central to remembering and reclaiming home place (nation of origin) and re-imagining Americana.

LUCIANO J. IORIZZO, "THE CASE FOR THE ETHNIC IDENTITY OF WILLIAM PACA, SIGNER OF THE DECLARATION OF INDEPENDENCE"

This paper reflects diligent searching for a definitive finding as to whether William Paca, who in fact signed the Declaration of Independence, could be said to be of Italian origin. The author examines many published and unpublished sources and also conducted searches on the Internet highway. Personal follow ups were also made to scholars in the field who are currently researching Paca or had done so in the past. According to this author, at present the findings are inconclusive and a final judgment must wait for the results of further study.

JEROME KRASE, "SEEING ETHNIC SUCCESSION IN LITTLE AND BIG ITALY."

This essay on urban neighborhoods in the United States and Italy attempts to demonstrate how Italian American neighborhoods in United States are similar to Italian neighborhoods in Italy in the way that they have been changed by the invasion of new and different ethnic groups. The spatial and semiotic logic of diasporic/transnational processes is discussed here as images; especially of changing commercial vernacular landscapes. In the Italian American case this process of what the classic urban ecologists called "ethnic succession" is analogous to the aphorism of fish swallowing other fish. For more than a century Italian immigrants to the United States have been changing the meanings of central city spaces. Most stereotypically they created Italian Colonies and Little Italies in one form or another. They accomplished this not merely by the power of superior numbers of local inhabitants but by the momentum of spatial semiotics, i.e. changing the appearances of spaces and places and thereby changing their meanings as well. By the 1970s the demography as well as the meanings of many of those Italian American ethnicized spaces was being challenged by the influx of new groups. As we can consider how American urban spaces became Italianized and subsequently became less so, we should be able to consider how Italian spaces lose their own, indigenous *Italianita* in response to immigrant settlements and local commercial practices.

In order to demonstrate how Italian central cities have become as American ones cities, an idea once rejected as almost absurd, both old and new approaches are needed. The old is represented by Robert Ezra Park and Ernest Burgess' classical ecological theory of invasion and succession of urban neighborhoods. The new is represented theoretically by Spatial Semiotics and methodologically by Visual Sociology.

Nicole T. Librandi, "Study Abroad in Italy Brings History to Life"

At the Community College of Vermont (CCV), I recently developed and taught "Special Topics in Vermont History: The Stories in the Stone of Italy and Vermont/Study Abroad in Italy", a course which focuses upon the unique contributions and heritage of the Italian stoneworkers and artisans who came— in the late 1800s through the early 1900s—to work in the marble and granite industries of Vermont.

CCV's innovative Study Abroad program provides a unique opportunity for students, who traditionally lack the time, resources and—in some cases—the academic preparation for study abroad. However, the profile of the community college student is changing and, thus, so are the academic offerings. I wanted my students to be prepared to fully absorb experiences in the world which engendered the artistry of generations of stoneworkers. This happened! . . . one student's reaction is indicative: "My memories of this study will last a lifetime . . . I feel like I have learned a lot about something very important to Vermont's history and I know I would not have learned it elsewhere . . . "

The course design included pre-departure seminars, research and discussion via a seminar at the Socialist Labor Party Hall in Barre with historians, sculptors and descendants of the men of stone, through reading, research, and discussion, students explored this unique social, economic and artistic legacy.

In Italy, we traced the path taken by thousands to the quarries of Vermont. The students' growing awareness of what they were seeing and experiencing was enriched by daily focusing questions, journaling, reflection and group discussion. We began with explorations in the north, near Lake Como, an area rich in artistic heritage, natural beauty—and granite. In Carrara (sister city to Barre), through discussions with sculptors, quarrymen, scholars in art and political history, students deepened their understanding.

A typical student reaction: . . . at the (marble) quarries in Carrara (Walter Danesi) painted the most vibrant images of the life of the stoneworker . . . he showed us a typical house for the stoneworker in the time of his childhood and before, and explained what home life was like. He also demonstrated how to move a huge piece of stone with two little crowbars and a song. I saw firsthand the excitement and pride that these stoneworkers have . . . in every single person that I spoke with at the quarries in Carrara."

The experiences in Lombardy and Carrara prepared the students intellectually and spiritually to appreciate the masterpieces of Florence and Siena.

Reflection . . . history came alive . . . goal accomplished. It was unanimous— the trip had been a resounding success! At our final meeting, students were delighted to share their pictures, memories and reflection. We had come full circle.

Everyplace we went had a connection with Vermont, not only in the stone but also in the people. The heritage and culture seems different at first, but in reality it is about the same. We take pride in what we do, and we pass this on to our children.

STEPHANIE LONGO, "THE ITALIANS OF NORTHEASTERN PENNSYLVANIA"

"Chi lascia la via vecchia per la nuova
sa quello che perde ma non sa quello che troverà."

"Whoever leaves the old way for the new
knows what he is losing but not what he will find."

It is perhaps this proverb that best articulates the collective experience of Italian immigrants arriving in the United States during the latter part of the 19th and the beginning of the 20th centuries. These people were well aware of what they were leaving behind in Italy: their families, their friends, and their birthplaces. In short, these people left behind the only lives that they had ever known in search of something more. These brave souls did not know what was in store for them in America; yet they were all willing to do almost anything to ensure the survival of their families; the descendants of whom are scattered across the United States and, quite possibly, are unaware of the sacrifices their immigrant ancestors made for them due to the process of Americanization and the more recent generations' subsequent loss of their ethnic identity.

When one thinks of the "Italian" regions of the United States, Northeastern Pennsylvania rarely comes to mind. Northeastern Pennsylvania is typically associated with the boom in the anthracite coal industry that was a direct result of the Industrial Revolution; which, incidentally, occurred in the United States at around the same time as the beginning of the first wave of immigrants that brought the Welsh, Irish, and Germans to Northeastern Pennsylvania. The first recorded Italians living in Northeastern Pennsylvania were a group of seven individuals living in Scranton and its surrounding areas in 1870. Statewide, roughly 784 people living in Pennsylvania in 1870 were born in Italy. In 1900, this number had risen to 484,207 Italian-born people living in Pennsylvania with 1,312 living in Scranton. This increase in Scranton's Italian population is due to the abundance of jobs that became available in Northeastern Pennsylvania by virtue of the growth in the rail and coal industries in the region.

"The Italians of Northeastern Pennsylvania" is an attempt to acknowledge Northeastern Pennsylvania's rich ethnic history while preserving it for future generations in an easy to read and follow format. It is also an attempt to recognize the Italian community of Northeastern Pennsylvania as one of the region's largest and most visible ethnic groups; since, according to the 2000 United States Census, Italian Americans are the second-largest ethnic group in Lackawanna and Luzerne Counties, the central counties of Pennsylvania's Northeastern region. It should also be mentioned that "The Italians of Northeastern Pennsylvania" ventures to fill the void that exists in the knowledge that Americans of Italian descent have of the lives their ancestors lived in the "madrepatria" as well as the void that exists in the information that various towns in Italy have that shows what their emigrants' lives were like upon arrival in America.

STEFANO LUCONI, "ITALIAN AMERICANS FOR ULYSSES S. GRANT: THE 1872 CAMPAIGN AS A CASE STUDY OF POLITICAL MOBILIZATION BEFORE MASS MIGRATION"

A few thousand Italian Americans lived in New York City in the early 1870s. This, however, did not prevent party organizations from trying to mobilize them politically. Focusing on the articles published by *L'Eco d'Italia* and the activities of prominent leader of Italian origin Luigi Tinelli on behalf of the GOP, this paper examines the strategy that was used to lure Italian American voters into the Republican camp in New York City during the 1872 presidential campaign. It identifies primarily a series of ethnic issues that were exploited to such an end, including the alleged anti-Italian bias of Horace Greeley—incumbent Republican President Ulysses S. Grant's opponent in the race for the White House—and the Irish hold of the Democratic Party. The year 1872 witnessed an early example of the attempts at bringing out the Italian American vote in the United States. These endeavors were to gain momentum after the turn of the twentieth century when a massive influx of immigrants from Italy made the newcomers from this country a significant cohort of the eligible electorate. Yet an analysis of the 1872 election campaign shows that, even before mass migration, the ethnic determinants of voting behavior were already key to Italian Americans' political mobilization.

LAURA MACALUSO, "THE FIRST ONE HUNDRED YEARS: ITALIAN ARTISTIC CONTRIBUTIONS TO AMERICA, 1776 TO 1876."

This paper is a survey of Italian American artistic contributions before the period of mass migration or the end of the nineteenth century. Though Italian artistic contributions to the United States are most often associated with the Gilded Age and Progressive Era and its large numbers of craftsmen (such as sculptors and stone masons), the first one hundred years (1776–1876) of American history offer a wide range of evidence that Italian Americans and Italian culture played a significant role in the shaping of visual art in America. The integration of Italian visual culture in America occurred in multiple forms and strategies, such as in paintings of Italy, and in collecting Italian art at mid-century. A brief survey of these contributions will allow for further recognition of Italian culture in America before 1880.

MARY ANN MANNINO, "DO WHAT PRESENTS ITSELF": SISTER BLANDINA SEGALE'S: *AT THE END OF THE SANTA FE TRAIL*

Sister Blandina Segale, missionary, frontiers woman and Italian immigrant is one of the earliest Italian American woman writers. She kept a journal of her life as a missionary to the Southwest from 1872 to 1892, which was published in 1932 under the title, *At the End of the Santa Fe Trail*. Born in northern Italy, she was living and writing in America before the mass migration of Italians and, in fact, after she returned to Ohio from the Southwest she was assigned with her sister, Sister Justina, to begin work among the Italian immigrants in Cincinnati. By 1897, she founded Santa Maria Italian Educational and Institutional Home where she continued to work until she died at ninety-one in 1941.

My paper discusses her journal as a representation of her personality, attitudes, behaviors and values. I argue that her Italian heritage is unmistakingly the force that directs her. Ann Cornelisen in her study of southern Italian women living in small villages after World War II, *Women of the Shadows*, published in 1976, suggests that the Italian women she lived with possessed strength, inventivness, endurance and courage what she calls "a certain moral fortitude" in the face of abject poverty and limited opportunity. Chichella, a woman Cornelisen interviewed is quoted as saying "As for the women. Put any label you want on it. It amounts to the same thing: we do whatever no one else has done. That's what we're taught; that's what we're supposed to do. Men work and talk about politics. We do the rest . . . That's what our lives are. We're born knowing it . . . It's a world of work. It's that simple. If you want something, you work" (Cornelisen, 227–228).

In my paper I suggest that Sister Blandina's life in Trinidad, Colorado and Santa Fe, New Mexico reflected this same philosophy. When she arrives in Trinidad she is not pleased with the small schoolhouse and she sets about building a new one. She has no money. The missionary sisters were not subsidized by the priests, their order or the diocese but were on their own to pay for themselves. Sister Blandina begins to take the adobes off the roof of the old schoolhouse and is helped by a Spanish woman who offers to send her six workers and other supplies. Other people offer to work in building the school in exchange for free tuition for their children. Sister herself assists the plasterer of the new school by carrying the mortar so he could continue to work after the other men had left.

Like Chichella, Sister is daunted by nothing. Her journal records successful encounters with the poor, the neglected, criminals, and even Billy the Kid. Of her attitude to work she says "Do whatever presents itself, and never omit anything because of hardship or repugnance." Sister founds the first hospital in Santa Fe, buries the dead and all the while supports and loves the native population. Her spunk and her compassion connect her to an Italian value system learned from her parents.

ROB MARCHESANI AND ELIZABETH MESSINA, "HISTORIES IN OUR FAMILIES AS THEY OFTEN UNFOLD ON THE COUCH IN PSYCHOANALYSIS"

The couch in psychoanalysis has become a story-telling stage for the histories we carry. Much like the kitchen table, that icon of human battles and passionate interchanges in the Italian American home, the couch has become another place to "let it fly." And what flies includes everything from simmering to hot tempers, creative imaginations and great senses of humor to profound sorrows. There the life of the teller gives birth to the life of the culture of the family and its legacies. Stories of pride emerge as well as those of shame. Family portraits are woven with words, with silences, with recreations through the character of the story-teller. However many the fragments, what takes form in the jigsaw puzzle is often the springboard for fascinating material, having implications for the most personal of transformations as well as holding great potential for artistic and scientific productions and discoveries be they paintings, poems, plays, novels, motion pictures, inventions, or just a good story to tell as grandma first told it at the table. In each production, each discovery, the word is key, the key to unlocking the door to the mansion of human experience.

ROB MARCHESANI, "FROM THE KITCHEN TO THE COUCH: HISTORIES IN OUR FAMILIES AS THEY UNFOLD IN THE ANALYTIC NARRATIVE"

This short essay examines the history of one Italian American family as it affected the development of the professional choice of the author. Integrating the qualities of each parent's contribution to the author's development, the author argues for the emergence of his vocation as something that was present in the family even without any mention of it as a profession. The journey of self discovery finds its roots in the parental legacies as they are inherited and transformed into new works and productions. Not only have we always been here, but our work has also always been here. The author highlights the influence of an Italian American professional and his importance in bringing that professional choice to fruition. In a world where few seem to have the time of day for another, the author makes the case for the role of the spoken word that was first transmitted around the kitchen table, then on the couch of the analyst where the history unfolds and becomes the source of other creations. This paper was part of a larger panel examining the psychological and psychoanalytic dynamics of literature and personal experience.

ELISABETTA MARINO, "PSYCHOANALYTIC THEMES IN ROBERT VISCUSI'S *ASTORIA*"

*Astoria*, the 1996 American Book Award-winning volume by poet, critic, university professor Robert Viscusi, has been the subject of several essays since its first publication in 1995. Two of them explore some themes that prove to be particularly remarkable for the present analysis: a 1999 article by Peter Carravetta, and a 2001 contribution by George Guida. Carravetta focuses his attention on the particular nature of Viscusi's text, which cannot be "labelled" simply as a novel (if not for merely editorial reasons), since it is able to display a perfect fusion of all the different literary genres (an essay, an autobiography, a memoir, a "biographia literaria", a "metanovel", a poem, and revisionist historical fiction, just to mention a few). George Guida, on the other hand, points out how Viscusi's *Astoria* enables the Italian American male identity to be finally released from the shackles of the stereotypical representation to be seen in many of Coppola's and Scorsese's movies: the "Mafioso", trapped in his code of silence and honor. In

Viscusi's volume, in fact, the narrator is primarily a "speaking subject" (3) and, thus quoting the title of one of Viscusi's seminal essays, he "breaks the silence".

This paper aims at showing that Carravetta's intuition of the author's urge to combine what is commonly disjoint, and the importance attached by Viscusi to speaking, as shown by Guida, can be successfully reinterpreted through the writer's deep interest in psychoanalysis, which permeates the whole volume, as the author himself points out by defining it as his "contribution to psychiatric literature" (15). This paper sets out to demonstrate that the language (through speaking—as a kind of Freudian "talking cure"—and therefore writing) becomes the means through which Viscusi manages to heal and recompose his and many Italian Americans' "fragmented self" (a condition typical of schizophrenia), scattered by a personal and a collective trauma: respectively, the death of his Italian mother (signifying the tangible loss of his—up to that moment—never fully acquired Italian identity) and the harsh experiences of isolation, silence and paralysis shared by many first generation Italian immigrants to America, often leading to the amnesia of one's past in order to blend in. In this paper, therefore, I will also try to show how in his volume Viscusi seems to aim at joining together the two halves of the psychoanalytic process which are commonly disjoint, by acting, at the same time, as a "patient", unfolding his own repressed memories through his reasoning, free associations and dreams (of which the narrative is rich), and as an "analyst", trying to remove mental blocks in his patient (himself and many first generation Italian Americans), thus re-establishing a flow of thoughts, as the volume itself seems to testify by employing the "stream of consciousness" technique, which refuses to accept any chronological order and binary logic of mutual exclusion, an example of which may be "the American vs. the Italian identity".

CESARE MARINO, "COUNT PAOLO ANDREANI IN AMERICA: NO LONGER 'FORGOTTEN TRAVELER'"

In 1790–1792 a young, aristocratic naturalist-explorer from Milano, already famous in Europe for having successfully executed on March 13, 1784, the first manned, hot-air balloon flight in Italy, visited the United States of America and the Dominion of Canada. He met with the leading political and intellectual figures of the two countries, traveled extensively along the Atlantic Coast, through Pennsylvania and New York State, explored the St. Lawrence River and Niagara Falls, and ventured in the interior region of the Great Lakes. This first intense American stay was followed, after a fourteen year hiatus, by a second and longer voyage to the Caribbean and again to North America in the years 1806–1812. Afterwards, the restless and eclectic traveler returned to Europe. He wandered from city to city and finally took up residence on the French Riviera where, exiled from his hometown of Milano due to the large debts he had accrued in the course of his unsettled and dissipate life, he passed away in 1823. His name was Count Paolo Andreani, and until recently he was one of the lesser known and least understood of the early Italian visitors to America.

YVONNE MATTEVI, "ITALIAN AMERICAN CHILDREN'S LITERATURE: TEACHING
CHILDREN TO REMEMBER"

Italian American children's literature is a small but exciting field that counts some great writers like Tomie de Paola, Angelo Valenti, George Panetta, and Paul Gallico. This unique literary genre is far from being only a light and amusing subject. Immigrant children's literature, often erroneously defined marginally, addresses important and difficult topics such as homesickness, family issues, identity crisis, racism, war, and poverty—all of which constitute reality and lived experience. Children's literature written by Italian American writers serves several purposes such as explaining various aspects of Italian culture (even through the use of the magic), exposing Italian American children to their origins, teaching them the traditional values (including love and respect for the family and religion), help them to remind the first Italian American immigrants' difficulties and sacrifices, and comparing different cultures without rating them. Both the content and the functions of Italian American children's literature show how today we still strongly need to assess our ethnicity, and how we fight not to forget our roots. The survival of both culture and values is possible not only to the reminiscing of our past, but above all to the teaching of it to the future generations: our children. Italian American children's literature is a rich and stimulating field that fully deserves the attention of the academic world.

GERALD MCKEVITT, "'SE HABLE ESPANOL': ITALIAN JESUITS AND HISPANICS
IN THE NINETEENTH-CENTURY FAR WEST"

One of the characteristics of Roman Catholic clergy from Italy in the period before mass migration was that they worked primarily among fellow immigrants. In an earlier era, however, Italian clergy and religious congregations served a more diverse clientele. This was true of the Jesuits, who began emigrating from Italy in 1848 after their expulsion during the *Risorgimento*. In the United States, members of the Society of Jesus ministered not only to Italian immigrants, but also native-born Americans Catholics, Native American converts, and a host of newly-arrived immigrants from such diverse locales as Ireland, Germany, and, Italy. In regions of the United States acquired as a result of the Mexican War, they were also active among Hispanic Americans.

This essay analyzes the relationship between the Italian missionaries and Hispanics, particularly in California and New Mexico where they founded schools that attracted large numbers of Spanish-speaking students. The typical Italian Jesuit school served as a mediating influence between old and new cultures. By providing continuity with pre-conquest society, it filled much the same function for young californios and nuevomexicanos that the Catholic parish did for European immigrants in the era of mass migration. It offered a familiar experience in a unfamiliar environment, thereby easing accommodation to a changed world.

The Jesuit ministry to Hispanics is instructive because it sheds light on the Italians' approach to ministry in immigrant America. On the one hand, the priests were Americanizers in both the active and passive sense. The émigré clerics hastened the assimilation of many populations with whom they were closely linked—not just Hispanics, but also Native Americans and a host of European immigrants. And yet, the Jesuits themselves were never so transformed by America that they forgot Europe. Clinging to the traditions of *la patria*, they remained outside the mainstream insofar as they employed many Italian strategies in the running of their colleges, parishes, and Indian missions. Moreover, they resisted aspects of Americanization that they found objectionable. No less important, the Jesuits furthered the Europeanization of American Catholicism through their promotion of ultramontanist religious piety and Church centralization. But there was another important aspect of immigrant assimilation that also typified the approach of the Italian clerics. As ministers to varied ethnic communities, they promoted pluralism. When mediating between Anglos and Hispanics, for example, the Jesuits encouraged the latter to preserve their language and culture as members of a subgroup within the larger society. In these instances, these Italian missionaries functioned neither as Americanizers or Europeanizers, but as brokers of multiple cultures.

ERNESTO MILANI, "GENOA, WISCONSIN AND THE CIVIL WAR: THE GUSCETTI BROTHERS FIGHT FOR THEIR NEW COUNTRY"

This is the case of the hamlet of Genoa, Wisconsin that is almost non-existent in the geographical atlases, but has an interesting history. The settlement was established by Joseph Monti, a Swiss-Italian who sailed to the USA in 1830. He had been in Baltimore, New York and then Galena, Illinois. Galena was booming due to the lead mines and its strategic shipping location. He took advantage of the Homestead laws and moved to the area along the Mississippi River that would become Genoa in 1853. Father Samuele Mazzucchelli was very active in Galena and nearby territories and would eventually die in Benton, Wisconsin in 1864. The family of future President Ulysses S. Grant also had a business in Galena. Soon after settling in Genoa, Joseph Monti induced some friends Swiss friends who lived in Scales Mound, Illinois to join him. Among other settlers, the Guscettis took part to the growth of Genoa.

When the Civil War started the three Guscetti brothers, Ferdinand, Jeremiah and Benjamin, enlisted in the Union Army. The only records of their participation were either confined to family stories and a simple mark on the grave of Ferdinand Guscetti.

The search for the Guscetti brothers eventually led to Frederick Guscetti. He had emigrated to New York from Egypt where he was born. He had enlisted in the Army and fought at Olustee, Florida and was interned in Andersonville. Gravestones in Genoa also record John Buzzetti from Isola, Sondrio. He fought for the Confederation and was married in Louisiana. The end of the Civil War brought more Italians from Valchiavenna to Genoa and gave it distinctive Italian traits. The influx continued through the 1880s with Italian families from Cuggiono, a village near Milan and stopped around 1900.

Today, Genoa is just another American village with a past that is little remembered.

FRED MISURELLA, "WHY COLUMBUS MATTERS: THE EVOLUTION OF AN ICON IN LITERATURE AND HISTORY"

Being the first Italian in the New World, Columbus experienced many of the disappointments, opportunities, and defeats we traditionally associate with exile and immigration. As a result the prevailing view of his character and achievements has evolved through the centuries, in many ways reflecting complex and often contradictory views of immigrants in contemporary life. An explorer is an adventurer, a seeker of new lands and experiences (along with possible riches) who has played a central role in the myths of human communities since their very beginnings. In Canto XXVI of "The Inferno" Dante portrays Ulysses as a false counselor who has sinned in urging his men to disregard God's ordained limits on man's experience. As a result Ulysses' ship sails beyond the known boundaries of the world (virtually the same passage Columbus would follow nearly 200 years after Dante wrote), and after the crew sees the forbidden mountain of Purgatory, they fall victim to the vagaries of God's weather and sink to the bottom of the sea.

Well-known in Dante's day as a supreme strategist, daring warrior, and classical hero touched by the flaw of hubris, Ulysses represents many of the same qualities we now see in the figure of Columbus as he is brought before our eyes in historical essays, poems, statues, and biographies that reflect the social thought of our country during the past century and a half. In my paper I will explore the portraits of Columbus that have emerged in such works as Walt Whitman's "Passage to India" and "Prayer of Columbus," Daniel J. Boorstin's chapter "The Enterprise of the Indies" in *The Discoverers*, Samuel Eliot Morison's Admiral of the *Ocean Sea*, the standard biography, and in various artworks such as the statue in Columbus Circle in New York City. I will show how the portrayal of Columbus has reflected the contemporary society's view of human ambition and its toleration of immigrants generally. When we feel confident and proud (as at the end of the 19th century), the daring, heroic view of Columbus comes to the fore. When we feel less secure and need to consolidate the status quo (as we have since the 1970s), we see him as having gone too far and exhibited too much ambition.

Whatever the view, however, Columbus remains important as a representative of global humanity struggling to understand and control its geological home. Of course, he is also a cautionary figure reminding us that there are limits to control that we must heed. As such, Columbus is more than an Italian American hero; rather he represents Western Humanism in search of its proper ideal: an individual who can achieve important things but who must never forget forces, for good as well as evil, much bigger than he and far longer lasting.

JAMES PASTO, "NORTH ENDERS VS. YUPPIES: DYNAMICS OF IDENTITY IN A CHANGING NEIGHBORHOOD"

This paper is based on research in progress in Boston's North End neighborhood. Once a predominantly Italian neighborhood, the North End is now about 20% Italian and American Italian, with the remainder of the population consisting of professional workers attracted to the neighborhood because of its deserved reputation for safety and its prominent Italian themes: restaurants, cafes, butcher shops, and street corner life. The paper will present an overview of the social history of the North End, with attention to the changes that began in the late 1970s and the transformation of the North End into an Italian "theme park." Special attention will be given to the prominent categories of "North Ender" and "Yuppie" as foci of identity and identification. The paper will also situate these internal identity dynamics within the broader context of Boston ethnic politics and the display of ethnic heritage during the Democratic National Convention.

PAMELA POTTER- HENNESSEY, "BRIEF ENCOUNTERS IN THE NEW WORLD: ITALIAN SCULPTORS IN THE EARLY YEARS OF THE REPUBLIC"

Italian sculptors traveled to America in the early years of the Republic to fill an artistic void and in search of government commissions. Most arrived with an enthusiasm for American politics and a deep passion for a cause in which they believed. Their plan was to help formulate an American iconography that would define the new nation and the artists' neoclassical style provided the perfect vehicle. The simple planar surfaces and the abstract nature of neoclassicism offered the founding generation an ideal template through which to mobilize ideas.

Many of these long-forgotten sculptors brought their families and studio assistants with them on shipboard, along with their tools and materials. This belies the commonly held belief that Italian artists ventured to America simply to make their fortunes, before moving on to other lucrative venues. Despite their commitment, a good number were forced to find consistent work elsewhere. They left America disappointed and bankrupted and unable to support their families in a country with restricted funds and a limited interest in the arts. However, the Italian legacy remains—spread throughout the landscape from New York, to Philadelphia, to Baltimore and Washington D.C. We owe a debt to these adventurous Italians who provided their services at a crucial time in our history. They stepped in when we had no trained artists to create the much needed icons capable of memorializing virtues, persons and events most representative of the nation's ideals.

JAMES PERICONI, "LORENZO DA PONTE AND THE ITALIAN COLONY IN NEW YORK FROM 1805–1838"

While the life and works of Lorenzo Da Ponte have been examined and reexamined with some frequency in the 167 years since his death, Italian Americanists have little studied him, even in the periodic "reassessments" in this country, such as those at Columbia University in 1938 on the centenary, and again in 1988, on the 150th anniversary, of his death. The maturation of Italian American studies argues for a fresh look.

First, beyond his private teaching of Italian, Da Ponte's writing, book publishing, buying and selling encouraged the spread nationally of Italian literature and culture; and his large library formations at Columbia and elsewhere, in part for his beloved Italian Library Society, were significant (Da Ponte, Fido, Keep, Ragusa). No theory of what these activities really amounted to has been advanced.

Second, Da Ponte played an important role in the development of American—specifically, New York's—cultural institutions, through his teaching of leading intellectuals trying to assist in the formation of a real American culture (Fucilla, Bender, Hodges). That movement occurred in an emergent era of great respect for Italian contributions to culture generally in America (La Piana). Da Ponte's own writing on Dante, and other subjects, in (and reviews of his work in) important journals of the time, in New York enhanced that cultural development.

Third, Da Ponte played an important role in the formation of a pre-mass migration Italian American "colony" or community in New York, albeit clearly small. He rightly called himself the "oldest Italian resident" of the City (Da Ponte), as no other Italian matched his longevity in the City; he was known for the social gatherings at his house (Livingston, Gallenga); and he may well have earned the greatest respect and authority among New York's Italians as a result of his spirited defense of Italy and Italians against slurs about their being "criminal in nature" (Francis). The City was itself in mourning at Da Ponte's death, with a blend of "Americans" and Italians converging to show their respect (Francis, Ward).

Finally, apart from Da Ponte's leadership role, his life and writings contain an immigrant story that has not been much examined by Italian Americanists. His pre-mass migration story is so atypical, and therefore is believed, unfairly, not to shed much light on the central concerns of Italian American history.

In fact, Da Ponte was a one-man Italian diaspora, with everything that implies about a complex relation to the land to which and from which he emigrates. Even after becoming an American citizen, in 1828, for example, Da Ponte carried an immigrant's ambivalence about his move: he complains to friends abroad that he wants to return to Italy, for there is "so little" that attracts him about America, yet he never makes such a trip back. There is much that is unmined in his writings that sheds light on his proto-Italian American "immigration story."

LEONARD NORMAN PRIMIANO, "'HER GREATEST GIFT TO ALL OF US': THE NEGOTIATION OF INSTITUTIONAL AND VERNACULAR CATHOLICISM IN THE RELIGIOUS TRADITIONS OF ITALIAN AMERICAN WOMEN IN GLOUCESTER, MASSACHUSETTS"

Working with professional photographer, Dana Salvo, I have been doing ethnographic work for the last two years on the "Mother of Grace Club." The Club represents an extraordinary social and religious alliance of Italian American women who are primarily the wives of fisherman in Gloucester, Massachusetts. The Mother of Grace Club had its genesis as a support group for women anxious about the safety of their husbands and sons during World War II. With its traditions of pageants, parades, feasts, and novenas, the Club members played a significant role in the civic, social, ethnic, and religious life of Gloucester as the organization evolved from a war-time activity to a robust cultural outlet for these women. Sixty years later, the members still gather to eat, sing, socialize, and pray. Their prayers and hopes for blessings—for their young families; alcohol and drug problems; sickness; and for an abundance of fish—remain an integral reason for this organization's existence. Many of their domestic religious activities, such as the building of elaborate altars to honor St. Joseph on 19 March, continue vernacular religious traditions no longer found among Catholics living on the East Coast of the United States.

My paper, accompanied by Dana Salvo's remarkable photographs will note the relationships of the institutional Church to these women's vernacular religious traditions in a community that has never been served by an Italian "national" or ethnic parish for over 100 years, and especially how the local clergy respond to and participate in the St. Joseph's domestic altars which they are called on to bless every year.

ROSEANNE GIANNINI QUINN, "(EN)COUNTERING CRIME: CRIMINALITY, FEMININITY, AND ITALIAN AMERICAN LEGACY IN THE LEGAL THRILLERS OF LISA SCOTTOLINE"

*"Italian Americans, accustomed historically to regard ourselves as perpetual oudsiders, have had to adjust and recalibrate our written work to adapt to our changing place in the American landscape."*    —Regina Barreca

*"'You're not in Naples anymore. It was 1900 a long time ago. You're in Philadelphia, in the new millennium. We have the Internet now, and e-books, and boy bands. Microsoft and Britney Spears. Nobody has to go to the well for water in this town, or pound their socks with rocks. If somebody comes [after you] we'll call the friggin' police.'"*    —The Vendetta Defense, Lisa Scottoline

Given the centrality of "The Sopranos" in the recent popular imagination, I wanted to ask the question: What do Italian American women writers construct when they write from the positionality of crime fighter rather than criminal? In the novels of Lisa Scottoline, I found a series of complex counter-narratives to traditional version of Italian Americans and the normalization of crime. Particularly, in her last three works, The Vendetta Defense, Dead Ringer, and Killer Smile, Scottoline addresses the legacy of Italian Fascism and Italian American internment by setting double plot narratives moving from the geopolitics of World War II to a current Philadelphia law firm run by Italian American women. Surprisingly, perhaps, Scottoline's novels are enormously popular, quite literary, and widely read both inside and outside of Italian American circles. In my paper, I will argue that these latter novels provide insight into the changing cultural psyche of any lingering immigrant attachment to criminality as a vital component of Italian American identity versus the new gendered generation, and of Italian American women particularly, providing a distinct cultural bridge: between the old and the new, the historical and the technological, the patriarchal and the feminist.

Though my paper does not literally fit into the theme of "We've Always Been Here," through my examination of Scottoline's work, I hope to follow the spirit of the conference theme by showing her writing as a current literary example of the Italian American feminist historical counter-narrative. In Scottoline's work, "We have always been here" and we still are—in old valuable ways and in those expansive and perhaps need ones, especially for Italian American women. In so doing, crime gives way to culture gives way to gender gives rise to opportunity while mindfully preserving legacies of Italian American life.

GAETANO RANDO, "ITALIAN MIGRATION TO AUSTRALIA IN THE 19TH CENTURY"

Although significant numbers of Italians did not begin to emigrate to Australia until the end of the 19th century, persons from the Italian peninsular are found in the island continent since the beginning of colonisation in 1788 and feature among the convicts, missionaries, craftsmen, musicians, artists, architects, businessmen and political activists that found their way to Australia before federation. Relatively small in number—the dominant groups of non angloceltic origin in Australia during the 19th century were Chinese and Germans—Italians nevertheless were able to make their mark on some aspects of Australian life. This paper proposes to survey the Italian presence in Australia and their contribution to its development at a time when the country was undergoing a process of transition from a fledgling British colony to a self-governing member of the British Commonwealth.

JOANNE RUVOLI, "WORK, VENGEANCE AND THE (UN)AMERICAN WAY: GUIDO D'AGOSTINO'S MY ENEMY, THE WORLD"

In perhaps all immigrant novels, work is the prime way of achieving the American Dream and self-fulfillment. In many Italian American novels, the work a character chooses to do is often characterized as destiny and becomes part of the character's identity. In Guido Agostino's My Enemy, the World, the main character Philip Bancatti is caught between the Italian class structures of his Sardinian schooling, and the new world business practices of his father's New York Olive Oil importing business. D'Agostino's secondary assimilated characters have jobs they love which define who they are. But Philip can't understand this because D'Agostino has drawn him between the worlds of America and Italy. Traveling across the ocean three times during the novel, Philip literally straddles the old world notions of landed class and gentility to which he has no access and the American ideas of self-fulfillment and opportunity neither of which he accepts. Instead of taking the engineering job he has always wanted, he pursues business to make as much money as quickly as possible to avenge his father's secret Italian dishonor and buy a Count's Sardinian estate where his father was a poor servant. Like other American characters such as F. Scott Fitzgerald's Jay Gatz, Philip is doomed by

D'Agostino. Despite his business successes, Philip cannot see beyond the wrongs committed against his father. For Philip, it is the past that defines a person, not the present deeds or future accomplishments, and for this, D'Agostino alienates Philip miserably from all the other characters. D'Agostino's thoughtful and nuanced 1947 portrayal of Philip Bancatti's rage against both the American and Italian system deserves a closer look especially in comparison with Michael Corleone and Tony Soprano.

Joan Saverino, "Dissonant Discourse, Hidden Histories: Color and Class at Play in a Philadelphia Landscape"

This paper explores the intertextual interpretations on multiple levels involved in an ethnohistorical public history project. Pastorius Park is located in the tony upper northwest neighborhood of Chestnut Hill in Philadelphia. This park encapsulates how a publicly memorialized place can have a duplicitous history. The physical transformation of the parkland and its contemporary popular usage masks a veiled history. Initially indicated through oral interview sources, the transformation of the land into park space involved the interplay of local power, ethnic, racial, and class tensions, a lawsuit, and finally forced displacement of two historically marginalized groups—Italian Americans and African Americans—who cohabited the land. This paper contributes to the ongoing discussion of how culture, place, and space are "mutually constitutive forces" and the park is a good example of the competing ideological forces at play in the culture and politics of historical and contemporary Chestnut Hill.

Charles J. Scalise, "Retrieving the "WIPS": Exploring the Assimilation of White Italian Protestants in America."

Italian Americans who converted to Protestantism in the nineteenth and twentieth centuries have been rendered invisible to most critical historical studies. Assimilated racially and religiously into white Protestantism, their distinctive stories have often been overlooked or ignored, obscured beneath a dichotomy that stereotypes Italian immigrants as either superstitious Catholics or as anticlerical secularists. In this study I have christened this group with the acronym "WIP"—White Italian Protestant.

This research explores the assimilation of the WIPS into American culture and seeks to offer some possible explanations for their general invisibility in historical studies of Italian Americans. After a brief survey of the problem of invisibility, I examine the contexts of religious and ethnic conflict in which the WIPS emerged and the ambivalent dynamics of the Protestant missions to Italian Americans. Then I briefly discuss the goal of gradual assimilation into American society advocated by leadership of the WIPS and explore the reinterpretation of American history that accompanied this assimilation.

WIPS emerged within a context of significant ethnic conflict in the American Catholic Church and were immediately involved in Protestant-Catholic religious hostility. Their origin in ethnic and religious conflict helps to account for the invisibility of the WIPS, as well as the ambivalent dynamics of the Protestant missions toward Italian Americans. Established Protestant congregations, especially upper and upper-middle class churches, did not always welcome and accept the products of their own missions. So, the WIPS played a catalytic role in the formation of new groups within denominations and sometimes even of new denominations. A.B. Simpson's founding of the Christian and Missionary Alliance offers a parade example of this catalytic process.

As agents of assimilation, Protestant churches and missions used the practices of the Christian tradition to teach survival skills for life in America. Religious leaders of the WIPS saw some dangers in the rush to embrace the American dream. Instead, leaders advocated a gradual process of Americanization that would retain selected elements of the WIPS' Italian heritage and traditions. Protestant evangelical hymnody offers one outstanding example of this pattern. Familiar hymns were translated into Italian for immigrants; then later, as WIPS began to attend English-language services, they were already well-acquainted with the tunes and the themes of the songs.

Identifying themselves as biblical Christians, WIPS grafted themselves into the line of the Puritans. They accepted the Protestant myth of American origins, which equated primitive American ideals with Christian principles. Aligning their Italian ethnicity with the famous Italian explorers of the fifteenth and sixteenth centuries, they created a key place for themselves in a religious recasting of the American story. Through God's providence they sought to fulfill the heritage of Columbus through the biblicism of the Puritans. Protestant patriotism replaced both traditional Catholicism and disillusioned anarchism, offering a vehicle for effective assimilation into the American ethos.

JOSEPH SCIORRA, "OF DREAMS AND PHOTOGRAPHS, OF SAINTS AND THE DEAD: VISUAL PIETY IN THE RELIGIOUS AND SOCIAL LIFE OF SICILIAN GLOUCESTER, MASSACHUSETTS"

Since 1992, art photographer Dana Salvo has been photographing the religious life of Sicilian American Catholic women in Gloucester, Massachusetts. His work include images of devotional altars to St. Joseph and St. Anthony assembled annually in private homes and the celebrations of the Our Mother of Grace Club, a lay religious association founded by women during World War II.

Women's reception, use, and interpretation of Salvo's images, as well as family photos, paintings, souvenirs, religious prints, and dreams, are based on local knowledge and practices concerning the supernatural, family obligations, and social dynamics. Like the ceremonial altars themselves, collage, concentration, and redundancy are the aesthetic and social principals in the everyday display of images that articulate a heightened sense of the sacred in what folklorist Kay Tuner notes is the "symbolizing and enacting [of] the moral righteousness of relationship." This "visual piety," to use art historian David Morgan's term, helps us understand "the visual formation and practice of religious belief" of Gloucester's Catholics and, in particular, what Michael Carroll notes is the southern Italian Catholic "predisposition" to infuse two-dimensional images with supernatural power. Images, like the altars themselves, are portals where the sacred and the mundane communicate.

MARY ANNE TRASCIATTI, "LITERACY, CITIZENSHIP AND AMERICANIZATION: AMERICAN AND ITALIAN AMERICAN VIEWS FROM THE EARLY TWENTIETH CENTURY."

This paper offers an analysis of early twentieth century debates over a literacy test for immigrants among Americans and Italian Americans as a way to explore the various ways that participants in these debates imagined citizenship and the process of Americanization. Based on a sample of articles from English and Italian-language newspapers, popular journals, and congressional proceedings, she will argue that although they differed sharply in their assessment of the merits of a literacy test as a means to discourage so-called "undesirable" immigration, both proponents and opponents of the test characterized literacy as a key factor in determining whether immigrants could become worthwhile American citizens with the differences in their arguments breaking down along ethnic lines.

LINA UNALI, "PSYCHOANALYSIS OF THE UNCONSCIOUS AND THE VITALITY OF ITALIAN LANDSCAPE IN D.H. LAWRENCE'S "THE BIRTH OF CONSCIOUSNESS."

The study of the psychoanalytic works of D.H. Lawrence and, more generally, of that part of his literary production which was either set or written in Italy, may throw light on certain aspects of Italian American literature and even explain some of its characteristics. One reason is that the English writer revealed the greatest possible interest in North America and in Italy, in American and Italian literatures. It can also be said that his literary genius thrived at the intersection between several borders, thus offering a suitable model for writers acting in multicultural societies.

There are several references to D.H. Lawrence in Italian American literature. We may remember some passages from *Mount Allegro* in which Jerre Mangione, in contemplation of *Mount Etna* and the plain of Girgenti, seems to be quoting from Lawrence's Sea and Sardinia, precisely from the first pages in which the writer describes his trip from Messina to Trapani and thence to Palermo, where he embarked for his new destination: Sardinia. This paper compares two apparently heterogeneous interests by D.H. Lawrence: the Italian landscape and the development of the psyche as presented in "The Birth of Consciousness," a chapter of *Psychoanalysis and the Unconscious*, published in the United States in 1922.

In many of Lawrence's works the Italian landscape is seen as capable of expressing a special energy and vitality. It can moreover encourage research about the nature of the universe and the spirit that informed the first human societies; it can help establish, for example, the moment in which a certain deviation had occurred from a point of harmony and perfection. The kind of investigation that

D.H. Lawrence follows in *Psychoanalysis and the Unconscious*, can be read as another search for origins. The author wishes to retrace the process of the psyche's development in order to ascertain its nature. In so doing he draws an ideal line that goes from the navel to the brain, along which the fetus and the brain develop.

If we consider Lawrence's concept of psyche, the simile that comes more easily to the mind is that of a physical entity, the first presence of which is detected from its smallest appearance, a cell, an embryo that slowly enlarges and extends, biologically, physiologically, as does the corporeal substance of the body itself6, moving in its progress from a spot in the lower part of the body, from the navel to the solar plexus, from the solar plexus to the brain. Going now back to the comparison between the way the writer deals with the Italian landscape and with the progress of consciousness, we may say that to the appreciation of both based on the writer's research for origins, the realization can be added that their respective powers are hidden, inner, latent, that their discovery and appraisal might possibly save humanity from self- destruction.

RUDOLPH J. VECOLI, "CELSO CAESAR MORENO (????-1901): EXPLORER, REFORMER, MONTEBANK."

Moreno came to my attention over forty years ago when I found a death notice in *L'ITALIA* of Chicago. I have since kept an eye out (and actively searched) for information about him. His is not a great name in history, nor should it be. But he is one of those picaresque and picturesque figures who are intriguing for their adventurous lives. Celso was born in Chivasso, Piedmont, date unknown; fought in the Crimean War; assumed the title of Captain by which he was henceforth known; lived in Sumatra where he organized an insurrection of the natives against the Dutch; fled to China where he organized the first navigation company under the Chinese flag; next appeared in San Francisco, lobbied for "Legge Moreno" to restrict coastal fisheries; next surfaced in the Sandwich Islands where he won the confidence of the King who appointed him Prime Minister (a post which he held for four days); accompanied three youths of the Hawaiian royal family to Europe to supervise their education; carried on a campaign against Italian slavery" for three decades, charging the Italian ambassador and consuls with complicity with his *padroni*. I have located several of his rare publications and diplomatic correspondence relating to Moreno in the Archivio del Ministero degli Affari Esteri. I am still engaged in research on Moreno (I need to explore archives in Hawaii), but have enough on him to "convict" him—or at least present an interesting paper.

HENRY VEGGIAN, "GIUSEPPE GARIBALDI AND HENRY ADAMS."

The essay examines how Henry Adams's writings, and in particular *The Education of Henry Adams*, engaged the Italian revolutionary leader Giuseppe Garibaldi and the Italian *Risorgimento* in a proper modern historical context. Drawing upon a tradition of rhetorical criticism that includes Northrop Frye and Paul DeMan, the essay introduces how Adams devised a particular, non-anthropomorphic style by which to separate Garibaldi from Romantic rhetoric and also the cliché' perception of Italy then current in the United States.

Adams recognized in his early encounters with Garibaldi that Italy was not a nation but rather a series of divided territories torn between warring empires during this period, as Austria, Spain, and France clashed for control of the peninsula. Adams situated Garibaldi within the strong Italian revolutionary nationalism that quickly swept Italy towards political unity, and gradually expelled France and Austria. The Italian revolutionary Giuseppe Garibaldi embodied the political nationalism of this movement and period, which is known to history as the *Risorgimento*.

There existed in mid-19th century America an essentially primitive understanding of Italy. It was a perception that circulated in the visual arts through the major paintings of the Hudson River School painters, in literary study groups of the Boston salons, and with the strong strains of academic and popular humanism that influenced American education. Italy was presented to the American public as a land of ruins, renowned poets, and wondrous architectural ruins.

The essay draws upon these diverse examples to illuminate a comparative reading of Adams' writings on Italy and Garibaldi's memoirs. The contrast first demonstrates how Adams methodically eliminated the idyllic representation of Italy in American culture, then it proceeds to render Garibaldi as a tragic figure who was defeated ultimately by the political forces that he himself led to victory in war.

The "tragic" conception of Garibaldi in Adams' writings represents an alternative view of the American perception of pre-immigration Italy. Henry Adams' original analysis of the figure of Garibaldi offers an opportunity o understand the pre-migration period in a different context and to understand the disillusion and rejection experienced by Italian immigrants as a disappointment of American popular expectations of Italy, to which Henry Adams' analysis of Garibaldi stands as a powerful corrective.

MICHAEL T. WARD, "*LA TRIBUNA*: A CELEBRATION OF ITALIAN IDENTITY"

*La Tribuna Italiana* was published, principally in Italian, from 1914 until 1940, and was of great significance to the immigrant populations of Texas and surrounding states. Its founder was Charles Saverio Papa, a native of Cefalù, Sicily, who struggled financially until the paper achieved success. He collaborated with another Italian American, Louis Adin, who served as the journal's linotyper and editor. When the Fascists declared war on the Allies in 1940, the newspaper changed virtually overnight to an all-English format, assuming the name *The Texas Tribune*. In preparation for my analysis, I examined in detail some twenty issues spaced evenly over the Italian-language organ's history, beginning in 1918, giving attention both to "normal" editions and to those special printings commemorating Columbus Day. Throughout its existence, the *Tribuna* consisted in large part of contributions borrowed (and often translated) from other publications, incorporating those of local correspondents—from various communities, mainly within Texas—as well as pieces by journalists from Italy. Each issue offered a wealth of advertisements, many of which were designed specifically to appeal to an immigrant population; they abound particularly in those numbers celebrating the arrival of *The Navigator*. Always reflecting a lively interest in events across the Atlantic, the editors demonstrate their esteem for Mussolini's accomplishments beginning especially in the 1930s. Nonetheless, the *Tribuna*'s pro-American stance is also made patent, as we are shown undeniably that Papa and Adin were as concerned with their adoptive land as with that from which they came. The balance struck between reverence for the patria and love of the New World comes through decidedly in a series of editorials printed during the paper's last half-year of existence. The even-handed approach taken in these commentaries—and, indeed, by the journal as a whole—shows a notable ability to celebrate the best of both worlds. An Appendix to this article contains excerpts from the last issue of *La Tribuna Italiana* and the first volume of its successor, passages which accentuate continuity despite modification and confirm the possibility of maintaining affection for both old and new loved ones.

BARBARA A. WOLANIN, "THE CONTRIBUTIONS OF ITALIAN ARTISTS TO THE UNITED STATES CAPITOL, WITH A FOCUS ON CONSTANTINO BRUMIDI."

Italian sculptors were first recruited to work in the United States Capitol when it was first being constructed in the early 1800s. During its expansion in the 1850s, numerous Italians contributed to its decoration. Foremost among them was Constantino Brumidi (1805–1880), who painted murals in the United States Capitol over a twenty-five-year period. This talk will provide an overview of the contributions of Italian artists and an introduction to Brumidi's art/Belles Lettres.

In Rome, he studied at the Accademia di San Luca and then painted murals for the Vatican and for Prince Alessandro Torlonia. Brumidi was a captain in the civic guard during the republican revolution in 1849 and was later imprisoned after the Pope was restored to power. Although sentenced to eighteen years in prison, he was pardon and soon after emigrated to the United States in 1852.

Beginning in 1855, Brumidi worked at the Capitol under Captain Montgomery C. Meigs, who superintended construction and decoration of the Capitol extensions and dome designed by Thomas U. Walter. His sample fresco in room H-144, which was to be assigned to the House Agriculture Committee, was well received, and Brumidi was hired to complete the decoration of the room and to make designs for the most important of the other new rooms. He worked with teams of artists of various national origins to carry out his designs, executing all of the true frescoes himself. His murals throughout the building combine classical and allegorical subjects with portraits and scenes from American history and tributes to American values and inventions. Brumidi designed and executed murals for the Hall of the House of Representatives, the Senate Committee on Naval Affairs room (S-127), the Senate Military Affairs Committee room (S-128), the Senate Library (S-211), the office of the Senate Sergeant at Arms (S-

212), the Senate Reception Room (S-213), the President's Room (S-216), and the Senate first-floor corridors.

Brumidi worked intensively at the Capitol through the early 1860s. He continued to add frescoes in the 1870s. His major contributions are the monumental canopy and frieze of the new Capitol dome. In the canopy over the Rotunda he painted The Apotheosis of Washington in 1865. Brumidi began painting the frieze depicting major events in American history in 1878 but died in 1880 with the work less than half finished.

# NOTES ON PRESENTERS

CAROL BONOMO ALBRIGHT is editor-in-chief of *Italian Americana* and Vice-President of the American Italian Historical Association. She teaches Italian American Studies at Harvard University Extension School and a visiting lecturer at Harvard University. She co-authored an annotated edition of Joseph Rocchietti's works. She is series editor of *Italian American Autobiographies* and published essays in *The Dream Book*; *Voices of the Daughters*; *Social Pluralism and Literary History*; and the *Journal of American Ethnic History, LIT*, and *MELUS*. She is co-editor of *Italian Immigrants Go West*. She has received numerous grants and awards, including Associate Fellow of the Danforth Foundation of Higher Education and a university-to-community outreach grant from that foundation.

FRANK ALDUINO is a professor of history at Anne Arundel Community College in Arnold, Maryland, where he teaches classes in American history, and Italian American history and culture. Dr. Alduino earned his bachelor's, master's and doctoral degrees at Florida State University. He has authored several articles on Italian Americans in the American Civil War and the Prohibition Era in Florida. He has also participated in the "Italians of New York: Five Centuries of Struggle and Achievement," sponsored by the New-York Historical Society in October 1999. In 2001 Dr. Alduino received the NISOD Teaching Excellence Award and was named "Professor of the Year" in 2005. His book, *The Sons of Garibaldi: Italians in Blue and Gray*, co-authored with David J. Coles, will be published in November 2007.

EMELISE ALEANDRI (M.A. Theatre, Hunter College; Ph.D Theatre CUNY) is member of the AIHA Executive Council, and President of its New York Metropolitan Chapter. She has published and lectured extensively on the history of the Italian American immigrant theatre, about which she lectures for the New York Council on the Humanities, and also nationally and in Italy. Arcadia published her photographic histories, *The Italian American Immigrant Theatre of New York City and Little Italy*. She produced video documentaries: *Teatro: the Legacy of Italian American Theatre*, and *Festa: Italian Festival Traditions*. She is Artistic Director of Frizzi e Lazzi–the Olde Time Italian American Music and Theatre Company.

B. AMORE is an artist, educator and writer who has spent her life between Italy and America. She studied at Boston University, University of Rome, Accademia di Belle Arti di Carrara and received a Fulbright Grant for independent study in Carrara. She is founder of the Carving Studio and Sculpture Center in Vermont and has won major sculpture commissions in the US and Japan and most recently created the multimedia exhibit, "LIFELINE–filo della vita," an Italian American Odyssey, which is traveling in the US and Italy. *Filo della Vita* will soon be published by the Center for Migration Studies.

TERI ANN BENGIVENO graduated with honors-Phi Kappa Phi (BA) and (MA) from San Jose State University. She received her Ph.D. in American Studies from the University of Hawaii at Manoa and teaches U.S./Women's History at Las Positas College. Dr. Bengiveno is the Vice President of the AIHA Western Regional Chapter. She presented a paper on Title IX at the 2003 Oxford Roundtable. Current research includes the 30th Anniversary of Title IX and Con Le Nostre Mani—a photo/text exhibit of Italian Americans at Work in the East Bay. An article resulting from the exhibit was recently published in the AIHA proceedings *Italian Immigrants Go West: The Impact of Locale on Ethnicity.*

JUDITH PISTACCHIO BESSETTE has a Graduate Certificate in Museum Studies from Tufts University, Medford, Massachusetts and a BA in Art/Art History Concentration, French Minor from UMass/Lowell. Ms Bessette spent four summers in France participating in a medieval archeological dig. Ms Bessette has been conducting research on the historic textile mill village of Lymansville (North Providence), Rhode Island, including oral history interviews with members of the Italian American community who lived in the village and worked in the local textile mill.

MARY BUCCI BUSH is Professor of English and Creative Writing at California State University. Her book of short stories, *A Place of Light* will be reprinted by Guernica Press in 2004. She is working on a novel, *Sweet Hope*, about Italians in the Mississippi Delta to work on cotton plantations alongside African Americans. Chapters have appeared in *Growing Up Ethnic in America* (1999) and *From the Margin: Writings in Italian Americana* (1999). "Planting" appeared in *The Voices We Carry* (1994). Her short stories have appeared in *The Missouri Review*, *Ploughshares*, and *Story*. She received a National Endowment for the Arts Creative Writers' Fellowship in 1995.

DR. MICHAEL BUONANNO is Professor of English and Anthropology at Manatee Community College, Bradenton, Florida. He holds the Ph.D. in English and an M.A. in Anthropology from the University at Buffalo, SUNY. He has conducted extensive fieldwork in Italy and in the U.S. among Italian Americans. Among his publications are a study of *mal'occhio* (evil eye practices) and the commedia dell'arte in Sicilian theatre. Professor Buonanno has extensive experience teaching on-line in the Florida university system.

DR. LAURIE BUONANNO, Associate Professor of Political Science, SUNY Fredonia and 1995 recipient of the SUNY Chancellor's Award for Excellence in Teaching, holds the Ph.D. in Political Science from The Johns Hopkins University and an M.A. in Geography from the University at Buffalo, SUNY. She studied Italian literature and culture (including Italian American) as part of her graduate work at Buffalo. Her principal area of research is the European Union. She is currently co-authoring a book on policymaking in the European Union (Palgrave/Macmillan). She has taught the Italian American Experience at SUNY Fredonia. Dr. Buonanno has been teaching courses (American Politics, the European Union, World Political Geography) via the SUNY Learning Network since January 2001.

ALESSANDRO BUFFA graduated (Laurea Degree) at the Istituto Universitario Orientale of Naples, Italy, in Histories, Cultures and Literatures of English Speaking Countries. He obtained his Master in Media and Historical Studies from the Department of Communications at the Goldsmiths College, University of London. At the moment, he is pursuing a PhD in History from SUNY at Stony Brook. He is working on a dissertation on Italian American youth culture in New York in the 1950s and 1960s, and on the contact zones opened up between Italian Americans and African Americans youths in music and urban space.

ILARIA BRANCOLI BUSDRAGHI received her Laurea in lettere from the Università di Roma "Tor Vergata" in 2001. She wrote her thesis in history entitled "Gli uomini di pietra: lavoratori italiani del marmo e del granito in Vermont tra il 1880 e il 1915" ("Men of Stone: the Italian Marble and Granite Workers in Vermont between 1880 and 1915"), which she is translating for publication in English. She is on the faculty of the Italian Department and of the Italian Summer School at Middlebury College, Vermont, where she has taught a class on the contributions of Italian immigrants to American culture.

LOUISA CALIO won the Connecticut Commission of the Arts award for writing, the Barbara Jones and Talisen prizes for Poetry, and the 1981 Women in Leadership Award, New Haven. She is a founding member and first executive director of City Spirit Artists, Inc. She has contributed to *Italian Heart American Soul*, and *She is Everywhere*. She is author and producer of *In the Eye of Balance*, and *Kindred Spirits*. She graduated Magna Cum Laude with Special Honors in English from SUNY at Albany, and has an M.ED from Temple. She is producing a series of poems with her photos into graphic arts pieces based on her journey to the Niles of Nubia and her ties to Eritrea.

ROSETTE CAPOTORTO is a poet and writer whose work has been published in numerous literary journals and in the current anthologies *Are Italians White? How Race is Made in America, Italian American Writers on New Jersey*, and *The Milk of Almonds*. She recently published a chapbook of poetry, *Bronx Italian*. Ms. Capotorto is an educator, consultant and Teaching Artist throughout the New York City metropolitan area and the creator of Poetry Live!© an innovative series of "comfort zone" writing workshops. A two-time recipient of the Edward

F. Albee Fellowship and honorable mention in the Allen Ginsberg Poetry Award, Ms. Capotorto has a BA (Summa cum laude/PBK), from Hunter College.

FRANK J. CAVAIOLI is a former president of the AIHA and is a member of its Executive Council. He has been a proud member since 1968. He has authored numerous articles and books and has developed and taught college level courses on the Italian American Experience. The Freedoms Foundation George Washington Honor Medal is one of many awards he has received. A resident of Pompano Beach, Florida, he is Farmingdale State University Professor Emeritus.

DAVID J. COLES received his Ph.D. degree from Florida State University. He previously worked as a supervisor in the Florida State Archives and is currently Associate Professor of History at Longwood University in Farmville, Virginia. Dr. Coles was the associate compiler of the six-volume *Biographical Rosters of Florida's Confederate and Union Soldiers, 1861–1865*, and associate editor of the five-volume *Encyclopedia of the American Civil War*.

JOSEPH M. CONFORTI is Distinguished Teaching Professor and chair of Sociology at the State University of New York, Old Westbury. He received a Ph.D. in sociology from Rutgers University. He has taught both sociology and urban studies at Ohio State University and Rutgers University. As a sociologist he has published widely on various aspects of urban affairs, race and ethnicity, poverty, human rights and education. Internationally, he has participated in academic programs in China, Korea and Italy. He has been active in the American Italian Historical Association for several decades and has served as a member of its executive council.

MARINA CORREGGIA has a B.S. in Public Administrations and International Organizations Law from the University of Turin. Her interest in history of the Italian American community in San Francisco began when she moved to the West Coast in early 2000, on the wave of the modern California Gold Rush: the rise and fall of the Internet economy. She earned her degree with a thesis on "Historical-Juridical Research on Diplomatic Relations between the United States of America and pre-unified Italian States in the mid-19th century: The General Consulate of San Francisco", under the guidance of Prof. Enrico Genta.

PETER COVINO was born in Italy and educated there and in the United States, where he earned an M.S. degree from Columbia School of Social Work. Currently, he is a Steffensen Cannon Fellow in the Ph.D. Program in English/Creative Writing at the University of Utah. Covino is the author of *Straight Boyfriend*, winner of the 2001 Frank O'Hara Chapbook Prize; his poems have appeared in *Colorado Review*, *Columbia*, *The Journal*, *The Paris Review*, *VIA*, and *The Penguin Anthology of Italian American Writing*, among other publications. He is one of the founding editors of Barrow Street and Barrow Street Press.

ANGELA D. DANZI, Professor and Chairperson, Department of Sociology and Anthropology at Farmingdale State University of New York, has a Ph.D. in Sociology from New York University and a B. A. in Urban Studies from SUNY Old Westbury. The University Press of America published her study *From Home to Hospital: Jewish and Italian American Women and Childbirth in New York City: 1920–1940 in 1997*. She is AIHA's Secretary and was President of its Long Island Regional Chapter. She received the Elena Cornaro Award, Grand Lodge of New York, Order Sons of Italy in America in 2003 and the Farmingdale State University of New York Alumni Association Excellence in Education Award in 2004.

GIOVANNA P. DEL NEGRO, author of *The Passeggiata and Popular Culture in an Italian Town: Folklore and the Performance of Modernity* (Mcgill-Queen's University Press, 2004) and *Looking Through My Mother's Eyes: Life Stories of Nine Italian Immigrant Women in Canada* (Guernica: Tornoto, 2003). She is assistant professor at Texas A&M University. Her work on performance, identity and piazza strolling has appeared in the *Journal of American Folklore, Midwestern Folklore,* and *Global Media Journal.* She also co-authored *Identity and Everyday Life: Essays in the Study of Folklore, Music and Popular Culture* (Wesleyan University Press, 2004). She has also been named the next editor of the *Journal of American Folklore.*

JENNIFER-ANN DIGREGORIO KIGHTLINGER is a former assistant editor of non-fiction trade titles and children's educational publications, and a former assistant dean of St. John's College of Liberal Arts & Sciences at St. John's University, Jamaica, NY. She is currently teaching writing and literature while pursuing a Ph.D. in English Literature at Stony Brook University with concentrations in 19th-Century American Literature, International Modernism and Italian American Studies.

LAWRENCE DISTASI has been the project director of the traveling exhibit Una Storia Segreta: When Italian Americans Were "Enemy Aliens" since its inception in 1994. A past president of the American Italian Historical Association's Western Regional Chapter and current Newsletter Editor, DiStasi is a board member of the Before Columbus Foundation. He is the author of *Mal Occhio: The Underside of Vision* (North Point Press, 1981), *Dream Streets: The Big Book of Italian American Culture* (Harper & Row, 1989), and *Una Storia Segreta: The Secret History of Italian American Evacuation and Internment During World War II* (Heyday Books, 2001).

MICHAEL DI VIRGILIO received an M.A. in American Studies from the State University of New York at Buffalo. His research focuses largely on emigration from the Province of Chieti, Abruzzo in Italy. Currently, he is an active member of Bricklayers Local 3, New York.

WILLIAM EGELMAN, is currently a professor in the Department of Sociology of Iona College in New Rochelle, NY. He is frequent participant at AIHA conferences and has published many articles, especially demographics, on Italian Americans. He co-edited with Jerome Krase the proceedings of the 1984 conference in Providence, Rhode Island: *The Melting Pot and Beyond:" Italian Americans in the year 2000.*

KATHARINE NICELY EMSDEN graduated from Swarthmore College with a B.A. in History with Honors, followed by an M.A. in English from the University of Denver. Teaching in schools and community colleges since 1963, she discovered Tonty while completing a National Endowment for the Humanities grant at Harvard. Publications include: *Voices from the West* (Discovery Enterprises, Carlisle, Massachusetts 1995) and *Coming to America* (op cit.,1993). She lives in La Veta, Colorado and is writing a biography on Tonty.

MICHELE FAZIO is pursuing a Ph.D. in English at the State University of New York in Stony Brook with a concentration in nineteenth- and twentieth-century American literature. Her interests include the study of class and ethnicity.

FRED GARDAPHE directs the Italian/American Studies Program at the State University of New York at Stony Brook. He is Associate Editor of Fra Noi, editor of the Series in Italian American Studies at State University of New York Press, and co-founding–co-editor of *Voices in Italian Americana*, a literary journal and cultural review. His books include *Italian Signs, American Streets: The Evolution of Italian American Narrative, Dagoes Read: Tradition and the Italian/American Writer, Moustache Pete is Dead!: Italian/American Oral Tradition Preserved in Print, Leaving Little Italy: Essaying Italian American Culture,* and the forthcoming *From Wiseguys to Wise Men: The Gangster in Italian American Literature and Film.*

EDVIGE GIUNTA is associate professor of English at New Jersey City University. Her recent publications include *Writing with an Accent: Contemporary Italian American Women Authors, Dire l'indicibile: Il memoir delle autrici italo americane, The Milk of Almonds: Italian American Women Writers on Food and Culture,* and *Italian American Writers on New Jersey* (Rutgers University Press, 2003). She has edited special issues of *VIA* and *TutteStorie* devoted to Italian American women, and *A Tavola: Food, Tradition and Community Among Italian Americans.* She is poetry editor of *The Women's Studies Quarterly* and co-editor of *Transformations: the Journal of Inclusive Scholarship and Pedagogy.*

CHICKIE FARELLA, native from Chicago transplanted in the California Desert after a career as singer/dancer/songwriter in the Chicago local rock scene and recipient of video music awards in the Chicago International and Athens International Film Festivals during the early inception of MTV 1981, 1982. An independent scholar/performance artist of Women's Spirituality, a recipient of a scholarship from the Italian American Cultural Foundation in 1997 for her work in progress, *Ciao Giulia,* published in part in *VIA* 1999 Dieci Anni . Her current anthology entitled, *Dialogues With My Mother's Guilty, Superstitious and Subservient Ways*, is published in Dr Lucia Chiavola Birnbaums, *She Is Everywhere* from i universe press August 2004.

GEORGE GUIDA is Associate Professor of English at New York City College of Technology, and Lecturer in Italian American Studies at the State University of New York at Stony Brook. He has published in *Poetry New York*, *The Paterson Literary Review*, *Italian Americana*, *Perspectives*, *Red Shift*, *The Columbia Journal of American Studies*, *MELUS*, and *PMLA*. Publications include the poem "Napolitan'" in *Voices in Italian Americana*'s Poetry-in-Performance section, "Las Vegas Jubilee: The Ethnic Semiotics of Louis Prima's 1950s Stage Show," in *The Journal of Popular Culture*, and his first book, *The Peasant and the Pen: Men, Enterprise, and the Recovery of Culture in Italian American Narrative*.

LUCIANO J. IORIZZO is Professor of History, Emeritus at the State University of New York at Oswego where he taught for thirty years. A past-President of the American Italian Historical Association as well as a founding member he has made many contributions to the field of Italian American history and is noted for his pioneering AIHA volume *An Inquiry into Organized Crime* (1970). He has also written *Al Capone: A Biography* (2003) and with Salvatore Mondello *The Italian Americans* (2006). Iorizzo has also published scores of scholarly and popular articles and lecturing extensively on Italian immigrants. A former chair of the Public Justice Department, he is also a recognized authority on the history of organized crime

JEROME KRASE is Emeritus and Murray Koppelman Professor, at Brooklyn College CUNY. He received a BA at Indiana University (1967) and his Ph.D. at NYU (1973). A "Public Sociologist" with a specialty in visual studies of urban neighborhood communities, he lectures widely on "Spatial Semiotics." Representative published works include *Self and Community in the City* (1982), *Ethnicity and Machine Politics* (1992), *Italian Americans in a Multicultural Society* (1994), and *Race and Ethnicity in New York City* (2005). He was President of the AIHA, and is active in the American Sociological Association, H-NET Humanities on Line, the International Visual Sociology Association, as well as the Polish Institute of Arts and Sciences in America.

NICOLE T. LIBRANDI, in her career as an educator, has advocated a collaborative, interdisciplinary approach. She received Master's degrees from Cornell University and the Scuola Italiana of Middlebury College, and studied Italian at UMass/Boston, Boston University, and the Universita` di Firenze. Finding linkages between psychology, psycholinguistics, bilingual education, and Italian American Studies has given her a unique perspective on the study and teaching of Italian. She has authored curricula in Italian and World languages, co-authored the workbook "*Ciao! Sono io!*", facilitated educational exchanges, and presents workshops on Italian language instruction and children's 2nd language learning.

STEFANO LUCONI (Ph.D. in American Studies) teaches at the Faculty of Political Sciences, University of Florence. He specializes in Italian immigration to the United States and the political experience of Italian Americans. He authored: *Teorie del comportamento di voto e crisi della democrazia elettorale negli Stati Uniti dal secondo dopoguerra a oggi; La "diplomazia parallela": Il regime fascista e la mobilitazione politica degli italo-americani; From Paesani to White Ethnics: The Italian Experience in Philadelphia; Little Italies e New Deal: La coalizione rooseveltiana e il voto italo-americano a Filadelfia e Pittsburgh; L'ombra lunga del fascio: Canali di propaganda fascista per gli "italiani d'America* (with Guido Tintori).

LAURA A. MACALUSO is a doctoral student in American art history at the Graduate Center, City University of New York. At the moment Laura is teaching a course titled "Italians in America and Americans in Italy: A History of Artistic Connections" at New York University's School of Continuing and Professional Studies. She holds a M.A. in Italian Renaissance art from Syracuse University's Florence program.

PROFESSOR ADELE MAIELLO is a professor of Contemporary History in the Faculty of Political Science at the University of Genoa in Italy and a frequent participant and presenter at the annual meetings of the American Italian Historical Association.

MARIA PAOLA MALVA is a Ph.D. Candidate at the University of Sassari. She is researching Female Writing in Italian American Literature. She has earned two undergraduate degrees at the University of Sassari: Foreign Languages and Literatures (English Major) and Letters and Philosophy, both with Honors. She has published "*Joyce's Dubliners: From Clock Time to Memory*" (1998) and "*Arturo Bandini in John Fante's Wait Until Spring Bandini*". She also has contributed to the AIHA Proceeding from Lowell, Massachusetts. She also attended the AIHA Annual Conference at Florida Atlantic University, Boca Raton, Florida, where she presented a paper titled: "Bringing Back Memories: An Epistolary Analysis."

DR. MARY ANN MANNINO is a Visiting Assistant Professor at Temple University. Her book *Revisionary Identities: Strategies of Empowerment in the Writing of Italian American Women* published by Peter Lang in 2000 discusses the work of leading writers such as Helen Barolini, Maria Mazziotti Gillan and Maria Fama. In 2003, along with Justin Vitiello, she edited a collection of essays by Italian American women writers and critics which explores the ways Italian heritage impacts writing choices for women. *Breaking Open* was published by Purdue University Press. Her poem "Jimmy Fahey" took first prize in the Allen Ginsberg Awards in 2001. She is both a fiction writer and a poet and her work has appeared in many literary magazines and anthologies.

ROB MARCHESANI, MSSc, is executive editor of *The Psychotherapy Patient* journal and book series for Haworth Press. His latest collection, *Saints and*

*Rogues: Conflicts and Convergence in Psychotherapy* (2004) is forthcoming following *Inhabitants of the Unconscious: The Grotesque and the Vulgar in Everyday Life* (2003), *Frightful Stages: From the Primitive to the Therapeutic* (2001), and *Awe and Trembling: Psychotherapy of Unusual States* (1999). He is also the executive editor of the newsletter of the National Association for the Advancement of Psychoanalysis. His essay, "Oedipus Revisited: Depictions of the Mother-Son Relationship" was featured in Elizabeth Messina's *In Our Own Voices: Multidisciplinary Perspectives on Italian and Italian American Women* (2003, Bordighera).

CESARE MARINO was born in Catania, Sicily and studied social sciences at the University of Padua, Italy, then transferred to the American University in Washington, DC, where he received his Ph.D. in Anthropology with a specialization in North American Indian ethnology and ethnohistory. Dr. Marino resides in Virginia and is on the staff at the Smithsonian Institution in Washington DC.

ELISABETTA MARINO is assistant professor of English literature at the University of Rome "Tor Vergata". She has published a book on the figure of Tamerlane in English and American literature (Rome 2000), she has edited the volume of the proceedings of 2001 Asia and the West Conference held at "Tor Vergata" (Rome, 2002). She has published extensively on Italian American literature, Asian American and Asian British literature. She participated in the 1997, 2002, 2003, 2004 AIHA Conferences and presented a paper in each of those years.

YVONNE MATTEVI is a Ph.D. Student at the City University of New York.

GERALD MCKEVITT, S.J., is professor of history at Santa Clara University where he teaches courses in Historical Writing, the American West, California History, Native Americans of the United States, and History of the Jesuits. He is the author of books and articles on the history of the American West, such as *The University of Santa Clara, A History, 1851–1979* and articles on aspects of missionary and frontier history that have appeared in *The Western Historical Quarterly*, the *Pacific Historical Review, California History*, and *U.S. Catholic Historian*. He is currently preparing for publication a book entitled, "Brokers of Culture: Italian Jesuits in the American Far West, 1848–1919."

ELIZABETH G. MESSINA is adjunct assistant professor of Psychology at Fordham University and a faculty member in the Department of Psychiatry at Lenox Hill Hospital. She has conducted cross-cultural research in Italy and the United States on gender egalitarianism and cancer pain. Her current research interests are culture and gender, and intergenerational migration trauma. She is the author of numerous articles. She is editor of *In Our Own Voices: Multidisciplinary Perspectives on Italian and Italian American Women* and author of a chapter of the forthcoming *Psychological Perspectives on The Stigmatization of Italian*

*Americans in the Media* in Robert Marchesani ed. *Saints and Rogues*. She is past Vice-President of AIHA.

STEPHANIE LONGO is pursuing a Masters in History at the University of Scranton focusing on Italian and Italian American History. She received her Bachelor of Arts, Magna cum laude in 2003. She won the Joseph G. Brunner Award for Excellence in Modern Languages (2003) and is a member, of Mu Rho: National History Honor Society (2003), Phi Alpha Mu: National Social Science Honor Society (2003), and Alpha Mu Gamma: National Foreign Language Honor Society (2001). She is Founding President, University of Scranton Chapter of the National Society of Collegiate Scholars (2000) and a member of the Royals Historical Society (1999).

GINA M. MIELE is Executive Director, Joseph and Elda Coccia Institute for the Italian Experience in America at Montclair State University. She received her B.A. from the College of the Holy Cross in Italian Studies, Magna Cum Laude and Phi Beta Kappa. At the University of Florence, she obtained a Master's Degree (1998) and a Ph.D. (2003) in Romance Languages and Literatures, both at Harvard University. In her time at Harvard, she taught Italian language courses and Dante's *Divine Comedy*, among other seminal texts, to undergraduates. While conducting research on Luigi Capuana's folktales in Mineo, she taught at Harvard's summer program in Calabria and Sicily in 2002.

ERNESTO R MILANI is an Ethnic Archaeologist who researches the migration from western Lombardy to the Americas. He recently coordinated the first Italian translation of *Rosa, the Life of and Italian Immigrant* by Marie Hall Ets (1999). His published essays span from Sunny Side Plantation, Jack Kerouac on the Italian literary scene, the "macaroni railroad", the Lombard presence in the Canadian Railway system and Alberta/British Columbia collieries, Lombard fraternal orders in Rockford, Illinois and Dorchester, Massachusetts. His thesis interest in mutual aid societies has evolved into a collection of badges and documents of a great number of Italian American fraternal orders.

FRED MISURELLA has published fiction and non-fiction in *Partisan Review*, *Salmagundi*, *The Village Voice*, *The New York Times Book Review*, *The Christian Science Monitor*, *VIA*, *Italian Americana*, and other journals. *Understanding Milan Kundera: Public Events, Private Affairs* was published by The University of South Carolina Press, and a novella, *Short Time*, came out from Bordighera, who will publish his book of stories, *Lies to Live By*, in June, 2005. He teaches writing and literature at East Stroudsburg University in Pennsylvania.

SUSAN BUCCI MOCKLER is a poet whose work has appeared in *Poet Lore*, *The Southwestern Review*, *Potpourri*, and *The Black Buzzard Review*. Her poem, Picking Strawberries, was a finalist in the Moving Words Contest, Virginia Cultural Affairs Division, 2004, and Susan will be the featured poet in the June 2004 issue of the

Arlington Artsletter. Susan's poetry was featured in an exhibit, Turning to White, with artist Bill Firestone at the Arlington County, Virginia, Public Library during August 2004. In addition, she gave a reading there on August 24. She and Bill are at work on a book that will include their rural-themed poetry and paintings.

PROFESSOR FRANCO MULAS teaches English and Anglo-American Literature at the University of Sassari, Sardinia, Italy. He has many of his papers published in the Proceedings of the Association, and he has also published a book *Studies on Italian American Literature* in 1995. He is also the author *Virginia Woolf: The Search for Greater Reality*, Ed. Dattena, Cagliari, 1993, the other, *An Investigation in Artistic Creation: John Keats and D.H. Lawrence*, Ed. EDES, Sassari, 1996. Recently, he has also published a book titled *Critical Essays on John Fante's Novels*, Ed. Edes/Tas, Sassari, 2003.

MICHELA MUSOLINO is a singer and actress who has performed at such New York City landmarks as the Rainbow Room, Rockefeller Center, the Cathedral of Saint John the Divine as a member of I Giullari di Piazza, and at Saint Mark's Church in the Bowery as a soloist in poet Paolo Valesio's The Square of Massacred Prayers. She studied Commedia dell'Arte with Enzo Aronica and Lydia Biondi,and movement and mime with Yass Hakoshima. She has also worked with Alessandra Belloni and Roberto Raheli perfecting Southern Italian drumming skills. After years of researching Sicilian folk music, Michela is now sharing these treasures with audiences.

JAMES PASTO holds a Ph.D. in Near East Studies from Cornell University and now teaches at Boston University. His later father Mario and mother Gilda were born in Boston to immigrant parents from Southern Italy. James has two daughters. He is forty-six and grew up in Boston's North End. Though his primary work is in Near Eastern archaeology and politics, he is currently carrying out research on the social history of the North End.

DR. POTTER-HENNESSEY is a former holder of Smithsonian and Winterthur Fellowships. She published several articles on the interchange between Italy and America in the eighteenth and nineteenth centuries as well as. two chapters in American Pantheon, Sculptural and Artistic Decoration of the United States Capitol, published by the United States Capitol Historical Society. These essays, "The Italian Influence on American Political Iconography," and "A New World," explore the Italian legacy in Washington, D.C. Her current research focuses on the impact of Italian sculptors working in the Philadelphia and Baltimore regions and she is also completing a manuscript for a book about Baltimore monuments.

JIM PERICONI has presented many papers AIHA annual meetings. He is on the Italian American Writers Association board of directors, and is a past member of the AIHA Executive Council. He was co-editor, with Fred Gardaphe, of the *IAWA*

*Bibliography of the Italian American Book*, the most complete such bibliography which is now fully searchable on the IAWA website. He essays as well as book reviews for *Voices in Italian Americana, Italian Americana, The New York Law Journal*, and *The Free Reed Journal*. Jim Periconi practices environmental law in Manhattan full time, and is former Chair of the Environmental Law Section of the New York State Bar Association.

LEONARD NORMAN PRIMIANO is Associate Professor in the Department of Religious Studies at Cabrini College and Lecturer in the Graduate Program in Folklore and Folklife at the University of Pennsylvania. With a Master of Theological Studies from the Harvard Divinity School and a dual doctorate in Religious Studies and Folklore and Folklife Studies from the University of Pennsylvania, he has worked as specialist in folk and popular religion for the national exhibition, "The Invisible Made Visible: Angels From The Vatican." His book on the Philadelphia branch of the gay and lesbian religious group known as "Dignity" is will be published by Indiana University Press.

ROSEANNE GIANNINI QUINN, Ph.D, teaches in the English Department, and the Ethnic Studies Program, at Santa Clara University in California.

GAETANO RANDO holds degrees from Italian and Australian universities and is Associate Professor in Italian and English Language and Linguistics at the University of Wollongong (Australia). One of his major research interests is in the area of Italian Australian studies and among his publications are: Letteratura e emigrazione. Il caso italoaustraliano, Pellegrini Editore, Cosenza, La Barricata dell'Eureka. Una sommossa democratica in Australia, Rome, Archivio Guido Izzi, 2000 and Stephen Castles, Caroline Alcorso, Gaetano Rando, Ellie Vasta (eds). Italo-australiani, La popolazione di origine italiana in Australia, Turin, Edizioni della Fondazione Giovanni Agnelli, 1992. A current research project is the production of a study on Calabrian Australian literature.

JOSEPH V. RICAPITO, born Giuseppe Ricapito, in Giovinazzo, Bari, Italy, came to America as a child and was raised in Brooklyn, New York, where he attended public schools up to and including Brooklyn College, CUNY. He holds the M.A. in Spanish and the PH.D. in Romance Languages from UCLA. Currently, he is professor of Spanish, Italian and Comparative Literature. He has been Chair of Spanish and Portuguese, as well as the Director of the Comparative Literature Program. He is the Section Head of Italian Studies. His field of study is the Renaissance and has written widely on prose works of the Renaissance.

JOANNE RUVOLI is a Ph.D. student in English at the University of Illinois at Chicago, where she studies writing, American Literature and Film. She has taught both high school and college for many years and is an assistant editor at the fiction magazine *Other Voices*.

JOAN SAVERINO is an Education Specialist at the Historical Society of Pennsylvania where she is developing content for a web site on Pennsylvania ethnic history funded by the Pennsylvania Department of Education. From 1998–2002 she was a Pennsylvania Humanities Council funded visiting scholar at the Germantown Historical Society to document the Italian American neighborhoods of northwest Philadelphia. She is working on a book that uses the lens of needlework and costume to investigate Calabrian and immigrant women's identities. Saverino has a doctorate from the University of Pennsylvania's Department of Folklore and Folklife and a Masters in Anthropology from George Washington University.

CHARLES J. SCALISE, Ph.D., professor of church history, Fuller Theological Seminary has an A.B. (summa cum laude) from Princeton University, an M.Div. degree (magna cum laude) from Yale University Divinity School, and a Ph.D. from The Southern Baptist Theological Seminary. His first two books focused upon the interface between the Bible and Christian theology: *Hermeneutics as Theological Prolegomena* and *From Scripture to Theology*. Recently, he has examined theological models for ministry in *Bridging the Gap*. Dr. Scalise has published in the *Scottish Journal of Theology, The Greek Orthodox Theological Review, Review and Expositor, Cross Currents*, the *Journal of Pastoral Theology*, and *Journal of Personality and Social Psychology*.

FOLKLORIST JOSEPH SCIORRA is Assistant Director of Academic and Cultural Programs at the John D. Calandra Italian American Institute. He has recently curated the exhibitions "'Evviva La Madonna Nera!': Italian American Devotion to the Black Madonna" and "Sacred Emblems, Community Signs: Historic Flags and Religious Banners from Italian Williamsburg, Brooklyn." Sciorra is the co-editor of a bilingual edition of verse by Sicilian American poet Vincenzo Ancona, *Malidittu la lingua/ Damned Language* and author of *R.I.P.: Memorial Wall*. He won the Anne and Henry Paolucci Prize in Italian American Writing for "'Italians Against Racism': The Murder of Yusef Hawkins (R. I. P.) and My March on Bensonhurst."

LINA UNALI, professor of English and American Literature at the Second Università di Roma, has published on the poetry of William Carlos Williams, cultural and theological movements in New England at the end of the nineteenth century, eighteenth century American autobiography and on cultural and literary relationships between the British and India. She has translated into Italian *Continuities in Cultural Evolution* by Margaret Mead and articles on the poetry of Marianne Moore. She has published poetry and three books of narrative, one of which won in 1995 the Alghero Donna Prize for narrative, another the Parola di Donna Prize in 2004.

RUDOLPH J. VECOLI, is Professor Emeritus of History and Former Director of the Immigration History Research Center at the University of Minnesota–Twin Cities. He received the Ph.D. from the University of Wisconsin. Vecoli has served as president of AIHA, the Immigration History and Ethnic History Society, and chair of the History Advisory Committee to the Statue of Liberty/Ellis Island Commission and Foundation. Among his many honors is the Cavaliere Ufficiale nell'Ordine al Merito from the Republic of Italy. He has authored or edited six books and over a hundred articles. Among his recent publications are: "The Making and Un-Making of the Italian American Working Class" in *The Lost World of Italian American Radicalism*.

HENRY VEGGIAN is a doctoral candidate in the Department of English at the University of Pittsburgh. Mr. Veggian has written articles on Italian American culture for *America Oggi* and he has translated several works from Italian into English, including Anna Maria Pellegrino's Italian best-seller *Diary of a Rapist* (*Diario di uno Stupratore*, Mondadori, 1992). Mr. Veggian is currently a visiting scholar at Columbia University, where he is writing his dissertation on Thomas Pynchon. He has been a member of the American Italian Historical Association since 2000.

MICHAEL T. WARD is Associate Professor of Italian and Spanish at Trinity University. He received his Ph.D. in Romance Philology from the University of Pennsylvania. His research interests include the history of linguistics, both in Renaissance Italy and nineteenth-century Latin America, and the history of linguistics in Italy and South America. Professor Ward is currently at work on a study of the scholarly contributions made by the Peruvian Carlos Prince. He has published in such journals as *Italica*, the *Hispanic Review*, and *Historiographia Linguistica*, and is currently completing a translation of Benedetto Varchi's *Ercolano*.

BARBARA ANN BOESE WOLANIN is an Art historian, curator, and administrator. Since 1985 she has served as Curator for the Architect of the United States Capitol in Washington, D.C. She received her Ph.D. in Art History at the University of Wisconsin–Madison, for her Dissertation: "Arthur B. Carles, 1882–1952: Philadelphia Modernist." She is listed in *Who's Who in American Art*, *Who's Who in America*, and *Who's Who of American Women* among many other honors and awards.

# INDEX

## AIHA PAST PRESIDENTS

Rudolph J. Vecoli 1967-1970

Salvatore J. LaGumina 1971-1974

Luciano J. Iorizzo 1975-1978

George E. Pozetta 1979-1980

Francis X. Femminella 1981-1982

Frank J. Cavaioli 1983-1984

Dominic Candeloro 1985-1988

Richard N. Juliani 1989-1992

Jerome Krase 1993-1996

Fred L. Gardaphé 1997-2000

Mario Aste 2001-2003

Anthony J. Tamburri 2004-2007

Mary Jo Bona 2008-

# AIHA CONFERENCES AND PROCEEDINGS

Adapted from Frank J. Cavaioli. *The American Italian Historical Association at the Millenium*, American Italian Historical Association, nd.: 12-13.

1. *Ethnicity in American Political Life: The Italian American Experience.*
Salvatore J. LaGumina, ed. 1968.
36 pages.
Casa Italiana, Columbia University, New York. October 26, 1968.

2. *The Italian American Novel.*
John M. Cammett, ed. 1969.
35 pages.
Casa Italiana, Columbia University, New York. October 26, 1969.

3. *An Inquiry Into Organized Crime.*
Luciano J. Iorizzo, ed. 1970.
87 pages.
Casa Italiana, Columbia University, New York. October 24, 1970.

4. *Power and Class: The Italian American Experience Today.*
Francis X. Femminella, ed. 1973.
58 pages.
Kosciuszko Foundation, New York. October 23, 1971.

5. *Italian American Radicalism: Old World and New World Developments.*
Rudolph. J. Vecoli, ed. 1972.
80 pages.
The North End of Boston. November 11, 1972.

6. *The Religious Experience of Italian Americans.*
Silvano M. Tomasi, ed. 1975.
133 pages.
Seton Hall University, South Orange, New Jersey. November 17, 1973.

7. *The Interaction of Italians and Jews in America.*
Jean A. Scarpaci, ed. 1975.
117 pages
Towson State College, Baltimore, Maryland. November 14-15, 1974.

8. *The Urban Experience of Italian-Americans.*
Pat. Gallo, ed. 1977.
177 pages.
Queens College, The City University of New York, Flushing, New York. November 14-15, 1975.

9. *The United States and Italy: The First Two Hundred Years.*
   Humbert S. Nelli, ed. 1977.
   242 pages.
   Georgetown University, Washington, DC. October 8-10, 1976.

10. *The Italian Immigrant Woman in North America.*
    Betty Boyd Caroli, Robert F. Harney, and Lydio F. Tomasi, eds. 1978.
    386 pages.
    Toronto, Ontario, Canada. October 28-29, 1977.

11. *Pane e Lavoro: The Italian American Working Class.*
    George E. Pozzetta, ed. 1980. 176 pages.
    John Carroll University, Cleveland, Ohio. October 27-28, 1978.

12. *Italian Americans in the Professions.*
    Remigio U. Pane, ed. 1983.
    290 pages.
    Rutgers University, New Brunswick, New Jersey. October 26-27, 1978.

13. *The Family and Community Life of Italian Americans.*
    Richard N. Juliani, ed. 1983.
    191 pages.
    Chicago, Illinois. October 24-25, 1980.

14. *Italian Americans in Rural and Small Town America.*
    Rudolph J. Vecoli, ed. 1987.
    204 pages.
    Landmark Center, St. Paul, Minnesota. October 30-31, 1981.

15. *The Italian Americans Through the Generations.*
    Rocco Caporale, ed. 1986.
    263 pages.
    St. John's University, Jamaica, New York. October 29-31, 1982.

16. *The Interaction of Italians and Irish in the United States.*
    Francis X. Femminella, ed. 1985.
    308 pages.
    Albany, New York. November 11-13, 1983.

17. *Support and Struggle: Italians and Italian Americans in a Comparative Perspective.*
    Joseph L. Tropea, James E. Miller, and Cheryl Beatti-Repetti, eds. 1986.
    312 pages.
    Washington, DC. November 9-11, 1984.

18. *The Melting Pot and Beyond: Italian Americans in the Year 2000.*
    William Egelman and Jerry Krase, eds. 1987.
    318 pages.
    Providence, Rhode Island. November 7-9, 1985.

19. *Italian Americans: The Search for a Usable Past.*
    Richard N. Juliani and Philip V. Cannistraro, eds. 1989.
    304 pages.
    Philadelphia, Pennsylvania. November 14-15, 1986.

20. *Italian Ethnics: Their Languages, Literature and Lives.*
    Dominic Candeloro, Fred L. Gardaphe, and Paolo A. Giordano, eds. 1990.
    478 pages.
    Chicago, Illinois. November 11-13, 1987.

21. *Italians Americans in Transition.*
    Joseph V. Scelsa, Salvatore J. LaGumina, and Lydio F. Tomasi, eds. 1990.
    283 pages.
    John D. Calandra Italian American Institute of CUNY. New York.
    October 13-15, 1988.

22. *Italian Americans Celebrate Life: The Arts and Popular Culture.*
    Paola A. Sensi-Isolani and Anthony Julian Tamburri, eds. 1990.
    180 pages.
    Fisherman's Wharf, San Francisco, California. November 9-11, 1989.

23. *To See the Past More Clearly: The Enrichment of the Italian Heritage, 1890-1990.*
    Harral E. Landry, ed. 1994.
    285 pages.
    New Orleans, Louisiana. November 1-3, 1990.

24. *Italian Americans and Their Public and Private Life.*
    Frank J. Cavaioli, Angela Danzi, and Salvatore J. LaGumina, eds. 1993.
    240 pages.
    New Haven, Connecticut. November 14-16, 1991.

25. *New Explorations in Italian American Studies.*
    Richard N. Juliani and Sandra P. Juliani, eds. 1994.
    256 pages.
    Washington, DC. November 12-14, 1992.

26. *Italian Americans in a Multicultural Society.*
    Jerome Krase and Judith N. DeSena, eds. 1994.
    302 pages.
    St. John's University, Jamaica, New York. November 11-13, 1993.

27. *Through the Looking Glass: Images of Italians and Italian Americans in the Media.*
Mary Jo Bona and Anthony Julian Tamburri, eds. 1996
290 pages.
Chicago, Illinois. November 10-12, 1994.

28. *Industry, Technology, Labor and the Italian American Communities.*
Mario Aste, Jerome Krase, Louise Napolitano-Carman, and Janet E. Worrall, eds. 1997.
291 pages.
University of Massachusetts at Lowell. November 9-11, 1995.

29. *A Tavola! Food, Tradition, and Community Among Italian Americans.*
Edvige Giunta and Samuel J. Patti, eds. 1998.
137 pages.
Historical Society of Western Pennsylvania. Pittsburgh, Pennsylvania. November 14-15,
1996.

30. *Shades of Black and White: Conflict and Collaboration Between Two Communities.*
Daniel Ashyk, Fred L. Gardaphe, and Anthony Julian Tamburri, eds. 1999.
378 pages.
Cleveland, Ohio. November 13-15, 1997.

31. *Italian American Politics: Local, Global/Cultural, Personal.*
Jerome Krase, Philip V. Cannistraro, and Joseph V. Scelsa, eds. 2005.
260 pages.
Hunter College CUNY. New York City. November 12-14, 1998.

32. *Italian Americans: A Retrospective on the Twentieth Century.*
Paola Sensi-Isolani and Julian Tamburri, eds.
Pending.
Fisherman's Wharf, San Francisco, California. November 11-13, 1999.

33. *Greece and Italy: Ancient Roots and New Beginnings.*
Mario Aste, Sheryl L. Postman, and Michael Pierson eds. 2005.
269 pages.
University of Massachusetts at Lowell. November 9-11, 2000.

Printed in the United States
201921BV00003B/94-393/P